NIC SHEFF was drunk for the first
time at age eleven. In the years that followed, he would
smoke pot regularly, do cocaine and Ecstasy, and develop
addictions to crystal meth and heroin. Even so, he had always
felt like he could quit and put his life together whenever he
needed to. It took a violent relapse one summer to convince
him otherwise.

In a voice that is raw and honest, Nic spares no detail in
telling the compelling, heartbreaking, and true story of his
relapse and his journey toward recovery.

PRAISE FOR *TWEAK*

"Raw, powerful, and honest."

—The Bookseller

"Full of jaw-tightening and occasionally grisly scenes of
shooting up, deals gone bad, guns and sex, Sheff's story
takes off like a shot in the arm with a terse, honest, and
spontaneous narrative."

—Kirkus Reviews

"The trajectory of drug addiction is nothing new, but Sheff's
lucid, simple prose makes the heartbreaking journey seem
fresh."

—San Francisco Chronicle

"The harrowing story of a decade of youthful drug abuse."
—The Seattle Post-Intelligencer

"Riveting." *—Playboy*

TWEAK

TWEAK

(GROWING UP ON METHAMPHETAMINES)

NIC SHEFF

atheneum

NEW YORK LONDON TORONTO
SYDNEY NEW DELHI

atheneum

An imprint of Simon & Schuster Children's Publishing Division
1230 Avenue of the Americas, New York, New York 10020
This work is a memoir. It reflects the author's present recollections of his experiences over a period of years.
For information about special discounts for bulk purchases, please contact Simon & Schuster Special Sales at 1-866-506-1949 or business@simonandschuster.com.
The Simon & Schuster Speakers Bureau can bring authors to your live event. For more information or to book an event, contact the Simon & Schuster Speakers Bureau at 1-866-248-3049 or visit our website at www.simonspeakers.com.
Also available in an Atheneum Books for Young Readers hardcover edition
Book design by Michael McCartney
The text for this book was set in Helvetica Neue.
Printed and bound in Australia by Griffin Press
This Atheneum Books for Young Readers media tie-in paperback edition September 2018
10 9 8 7 6 5 4 3 2 1
Library of Congress Card Catalog Number 2008923615
ISBN 978-1-5344-3657-2 (media tie-in pbk)
ISBN 978-1-4391-0333-3 (eBook)

For Lee and my friend in New York
who took me in. You are both
beautiful, inspiring, powerful women.
You are the two people I respect
and admire most in the world.

Thank you.

How can I go forward when
        I don't know which way
I'm facing?
                —John Lennon

PART ONE

DAY 1

I'd heard rumors about what happened to Lauren. I mean, I never even knew her that well but we'd sort of hung out a few times in high school. Actually, I was sleeping with her for about two weeks. She had moved to San Francisco when I was a senior and we met somehow—at a party or something. Back in high school it was just pot, maybe I'd do some acid and mushrooms on the weekend.

But I smoked pot every day. I was seventeen and had been accepted at prestigious universities across the country and I figured a little partying was due me. I'd worked hard those last three and a half years. Sure I'd had some problems smoking weed and drinking too much when I was younger, but that was all behind me. I was smart. I was on the swim team. My writing had been published in *Newsweek*. I was a great big brother. I got along with my dad and stepmom. I loved them. They were some of my best friends. So I just started smoking some pot and what harm could that do me anyway? Hell, my dad used to smoke pot. Most everyone in my family did. Our friends did—it was totally accepted.

But with me things were different. In high school I was rolling blunts and smoking them in the car as I drove to school. Every break in classes had me driving off to get high. We'd go into the hills of Marin County, dropping acid or eating mushrooms—walking through the dry grass and overgrown cypress trees, giggling and babbling incoherently. Plus I was drinking more and more, sometimes during the day. I almost always blacked out, so I could remember little to nothing of what'd happened. It just affected me in a way that didn't seem normal.

When I was eleven my family went snowboarding up in Tahoe, and a friend and I snuck into the liquor cabinet after dinner. We poured a little bit from each bottle into a glass, filling it almost three-quarters of the way with the different-colored, sweet-smelling liquid. I was curious to know what it felt like to get good and proper drunk. The taste was awful. My friend drank a little bit and stopped, unable to take anymore. The thing was, I couldn't stop.

I drank some and then I just had to drink more until the whole glass was drained empty. I'm not sure why. Something was driving me that I couldn't identify and still don't comprehend. Some say it's in the genes. My grandfather drank himself to death before I was born. I'm told I resemble him more than anyone else—a long face, with eyes like drops of water running down. Anyway, that night I threw up for probably an hour straight and then passed out on the bathroom floor.

I woke up with almost no memory of what I'd done. My excuse for the vomit everywhere was food poisoning. It scared me, honestly, and I didn't drink again like that for a long time.

Instead I started smoking pot. When I was twelve I was smoking pot every day—sneaking off into the bushes during recess. And that pretty much continued through high school.

Lauren and I really never got very close back then. When I heard later that she'd been put in rehab for cocaine abuse and severe bulimia, I guess it wasn't that surprising. We'd both been really screwed up all the time and I had a history of dating, well, not the most balanced girls. I remember being ashamed to bring her to my house. I remember not wanting my parents to meet her. We'd come in late, late and leave early in the morning—whispering so as not to wake up my little brother and sister. Maybe it was them I wanted to shield from Lauren the most. Or, not from Lauren so much as, well, the person I was becoming. I was ashamed of my behavior, but still I kept going forward. It was like being in a car with the gas pedal slammed down to the floor and nothing to do but hold on and pretend to have some semblance of control. But control was something I'd lost a long time ago.

Anyway, Lauren was not someone I thought about a whole lot. When she approaches me, I don't even recognize her at first. It's been five years. She yells my name:

"Nic Sheff."

I jump, turning around to look at her.

She is wearing big Jackie O sunglasses and her dyed black hair is pulled back tight. Her skin is pale, pale white and her features are petite and delicately carved. The San Francisco air is cold, even though the sun has broken through the fog, and she has a long black coat pulled around her.

So I think . . . think, think. Then I remember.

"L-Lauren, right?"

"Yeah, don't pretend like you don't remember me."

"No, I . . ."

"Whatever. What're you doing here?"

It's a good question.

I'd been sober exactly eighteen months on April 1st, just two days ago. I'd made so much progress. My life was suddenly working, you know? I had a steady job at a rehab in Malibu. I'd gotten back all these things I'd lost—car, apartment, my relationship with my family. It'd seemed like, after countless rehabs and sober livings, I had finally beaten my drug problem. And yet there I was, standing on Haight Street, drunk on Stoli and stoned out on Ambien, which I'd stolen from the med room at that rehab.

Honestly, I was as surprised by my own actions as anyone else. The morning of my relapse, I had no idea I was actually going to do it. Not that there weren't ominous signs. In the twelve-step program they tell you to get a sponsor. Mine was a man named Spencer. He was around forty, strong, with a square face and hair that stood on end. He had a wife and a three-year-old daughter. He spent hours talking with me about recovery. He helped me get into cycling and walked me through the twelve steps. We'd ride our bikes together along the Pacific Coast Highway, up Latigo Canyon, or wherever. He'd relate his own experience getting sober from chronic cocaine addiction. But I stopped calling him as often.

Maybe I felt like I didn't need his help anymore. I seldom went to meetings, and when I did, my mind would talk to me the whole time about how much better I was than everyone else—or how much worse I was, depending on the day. I'd stopped exercising as frequently. I'd stopped taking the psych meds they had me on—a mixture of mood stabilizers and antidepressants. I'd started smoking again. Plus there was Zelda.

Zelda was a woman I thought I was madly in love with. She was fourteen years older than I was and, well, she was also engaged to marry another guy, a wealthy real-estate broker named Mike. When I started sleeping with her, I tried to justify it to myself. I figured it was her decision and I wasn't really doing anything wrong and it was just for fun and blah, blah, blah. Basically, I thought I could get away with it. I mean, I thought I could stay detached emotionally.

I couldn't.

She came to represent for me everything I thought would make my life perfect. After all, she'd been married to this famous actor and was an actress and grew up in Los Angeles, raised by her famous uncle who was also in the movie business. Everyone seems to know her in L.A. She's sort of a celebrity, you know? Being with her became my obsession.

Ultimately, however, she wouldn't leave her boyfriend for me and got pregnant with his child. I was crushed. I mean, I just couldn't handle it. So yesterday I relapsed, driving up the 5, drinking from a bottle of Jäger.

So now I'm standing on Haight Street and Lauren, this girl I haven't seen or thought about in five years, is here, in her long black coat, asking me what I'm doing.

I'd driven up from L.A. the night before and slept in my old, falling-apart Mazda, parked in a lot on the edge of the Presidio—a great expanse of forest and abandoned army housing that stretches out to the cliffs overlooking the Pacific and the San Francisco Bay. A friend of mine, Akira, had once lived there. He occupied a basement apartment on the edge of the Presidio. I'd hoped to find him still living there, but after I wandered around the house some—looking into the dust-smeared windows—it was clear that the place was deserted. It was Akira who'd actually introduced me to crystal meth when I was eighteen. He was a friend of a friend. He did a lot of drugs and we immediately gravitated toward each other. Somehow that always seemed to happen—we addicts can always find one another. There must be some strange addict radar or something.

Akira was like me, but more strung out at the time. He had dyed red, curling hair and dark, dark eyes. He was thin, emaciated, with hollowed-out features and narrow, dirty fingers. When he offered me that first line of meth, I didn't hesitate. Growing up I'd heard, you know, never to do heroin. Like, the warnings were everywhere and I was scared—do heroin, get hooked. No one ever mentioned crystal to me. I'd done a little coke, Ecstasy, whatever—I could take it or leave it. But early that morning, when I took those off-white crushed shards up that blue, cut plastic straw—well, my whole world pretty much changed after that. There was a feeling like—my God, this is what I've been missing my entire life. It completed me. I felt whole for the first time.

I guess I've pretty much spent the last four years chasing that first high. I wanted desperately to feel that wholeness again. It was like, I don't know, like everything else faded out. All my dreams, my hopes, ambitions, relationships—they all fell away as I took more and more crystal up my nose. I dropped out of college twice, my parents kicked me out, and, basically, my life unraveled. I broke into their house—I would steal checks from my father and write them out to myself to pay for my habit. When I had a job at a coffee shop, I stole hundreds of dollars from the register. Eventually I got arrested for a possession charge. My little brother and sister watched me get carted away in handcuffs. When my then seven-year-old brother tried to protect me, running to grab me from the armed policemen, they screamed for him to "get back." His small body crumpled on the asphalt and he burst into body-shaking tears, sobbing and gasping for breath.

Then there were the treatment centers, two in northern California, one in Manhattan, and one in Los Angeles. I've spent the last three years in and out of twelve-step programs. Throughout all of it, the underlying craving never really left me. And that was accompanied by the illusion that, the next time, things would be different—I'd be able to handle it better. I didn't want to keep hurting people. I didn't want to keep hurting myself. A girlfriend of mine once said to me, "I don't understand, why don't you just stop?"

I couldn't think of an answer. The fact was, I couldn't just stop. That sounds like a cop-out, but it's the truth. It's like I'm being held captive by some insatiable monster that will not let me stop. All my values, all my beliefs, everything I care about, they all go away the moment I get high. There is a sort of insanity that takes over. I convince myself and believe very strongly that this time, *this time*, it will be different. I tell myself that, after such a long time clean, these last eighteen months, I can go back to casual use. So I walk down to the Haight and start talking to the first street kid who asks me for a cigarette.

This turns out to be Destiny. He is a boy around my age, twenty or twenty-one, with snarled dreads and striking blue eyes. He has the narrow face of a fox or coyote and he's hiding a can of beer indiscreetly in the sleeve of his oversize jacket. He is distracted and out of it as I'm talking to him. I keep trying to get him to focus on what I'm saying. Eventually, he agrees to introduce me to a friend of his who deals speed, so long as I buy him another beer.

"Dude," he says, his voice thick and strained, "I'm gonna tell you straight, man, I'm fo'realze. My boy's gonna hook you up fat, that's no joke. You ask anybody, homes, they'll tell you, Destiny is all right. Everyone's cool with me 'cause I be cool with everyone."

He rambles on like that, pausing only to high-five pretty girls as they pass. As for me, the vodka and sleeping pills have calmed me down enough to keep me breathing through all this—though the blind hungering for the high that only meth can bring has me pretty anxious. There'd been times, in the past, where I got burned copping drugs on the street. On Mission Street I tried to buy some heroin once and came away with a balloon filled with a chunk of black soap.

I smoke cigarettes, one after the other, trying to keep Destiny on point—getting the phone number of his connection. It was right before Lauren stopped me that Destiny told me to wait while he went and got his "boy's" number from a friend. He walked off down the street and then Lauren is standing there, asking me what I'm doing.

My first instinct, of course, is to lie. The wind is blowing the street clear and Lauren takes off her sunglasses, revealing those transparent green eyes of hers. What I say is, "Actually, I just moved back here from L.A. where I'd been sober over a year, but now I'm doing the whole relapse thing and I'm just waiting to hook up some meth. I heard you had some trouble like that too. Is that true?"

If she's surprised, she doesn't show it.

"Yeah," she says, her voice light and soft. "How much are you getting?"

"A gram, I hope. What are you doing here?"

"I was going to get my tattoo filled in. But, well, now I guess I'm going with you, aren't I? You need any money?"

"Uh, no."

She puts her glasses back on. "What about a car?"

"Uh, yeah, we could use your car. Mine's over on Lake Street."

"All right, then."

What I said about the money is sort of true. I have three thousand dollars saved up and, for me, that is a lot of money. I'm sure that it'll be enough to get me started on a life working and using in San Francisco. The rehab I'd worked at in Malibu catered to wealthy, often celebrity, clients. They paid well and, sober, I had few expenses. I can afford a sixty-dollar gram. In the next couple days, I'll start looking for work. I mean, I've got it all figured out. Really.

We stand watching the people on the street, walking from shop to shop.

"What've you been doing?" I ask. "It's been a long time."

"Five years. But, like you said, I had some trouble. I'm working now, though—for my mom. I have about four months clean."

"But you're over it."

"Hell, I've just been waiting for the right person to go out with."

"Really?"

"I don't know."

"You look good."

"Thank you. It's nice to see you, too."

"Yeah." I put a hand on her shoulder, feeling her body tense up. "Here he comes."

Destiny is sort of strutting or limping or something down the street. I introduce him to Lauren.

"Rockin'," he says. "We can go meet him in, like, half an hour. Here's his number." He hands me a crumpled piece of paper. "You gonna get me that beer, right?"

"Of course."

"I'll go get my car," says Lauren.

I walk into the liquor store on the corner and buy two 40s of Olde E and another pack of Export As. Lauren pulls her green Nissan around and we pile in—me in front, Destiny in back. I pass him one of the 40s and drink a bunch of mine down. Lauren refuses to take it when I offer her some, but she pops a few Klonopins 'cause she says she's gonna freak out if she doesn't. She gives me one and I figure it won't do anything since I used to take so much of it, but I chew it up anyway, hoping it might take the edge off or something.

Destiny directs us out of the Haight, and lower Haight, down Market and up into the Tenderloin. The rows of Victorian houses give way to corporate high-rises and then the gritty, twisting streets of the San Francisco ghetto—cheap monthly hotel rooms, panhandlers, small-time hustlers, dealers, and junkies. Neon signs, off during the day, advertise strip clubs and peep shows. The sky has blown completely blue, but the sun is blocked by the falling-down buildings, leaving everything cold and windswept and peeling.

We stop the car on the corner of Jones and Ellis, watching the scourge of walking dead as they drift down the street. One man—a skinny white guy with no hair on his head, but a lot on his face—stands in front of an ATM machine. He turns his head toward the sky every minute or so, screaming, "Please! Please!" Then he looks back at the ATM. Nothing comes out.

"Here they come," says Destiny, getting out of the car with the 40. "Thanks a lot, kids."

"Cool, man, thanks."

"Have fun," he says, nodding toward Lauren knowingly. She maybe blushes a little.

A young kid greets Destiny and then jumps into Lauren's backseat. He is accompanied by a tall, skinny white man with gray hair and a face that looks like a pile of pastry dough. The boy is thin, but strong, with a round nose and darting eyes. He wears a black bandanna tied around his head and ratty, baggy clothes.

"Yo, what's up? I'm Gack," he says.

The fat older man says nothing.

"Hey, I'm Nic. This is Lauren."

"Cool, cool. You wanna G, right?"

His voice comes out in quick, hoarse bursts. I just nod.

"Word," he says. "Yo, this is my dad, Mike."

Mike waves stupidly.

"Anyway," continues Gack, "you're gonna give me the money, and I'm gonna go get yo' shit. My dad'll wait here."

"Dude, there's no way. I'm not letting you walk outta here with my money."

"Come on, yo, there's no other way. My dad'll stay here and, look, here's my cell phone, and my wallet, and I'll leave my skateboard. Just wait two minutes, okay?"

I look at Lauren. She shakes her head, but I say, "Fuck, all right."

I hand him sixty bucks and he leaves. Part of me expects never to see him again, but he returns ten minutes later with our sack. He comes all out of breath.

"Yo, I'm hookin' you up so fat," he says, handing over a very not fat Baggie of white crystals.

"Dude," I say, "this is fucking pin as hell."

"No way, man."

I take out one of the pieces and put it in my mouth. The bitter, chemical sour makes me shudder, but it tastes familiar. "All right, fine," I say.

"Word."

"You have any points?" asks Lauren.

I'm proud of her. I hadn't even thought about getting rigs and there she is, coming right out and saying it.

"Uh, yeah. You all don't mess around, huh?"

"No," we both say at the same time.

Out of his pocket, Gack pulls a pack of maybe five syringes held together by a rubber band.

"Those are cleans?" I ask.

"Fo'sure."

"All right," I say. "We'll take those and we're cool on the short sack."

"Dude, that sack is fat."

"Whatever."

"All right, well, call if you need more."

"We will," I say.

And with that, Gack and his dad leave the car and Lauren and I drive off with fresh needles and about a gram of crystal methamphetamine.

———

I remember Lauren's dad's house from the time we'd been together back in high school—but I also remembered it from

when I was much younger. The place is a European-style mansion
in Sea Cliff. It is four or five stories high, sort of boxy, with giant bay
windows bordered by faded green shutters. Vines climb the gray-
washed walls and white roses grow along the sloping stairway. It
looks out on the ocean—rough and pounding, relentless. The top
story, a bright, sun-drenched loft, used to be the playroom of my
best friend and sort-of brother, Mischa.

See, the divorce went down like this: My dad had an affair
with a woman, Flicka, then left my mom for her. Mischa was her
son. We all moved in together when I was five. Mischa was my
age, with long, white-blond hair, blue eyes, and a famous actor
father. He threw tantrums and would bite me, but we were also
very close. His father was the one who had lived where Lauren's
father lives now. I would go over there and play video games with
Mischa, or build Lego spaceships, or draw, or whatever.

Walking in the door with Lauren—backpack full of drugs,
drunk and stumbling—I can't help but feel a tightness in my
stomach, thinking back to the child that I had been. I remember
going on walks with my dad out to Fort Point, a jetty that stretches
out underneath the Golden Gate Bridge. I remember eating sushi
and tempura in Japantown, playing on the ships docked off Hyde
Street, riding my bike through Golden Gate Park, being taken
to the old Castro movie theater, where a man played the organ
before every show. I remember my championship Little League
team in Sausalito, birthday parties at the San Francisco Zoo,
going to art galleries and museums. I'd been so small that my dad
would shelter me from the cold by hiding me in his sweater. Our
heads would stick out of the stretched-out wool neckline together.
I remember the smell of him—that indescribable smell of dad. He
was so there for me always—especially when my mom moved
down south. Sober and living in L.A., I'd talked on the phone with
him almost every day. We talked about everything—from movies,
to art, to girls, to nothing at all. I wonder how long it will be before
the calls start coming in—how long before he knows I've gone
out, relapsed, thrown it all away.

Lauren's room is in the basement—basically just a large canopy bed and TV and not much else. There are books and clothes and things all over the place. The shades are drawn over the windows, and Lauren plugs in a string of Christmas lights above the built-in shelves along the wall. She puts a CD in the player, something I've never heard before.

"Come on, let's hurry up," she says. "My parents will be home soon and I wanna get out of here before they come."

"Cool. You know, my parents' weekend house in Point Reyes will be empty tonight. We can go stay out there."

"I gotta work tomorrow morning," says Lauren.

"That's fine. We'll get you back."

"My parents are gonna freak out if I don't come home tonight."

"Make something up."

"Yeah, fuck, all right."

"Can I use this?" I ask, holding up a blown-glass jar, maybe an inch high, swirled with streaks of white and green.

"Sure, whatever."

"You gotta Q-tip?"

"Fuck, yeah, but let's go."

"All right, chill."

She rummages around and gets me the Q-tip. I rip off the cotton from one end. I go to the sink in her bathroom and fill the jar with a thin layer of water. I pour in a bunch of the crystal and crush it up with the back of a Bic lighter I have in my pocket. I hold the flame to the base of the jar until the liquid starts to smoke and bubble. I drop in the cotton and then pull it all up into two of the syringes. I pass the one with less over to Lauren and set about making a fist with my right hand, watching the veins swell easily. My body is so clean, so powerful—over a year needle-free and my veins reveal themselves instantly. I think back to how difficult it'd once been to hit—when the veins all began collapsing, hiding under the skin. But now the veins jump up right away. I pull back the plunger, watch the blood rush up into the mixture, and then slam it all home.

I cough.

The chemical lets off this gas as it reaches your heart, or brain, or whatever and it rushes up your throat, choking you.

I cough, choking like that.

My eyes water—my head pounding like maybe I'll pass out, my breathing going so fast.

"Goddamn, goddamn," I say, the lights dimming out and really, I mean, there's no feeling like it. The high is perfection.

I turn and see Lauren push off and as it hits her I kiss her without saying anything and she kisses back and it is all so effortless, not like being sober and consumed by worry and fear and inhibitions. I kiss her harder, but she pushes me back, saying, "Come on, let's go to the beach."

We get outta there fast and then we are walking in the sunlight, back toward Lauren's car. It is a different world, man, heightened, exciting. I light a cigarette and my fingers move spasmodically and I start talking, talking, talking. The waves of the drug keep sweeping through me and my palms turn sweaty and I grit my teeth. I tell Lauren about the book I've written and the job I want to get at this magazine in L.A. and suddenly it doesn't seem like these are impossible dreams anymore. I feel like it is all happening—that my book is getting published and I can get any job I want and I'm gonna take Lauren along with me in my new life. Nothing, I mean nothing, can stop me.

"You know," says Lauren, "my parents are going out of town next week, so you should stay with me in my house, unless you have somewhere else to go."

"No, no," I say, everything fitting together perfectly in my world, in my mind, in destiny, and fate and blah, blah, blah. "That'll be great."

"They're gone for two weeks."

I laugh.

Baker Beach is mostly empty. We pull into the parking lot and look out at the pounding shore break, sucking up the brown, coarse sand and dashing it to pieces against the slick, jagged rocks. The Golden Gate Bridge looms up to the right, and across the channel are the Marin Headlands—lush, green, rolling hills dotted with eucalyptus and oak, the red earth cliffs dropping down to the swirling water below. We get out of the car and I take Lauren's cold little soft hand in mine. We walk down along the dunes and the wind is blowing sand in my face, and suddenly I stop and strip off all my clothes down to my boxer briefs and run, headlong, into the surf. I hear Lauren giggling behind me, then nothing but the roar of the ocean and the cold, cold, cold.

The current is strong and I'm immediately struggling against it, ducking the swells and feeling the pull out the mouth of the bay. But I'm a good swimmer. I navigate past the rocks and begin paddling into the waves as they break along the beach. Growing up I'd surfed all along this coastline. My friends and I would stay out sometimes five or six hours. In the end I'd gotten very comfortable in the water, able to ride the big waves off Ocean Beach or down in Santa Cruz. I'd watch the pelicans riding the updrafts of the swells, or sea otters eating crabs, floating on their backs. I'd wake up early, heading out before the sun rose to get the morning glass. But as I got deeper and deeper into my using, my surfboards went untouched on their racks in the garage. I lost interest. There's something devastating about that, though I try not to think about it.

I mean, here I am, bodysurfing the breakers at Baker Beach, feeling my breath catch in my lungs from the frigid water. The muscle memory is all there, in my arms and chest. I look back at Lauren, stripped and lying in the warm sand. I take another wave in, then run up to her, kissing the white of her stomach and listening to her laugh and shiver. Then I run on, up and down the beach. Fast, freezing, but not feeling it, really. I look at everything, the trees, and shells, and tall sea grass. It all seems so new and exciting. My little sister, Daisy, never failed to point out the delicate flowers or intricately shaped stones as we went on walks together. She was so present and filled with wonder. Meth gives me that childlike exuberance. It allows me to see, to really see. The world appears miraculous and I laugh and run down the beach until I'm gasping for air—then back to Lauren.

She smiles at me and I kiss her some more.

That night I drive her car through the winding back roads out to our house in Point Reyes. The drive is so familiar. I know every turn. It's the same route I'd used to get back from school every afternoon. We pass the little towns of San Anselmo and Fairfax, curving beneath the redwood forest of Samuel P. Taylor State Park. Then we come out on the green pastureland, obscured by the darkness and fog. We turn up our street, steep, steep, bordered by dense woods on either side. The car sputters some, but makes it—taking me home.

My parents' house isn't huge or anything, but it is designed by some famous architect. It's sort of very Japanese and minimalist, with mirrors and windows all over the place. It looks out on maybe half an acre of garden—wild, tangled vines, hedges, oaks, poplars. Gravel paths twist through the brush and in the spring and summer there are flowers everywhere.

Seeing that the driveway is empty and the lights are out, I creep along to the different doors and windows and things. It's all locked. I climb the faded wooden gate, wander over to the back doors until I find one that isn't dead-bolted solid. I yank it open, breaking the base of the door where it has been secured to the floor. Turning on as few lights as possible, I go through the house to the front and let Lauren in.

"Jesus," she says. "I remember these paintings."

My stepmother is an artist. The walls of our house are covered with giant, swirling canvases. The oil images are dark yet organic—eyes, organs, branches, shapes repeated over and over.

"They're beautiful," I say. "So haunting, right?"

"Yeah."

We go up to the living room and I put music on the stereo—some electronic stuff I left the last time I'd been home. I open a bottle of sake I find in the closet and pour a glass. Lauren looks at all the art books and things on the shelves. I look at the photographs of my little brother and sister on the windowsill. There is one of Jasper in his lacrosse uniform, smiling. There is Daisy, who's just two years younger than Jasper, dressed as an elf, with a fake beard and her tangled hair pulled back. And there is the whole family together, my stepmom, her parents, brother, sister, my dad, my aunt and uncle, my brother, sister, cousins, and, on the far right, me. Walking through the house, I feel dirty—like I'm this charcoal stain polluting everything I touch. I can't even look at the goddamn photographs—it hurts too much. I drink the sake down.

"Let's go take a shower," I say.

"Yeah. You wanna fix some more first?"

"Definitely."

We shoot up and take a shower. We have sex in my old bed until my knees are rubbed raw. After that, I smoke cigarettes and look for stuff to steal. I take a guitar and a couple jackets, but nothing bigger than that. Oh, and I need a notebook, so I grab this black thing with Powerpuff Girls stickers on the cover. It turns out to be my sister's diary.

DAY 4

We spend the night in some kitschy Art Deco motel off Lombard—the outside all mosaicked with bright-colored tiles. Lauren doesn't actually stay past midnight. Her parents were worried and wondering where she is. I listen to her talking with her father on the phone. Her voice trembles—wanting desperately to sound . . . what, innocent? Something like that. Of course, there'd been times when I'd done the same thing—lying about being sober, trying to hide the fact that I'd relapsed. Lauren is able to convince her parents—at least for now. They believe her, I suppose, because they want to. My parents had been that way.

I got thrown into my first treatment center when I was eighteen. I had been doing meth for only about six months, but already my life had begun falling apart. I dropped out of college and ended up having a sort of breakdown—wandering the streets and talking to people who weren't there. I didn't really come out of it until a police car was pulling up beside me. The officer threatened to arrest me but eventually let me go.

My dad helped me get into rehab five days later—a large, Victorian-style, falling-down mansion on Fell and Steiner. I still remember walking in there that first day. It had threadbare red carpeting, a rotted, creaking stairway, and long, misshapen, warped hallways leading to room after room of beds, beds, beds. There must have been around fifty of us in that house—all men. We had groups all day where we were educated about substance abuse, twelve steps, and how to live life sober. Walking through those green-painted wooden doors, my whole body was shaking and I felt like maybe I'd throw up or something. My dad was there beside me, wearing that same old wool sweater he used to shelter me in as a child. His hair was clipped short, black and gray. His square glasses obscured his eyes, which were red from almost crying. Maybe he was shaking too.

"Dad, please," I begged him. "I'll stop, I promise. Please, I don't need to do this."

"You can't come home, Nic."

"But Dad, I don't belong here."

I was wrong. I knew it the first group I went to. One of the residents, Johnny, a squat little man with scraggy facial hair and a dyed black Mohawk, told his story. He talked about his descent into crack/cocaine addiction. What struck me wasn't so much the specifics of his story, but rather the feelings he described. He talked about how until he started using, he had always felt like some alien, different from everybody. I think what he said was, "I felt like everyone else had gotten this instruction manual that explained life to them, but somehow I'd just missed it. They all seemed to know exactly what they were doing while I didn't have a clue. That is, until I found drugs and alcohol. Then it was like my world suddenly went from black-and-white to Technicolor."

Of course that had been my experience too, but it didn't mean I was willing to change my behavior. I loved drugs. I loved what they did for me. They relieved me of that terrible sense of isolation I had always felt. They gave me the manual to life that Johnny had described. I could not, NOT give that up.

But my parents were so hopeful and the counselors would give you more privileges if you cooperated, so I did. I said what they wanted me to say. I shared about my commitment to repairing the damage I had caused. I talked about being willing to adopt the spiritual principles outlined in the twelve steps. And I suppose part of me meant it. I didn't want to become like some of the other men at Ohlhoff House, grizzled, toothless, having lost everything. But I still had this feeling like it could never happen to me. I had a 4.0 in high school, for Christ's sake. I was a published writer. I came from a good family. Besides, I was too young to really be an addict. I was just experimenting, right?

They released me thirty days later and I moved into a halfway house in the city. I stayed sober three days. Then, one night, I said I was going to a meeting, but drove to hook up crystal instead. The car just seemed to drive itself across the bridge to Oakland. I never came back that night. When my parents found out, I was forced to go into another thirty-day program in Napa. After that I managed to stay clean for over a month, but when I went away to college in Amherst, Massachusetts, I quickly relapsed again. This time, however, I was able to hide it from my parents. As my behavior grew more erratic (stealing credit cards, writing checks to myself) and my lies more improbable (I just wanted to buy presents for Jasper and Daisy), my dad continued to dismiss what was happening—I was wasting away in front of him.

By the time I finished my first year of school, my using had progressed to the point where I could no longer really hide it. At first it was just drinking and smoking pot, a little acid, but then I started asking around to get my hands on some meth. But since there was no crystal I could find in western Massachusetts, I started using heroin. I'd drive my girlfriend's car into the slums of Hollyhock and just walk around till the offers started coming in. There was little doubt as to what a young white kid was doing wandering those streets. But the drug was expensive and snorting the white granulated powder was a waste.

That was my excuse to start sticking myself with needles. Putting the drug straight into the vein allowed me to conserve it a little more. I stole the syringes from the science lab. I taught myself to shoot up by looking at a diagram on the Internet. It was a messy process. I'd miss the vein and pump the drug right into my muscles. It would burn so bad. I didn't realize the veins were just under the skin's surface, so I'd dig way too deep. Before long, my arms were covered in puncture marks and I'd lost a lot of weight.

When I came home for summer vacation, I had my first experience with opiate withdrawals. It was just like in the movies—I was throwing up, shivering, sweating, scratching at my skin like there were termites crawling underneath.

At first I tried lying to my parents, saying I had a stomach flu or something. The first moment I could get away, I went to get some meth from my friends in the city.

Once I started IVing that drug, well, that was pretty much the end. After being off crystal for so long, my tolerance had gone back to nothing. Shooting it, the effect was so powerful, I plunged immediately into a period of about a week where, to this day, I have no idea what I did.

I came to out of this blackout in my bed at my parents' house. I could hear crying from the living room. My little brother's voice was shattered by tears.

"Where is it? Where is it?"

I felt that familiar sickness in my stomach.

"Are you sure it was in there?" my dad asked.

"Yes," wailed Jasper. "I had five dollars in there. Daisy, you took it."

"NO, I DIDN'T!" She was crying too and screaming.

I got out of bed and started to pack. I didn't remember taking the money, but I knew I had.

There was nowhere for me to go, really, but I couldn't stay. I filled my bag with as much as I could carry. I hoisted it on my shoulder, put my eyes on the floor, and started walking out of there.

Out in the living room, my dad and stepmom stood blocking my exit—their faces red and contorted.

"Where are you going?" my father demanded, on the verge of yelling.

"I'm leaving."

"Nic, we know you're using again."

"Yeah," I said—my head down. "I'm not coming back."

"This is bullshit," my stepmom exploded, stomping across the room and slamming a door somewhere.

"You can't just leave," my dad said, the tears coming now.

"I have to."

"We'll get you help."

"No. I need to do this."

"Nic, no, stop." He reached out and tried to physically stop me. I pushed him hard.

"What the hell are you doing?" I screamed. "Jesus Christ, you people suffocate me."

The truth was, I didn't want to stop. It's not like I enjoyed stealing or hurting my dad, or whatever. I mean, I hated it. But I was so scared of coming off the drugs. It was like this horrible vicious cycle. The more I used, the more I did things I was ashamed of, and the more I had to use so I never had to face that. When I reached a certain point with my drug use, going back just seemed like too far a journey. Accepting responsibility, admitting guilt, making restitution, hell, just saying I'm sorry—it had become too daunting. All I could do was move forward and keep doing everything in my power to forget the past. So I marched out into the hot summer air. I hitchhiked to the bus stop and made my way to my friend Akira's.

After that my parents really stopped believing anything I said. But Lauren obviously hasn't taken things as far as I have. Her parents are still willing to give her the benefit of the doubt or something. So she leaves me alone in that motel room and I write and draw for a while, listen to CDs, then actually sleep a few hours. When I wake up, I'm hungry and almost out of meth. I call Gack and he agrees to meet me at twelve thirty in the TL. I drive to North Beach to get breakfast.

———

When I was little, maybe six or seven, my dad and I lived at the top of California Street. It was a high-rise apartment that looked out on the cable cars and the gothic towers of Grace Cathedral. It was across the street from a small park with a sandbox, swings, and a wooden play structure. My dad would take me there to play in the mornings, then we'd walk together down to North Beach—the Italian district of San Francisco. We'd go to Caffe Trieste, a rustic coffee shop on the corner of Grant. I would hold his calloused hand and watch the pigeons and the cracks in the sidewalk. Inside the café, my dad would order me hot chocolate and a raspberry pastry ring. We would sit at a corner table—me drawing and my father writing in a notebook. He would drink cappuccinos. Sometimes we wouldn't write or draw at all; we'd just talk. I'd run my fingers over the mosaicked tabletop and smell the coffee and ask my dad questions about things. He would make jokes and tell me stories. Opera would play from the jukebox.

After breakfast maybe we'd walk over to City Lights Books—a damp, earthy-smelling printing house and bookshop. We'd walk past the sex show parlors and strip bars. After dark, women in tight leather costumes would hang around in front of the entrances, luring in passing johns. I remember thinking they were superheroes—Wonder Woman, Catwoman, Supergirl. I would talk with them and they all knew my name.

Driving through North Beach this morning, I look out at the

streets of my childhood. I stop my car and walk up to Caffe Trieste. Men and women stand outside talking and smoking. The sky has opened up blue and clear—the wind blowing hard off the bay. I go inside and order some coffee and a sandwich. I sit in the back at the same old table—the same old music coming from the speakers. I shoot up the last of the gram in their bathroom. The place is small and poorly lit. Someone keeps banging on the door 'cause it's taking me so long to find a vein. Once I hit, I start to pump in the mixture, but my hand shakes and I shoot a bunch of it into the muscle of my arm. It burns something terrible and I groan in pain. My whole right arm goes numb and aches. I curse loudly and go to meet Gack. There is blood all over my arm when I walk outta there.

Gack has me meet him in front of the hotel where he lives with his dad. It is named after some saint, but it looks like hell—barred windows, the paint peeling down to nothing, stripped away. He has a teener for me. I ask him if he wants to shoot some up with me right then, since I pretty much wasted the last one. He agrees and we go inside.

The woman who runs the hotel is Indian and wears a traditional sari, with a bindi on her forehead and everything. She makes me give her my driver's license in order to go up. She scowls through her thick, oversize glasses, her hair pulled back tight.

"You stay only one hour. Otherwise you pay."

I follow Gack up the rotted-out, stained, carpeted stairs, to the third floor. Hollowed-out men and women pace the halls, smoking cigarettes and calling out to us with offers of different crap we can buy.

"Hey, kids," says a stoned-out-looking black man with a bald, shiny head. "I gotta get rid of this keyboard. You wanna buy it?" He holds up a small electric piano out for us to see.

"Does it work?" asks Gack.

"Yeah, man, it works good. You wanna try it out?"

"Sure. Nic, you gotta second?"

"Sure, sure, fine, whatever."

We follow the man back to his room. What it looks like is, **23** well, just trashed. The bed has no sheets or anything and it looks like it is covered in dried blood. The floor is all ash and wrappers and porno mags and beer cans and tinfoil and videotapes. The man introduces himself as Jim. He shakes our hands. He clears off some clothes from the bed. He plugs the piano in, switches it on, and plays a simple chord progression, singing some R & B love song. His voice is deep and moving.

"Right on. How much?" asks Gack.

"Twenty."

"Twenty?"

"All right, ten. Look, man, I just wanna get high, that's all. Ten bucks'll get me through the night."

"All right, ten bucks."

Gack hands him the money. Somehow he manages to pull exactly ten dollars out of his pocket, without exposing the rest of his wad. The man takes the money quickly and stuffs it in his jeans. "Right on, right on."

We walk back out into the hallway and into Gack's room.

"This is so great," says Gack, holding up the keyboard.

"Yeah, that'll be fun to mess around with."

"No, man, you don't understand. This is a start, a first step in recognizing my dream. I'm gonna start making music."

I don't know what to say about that.

Gack's room is even more trashed than Jim's was. Gay porn and cigarette butts and ripped paper and wrappers and shoes and jars of peanut butter and boxes of cookies are scattered all over the floor and bed. There is a washbasin in one corner filled with dishes. A computer put together with mismatching parts sits on the dresser. The fluorescent lights shine too bright and buzz overhead. Gack sets about clearing off a space to try out the keyboard.

"Hey, man," I say. "You got any more rigs or what?"

"Yeah. There are some cleans in that bag over there." He points to a brown paper bag on the bedside table.

I reach over and find the needles and set about making us two big-ass shots. Gack asks if I want him to shoot me up. I hold out my arm and he inserts the point effortlessly and efficiently right into my vein. There is something chilling and erotic about the whole thing. He pumps the drug up inside me and I cough and feel the rush and it is so lovely, I mean, really.

Gack shoots himself up and I say, "Hey, you wanna walk around with me or something?"

"Walk around?"

"Yeah, man, I've been away from the city for, like, over two years."

"All right, cool."

We walk back down the stairs. I get my ID back from the Indian woman and then we're out on the street, moving fast down toward the water.

"Was that really your dad the other day?" I ask, just trying to think of something to say.

Gack stuffs his hands in his pockets, his arms jerking convulsively. "Yeah, man."

"You live together?"

"Uh, yeah. I never knew him until a year ago. I was adopted when I was, like, two or something."

"Weird, man. How'd you all hook up again?"

"I guess he just decided he wanted to meet me, so he came and found me at my adopted parents' house."

"And you just went to go live with him?"

"Yeah. He's pretty cool. Sometimes he'll bring guys back to the room, which is kinda fucked up."

"Guys?"

"Uh-huh. He's gay."

We walk on. The clouds are blowing fast overhead and I keep smoking cigarettes and bumming them out to Gack. Gack talks a lot of nonsense about different things—his plans for the future, things like that. I'm not sure where the idea to ask Gack to help me comes from. Suddenly I just trust him completely and

I come out with it, walking down Market—toward the shadow of the Bay Bridge.

"Look, man," I say. "I'm just puttin' this out there—so hear me out for a second. I've got about twenty-five hundred dollars left, okay. I'd been sober eighteen months, working, and I saved that up. Now, with a habit like I've got, I'm gonna burn through that pretty quick, unless I can figure out some way to make some money. So here's what I was thinking. I don't really know you, right? And you don't know me, but you've been cool to me so far and I have this feeling about you."

"You felt it too, huh?" he says, stopping to pick up a crumpled bag on the sidewalk. He looks inside, finds nothing, and then throws it down again.

"Yeah," I say.

"I knew we were gonna be friends."

"What?"

"Yep, when I saw you that first day."

"Maybe I did too. Look, you know, I really respect you and all and I was just thinking we could buy, like, some big quantity of meth and then break it down and sell it together."

"Word. We should cut it."

"Cut it?"

"Yeah, man. We'll buy a bunch of really good shit, then cut it with, like, Epson salts or something. I'll sell that shit so fast, man, and we'll be able to use for free, maybe get a place to stay. I could, like, work for you. We could start our own syndicate, man. We'll get walkie-talkies and shit."

"Well, just think about it, man."

"Fo'sure."

"And you know someone that could get us quantity for pretty cheap?"

"I think so. Let me just make some calls. You wanna do this now?"

"Well, uh, all right, sure. And, hey, do you know where I can get some heroin?"

"No doubt. What you want me to work on first?"

"The H, I guess."

"Cool, brother. Let me see your phone. Bullet'll be able to help us out."

"Bullet?"

"Yeah. I'll page him."

"Word."

"Just let me get another cigarette."

I give him two.

———

Bullet is homeless. He is tall and thin, thin, with a carved-up face and greasy hair slicked back. His nose is sort of twisted and broken. There's an off-white scar running down his face and his Adam's apple sticks out dramatically. He wears a backward base-ball hat, loose-fitting pants, combat boots, and he smells like stale sweat and urine. His walk is clumsy, with those spindly legs of his and a head that is continuously bobbing back and forth.

"Gack, man, how come you never call me?" He whines when he talks—always.

"Dude, I've been busy."

"But you guys wanna score some dope, huh?"

"Yeah," I say.

"Well, I got a number—but maybe we could work out a deal or something before I give it up."

Gack and I drove to meet Bullet at the Safeway on Church and Market. It is a well-known hangout for street kids and run-aways. For one thing, you can go into Safeway and graze out of the dried fruit and nut bins without too much trouble. Plus there is one of those private, self-cleaning toilets out front that is great to shoot up in. It is already getting to be dark and the lights on Twin Peaks are flickering on and off, on and off.

"A deal like what?"

"Like you give me a nice fat shot in exchange for the hookup."

"No problem."

"The girl's name is Candy. Here's the number. Don't lose it." He writes it on the front page of my sister's diary that I've stolen. There is a drawing of a girl with pigtails pointing at blotchy squares on a wall. Underneath it, Daisy'd written: "We are in L.A. with Nic. We went to a museum. We saw Napoleon things." That had been this past January, just two months earlier. My family had driven down to see me and we'd all gone to the Museum of Jurassic Technology on Venice Boulevard. Daisy went on to describe the museum and what she ate for lunch. Then she wrote something about seeing me and how I looked sad. She said it made her stomach feel all "fluddery."

Reading it, I know just how she felt. My stomach feels fluddery. I wonder if there might be a way to get the diary back to her. It was the last thing I ever wanted to take from her and yet, well, I did it. That's always how it goes for me, isn't it?

Anyway, I call Candy. Her voice is so soft I can barely hear her, but I manage to convince her to meet me at the video store around the corner. She shows up in a yellow Cadillac with a tattered fur coat and dyed black hair that is light at the roots. She wears thick pancake makeup over broken-out skin. She is probably around thirty-something.

"You want two grams, right?"

"Yeah."

She hands me four tiny balls wrapped in colored wax paper. I give her eighty bucks.

"This is great," she says. "Do you always buy this much at one time?"

"I guess."

"Well, call me any time."

When I get back to my car, Bullet and Gack are hanging out, laughing and making fun of each other.

"Gack told me your plan," says Bullet. "You guys are gonna start your own little dealing syndicate, huh?"

"Sort of."

"Well," he says. "You'll never be able to do it without my help."

"Why?"

"'Cause every crime syndicate needs some muscle." And with that, he pulls out a giant bowie knife from somewhere and waves it through the air.

I suck in a bunch of breath all at once.

"You got that junk?" he demands.

"Yeah."

"Well, let's go then." He puts the knife away and we drive down some side street to shoot up.

Gack doesn't want any heroin, but he sits with us. I melt down half a gram of the sweet-smelling black tar in the jar I took from Lauren's. We suck up the syrupy brown liquid in two needles and push it all home. I wait: one, two, three, four. My head starts to tingle and I feel waves of pulsing calm sweep over me. My body goes slack and I look over at Bullet. He is smiling so big. I drift off somewhere for a minute. It is like everything is infused with this warmth and okayness. I laugh. "Shit's good."

"Word."

"So, Gack," I say. "Should we let Bullet in?"

"Hell yeah, man, he's a good kid."

"That what you want, Bullet?"

"I'm your boy."

"Awesome."

"We should come up with a name or something," says Gack. "We're gonna start the next big street gang in San Francisco. Before long, we'll have all the kids workin' for us."

We sit back, talking on like that. I nod in and out, not giving a damn about one goddamn thing—knowing, just knowing, that it is all gonna work out.

We drop Bullet off around two a.m. He has to meet some guys about a bike theft racket. Basically they just go around with bolt cutters, break all the locks, and pile the bikes into an old van. It's risky, but Bullet needs the money and he's strong and quick.

Gack and I have nowhere to go, so I ask if he wants to drive out to Point Reyes with me. We've shot a little more speed to clear my head from the H and I feel real balanced out. I'm having fun taking the tight, winding turns through the redwoods. We're listening to this Japanese punk rock music really loud and maybe Gack doesn't like it, but I don't care.

Gack has half a joint, which we split, and the weed on top of everything is making me hallucinate pretty good. The road is all green and pink tracers. The branches hanging down are twisting, knotted veins—spider lattices, a crawling insect sky. Every time a car passes from the other direction I'm swallowed in the bright, bright lights. I swerve, but hang on.

We're laughing and talking as we pull into the driveway, but then I see my parents' car there. The house is dark, but they must be inside.

"Fuck."

"I thought you said they wouldn't be here?"

"I guess my little brother and sister don't have school tomorrow."

I wonder if they can tell I've been there—if they've noticed the missing guitar and things, or the back door I broke open. I wonder about it for a minute sitting there, feeling sick to my stomach. I imagine them walking in, looking around—those first moments of doubt and realization.

"Did you leave that towel there?"

"Did you drink that bottle of wine?"

"Were you in Nic's room?"

"Whose shoes are these?"

"Oh my God, someone's been in the house."

I pull the car out of there quick, feeling more guilty and humiliated than anything else. I try to push that all out of my mind though, saying, "It's cool. I know where we can go."

We head out farther along the point, past the town of Inverness. The salt-crusted buildings are all nearly rotted through and breaking apart. The old, rust-colored Inverness Store sits in the middle of the town's only block. They have everything from groceries to clothing to videos. I remember going there with my friends after school, getting high, and playing the one arcade game they had for hours. We pumped so many quarters into that thing. I try to relate something along those lines to Gack, but he's actually fallen asleep for a minute, so I drive on.

Virginia and Adam's house is empty. They're like my parents in that they have a weekday home in the city, and a weekend home out on the coast. Seeing that there's no car in the driveway I really breathe for the first time since leaving my parents' house. I'm so tired suddenly and all I want to do is sleep. Gack and I get out and wander around the back of the creaking wooden house, trying to find a place to break in.

Virginia and Adam are my parents' best friends, or, at least, they're really close and all. I guess I'm pretty close to them too. They have two kids. The older boy, Jessie—with blond, blond hair, a long curious face, and wide-gapped teeth—is exactly my little brother's age and they're in the same class at school. His younger brother, Trevor—with equally blond hair—is exactly my little sister's age. Our two families would go to the beach together, build bonfires in the sand, barbecue hot dogs and things. I would tell stories to all the children. I was always telling stories.

We would play tag on the beach, swim together in the stinging-cold ocean. The kids would all attack me and I'd have to fight them off—but gently. I remember genuinely looking forward to those nights together. We'd all go back to our house and play music, like the Talking Heads or something, and dance, dance, dance.

Adam is in his early forties and is a brilliant graphic designer.

Virginia is a writer and so sweet. We talked about movies and
books and art and everything. I watched them take so much interest in their kids' lives. I watched them devote themselves to those
children. They gave so much, you know?

"Hey," says Gack. "Come in here." Somehow he's gotten
inside and has the back door open and is looking around, nervous,
like someone might see.

I go in and we turn some lights on. The house is small—all
wood floors, tattered throw rugs, and worn-out leather furniture.
It is sparse but elegant—simple. We eat some cereal they have
in the cupboard and spread out on the two couches. We talk for
a while, saying nothing important. Eventually I fall asleep. I don't
dream. It's all just black.

"Nic, quick, get up." Gack is shaking me hard.

"Wh-what?"

"There's someone here."

The blurred morning light softly fills the living room and
I look out on the thick bramble outside—wet and frosted with
dew. There are some birds making shrill noises somewhere and
then I hear it—heavy footsteps in the kitchen. Instantly I'm on my
feet and we're walking as silently as possible toward the door. I
feel sick and high from adrenaline and fear. Behind us I hear the
footsteps coming faster and then a man's voice calling out with a
thick Hispanic accent.

"Hey, you, kids, stop."

We don't. We run to my car and jump in fast, starting the
motor as the man keeps yelling after us. There's a whole crew of
construction workers standing around the front of the house and
they're all staring at us as we drive off, looking at us with unveiled
scorn—or is it pity? Either way, I'm not laughing and neither is
Gack.

We drive not saying anything, still out of breath. It's so cold
that I'm shivering and I crank the heat up all the way. The Tomales
Bay opens up gray and still in front of us, the sun just starting to
rise above the distant green knuckle of Elephant Mountain. The

sky is wrapped in thick white clouds. I smoke a cigarette and give one to Gack without him asking for it. I pull into the town of Point Reyes and stop next to the Bovine Bakery. Gack rolls his eyes. "Come on, man, let's get back to the city. This country shit is trippin' me out."

"I'm just getting some coffee. You want some?"

"Coffee, man, I don't drink that crap. Shit'll rot your stomach out."

I laugh at that and go inside. I bring Gack some hot chocolate instead and he seems pretty grateful for it. That bakery was where I used to get picked up for car pool every morning before school. I loved the croissants there, hot and fresh with chocolate insides that got all over the place. We'd meet there every morning at seven fifteen. The different parents of the kids who lived out in Point Reyes would take turns driving into the city. It was a long drive, so sometimes we'd listen to books on tape, or play guessing games, or whatever. When my little brother was born, he would be brought along on the rides and more often than not, he'd end up crying the whole time. We would take turns, the other kids and I, inventing different ways of distracting him—quieting him, making him smile, or getting his attention so he would just stare at you with his wide-open eyes. We had songs we'd sing to him. Everyone was so patient. He became the car pool mascot. I think we all missed him the days he wasn't there.

My stepmom drove a lot of the time. I'm not sure how it happened exactly, but one day she just invented this game called the "complaining game." Basically, it was sort of like therapy. We'd get five minutes to complain about what was bothering us. We'd give one another points from zero to ten, based on how honest, insightful, and revealing our shares were. Anyone who cried got an automatic ten. People cried pretty often.

The car pool consisted of three girls and me, all in sixth grade. We'd start playing the complaining game and talk about feeling excluded at a certain birthday party—or the way our teacher gave too much homework. Eventually, however, it would get increasingly personal, with each one of us opening up about our difficulties with our families and things like that. One of the girls, Teresa—who was always so quiet and shy and everything—started talking about her parents' divorce and the hardship of that and how her mom was drinking too much. We all started crying and she was proclaimed the "complaining game" champion of all time.

Of course, when we got to school, no one said anything about anything. I'd go off to play with my friends and the girls would all go play with theirs. We wouldn't talk. Sometimes I'd see one of them getting picked on and I'd do nothing to stop it. If someone in my group of friends was mean to them, I'd go along with it. And the girls were the same way. But in the car, with my stepmom driving, we were transformed—wide open, like my little brother's eyes.

So Gack and I pull out from in front of the Bovine with coffee and croissants and hot chocolate—when I almost hit this blue Volvo station wagon coming the other way. I slam on the brakes and lock eyes with the driver. She has black hair coming down over her face, but I recognize her. My stepmom. She sees me and I see her and I back out of there so quick. She honks her horn wildly and speeds off after me. I drive recklessly over the road, but she is behind me—chasing me down.

"What the fuck is going on?"

"Dude, that's my stepmom."

"Well, why the hell is she following us?"

"Fuck if I know."

"Maybe you should stop and talk to her."

"No way, man."

In the rearview mirror I can see her expression. It is strangely blank—resigned or something. I try hard not to meet her eyes, thinking about how disappointed she must be in me. My dad and Karen were married when I was eight years old. They'd met the year earlier. I've always respected Karen so much—as a person, as a parent to me, as an artist. I remember watching *Pollyanna* with her when my dad was out of town. It was the first time we were together, me and her, just the two of us. I think we both thought the movie was pretty stupid and we would crack each other up for months afterward doing Hayley Mills imitations. Karen took me on hikes with her and her friends around Marin. She took me to galleries and out to dinner. She read stories with me and bought me comic books. I respected her and, well, I've always wanted her respect, you know, just so badly. I've always wanted her to like me, mostly because I like her so much. But how can Karen respect me now? I am ashamed of myself and, for a moment, I can't even remember why I'm doing any of this. What is the point? I guess it's crystal meth. I mean, that's always the bottom line, isn't it? That's the ultimate trump card for me. It is more powerful than anything.

As we drive, I look out at the eucalyptus and buckeyes that line the road out to Stinson Beach. The grasses grow up wild and unkempt along Route 1. I'm giving my car everything it's got, screeching around the corners, but Karen stays pretty close. We pass the bat house—a white-painted shack in the middle of a field with the doors and windows all boarded up. They can't tear it down because it's been taken over by species of bats that exist nowhere else in the world. The sun is up and the clouds are all gone and the wet road is drying quickly underneath us. I take the next turn a little too quickly. My back tires slide out and I almost spin.

"This is so bad," says Gack. "This is so fucking bad."

"Relax," I say, but I'm anything but relaxed.

The gears of my car are grinding and I'm starting to smell the rubber burning. The heat gauge is way up there. We go through Dogtown, past the Horseshoe Hill Road turnoff. The coastal town of Bolinas sits off to the northeast. That was where I learned to surf. The waves there roll into the lagoon gently—perfect for beginners. We'd surf out at the point and then go eat pizza at the Bolinas Bakery. When my little brother and sister were old enough, we'd take them out in the water and push them into the

shore break on an old, heavy longboard. We'd play road tag on
the beach—where you'd draw trails in the sand that you had to
run in. If you left the trail you were out.

And here Karen and I are—playing road tag on the broken,
jagged highway. Smoke is billowing up from the hood of my car.
I round a bend and lose the Volvo for a moment, turning up a
heavily wooded driveway. I swing the car around and let it idle
there. We wait.

"I need a shot," says Gack.

"Yeah." My shirt is soaked through with sweat. My hair is wet,
sticking up.

"Should we wait here?" I ask.

"Okay."

I see my stepmom's car go by—slow, slow. She doesn't look
up at us. She keeps moving. I turn off the car. It hisses loudly.

Gack dissolves a huge amount of crystal in the jar. After he
pulls some up for himself, I add a bunch of heroin. I let Gack shoot
me up. He's so good at hitting me. Everything is all better after the
tar and meth enters my bloodstream. I'm not even sure if that car
chase was a dream—or real. But my smoking car answers that
question.

Everyone knows I've relapsed now.

———

I drop Gack off in the TL and we make plans to meet up in a day
or so. He says he'll start feeling out for people looking to sell some
quantity. I turn on my cell phone. I have twenty-seven messages.
I listen to the first second or so of each one, then delete them. My
stomach has dropped out completely and there's a cold tingling
up the back of my neck. I think about Spencer, my mom, my dad,
my job, and friends I left behind. I wonder if I really have come too
far to go back. Yes, I reason, I have. Besides, things aren't so bad.
It's not like I owe those people anything. This is my life to live—or
throw away. Isn't that true? I tell myself again that it is.

The only message I hear all the way through is one from Lauren. She wants me to come by after she has dinner with her parents. She says I can sneak in through the back gate and maybe no one'll see me. I have a while to wait, so I drive down to Baker Beach and go swimming again in the ocean. I bring my leather toiletry kit over to the men's room. I shower outside with my shorts on and then step into the sand-covered bathroom, setting up my shaving equipment along the dark-stained sink.

I have a nice razor and one of those bristled facial brushes from L'Occitane. I have a silver dish of shaving soap. I get the hair off my face and put lotion all over. I put on deodorant. I splash on some cologne and put some styling product in my hair. I cut my fingernails and toenails. Every once in a while a stunned-looking beachgoer will come in, stare at me, then walk out quickly. Still, by the time I step outta there, I look halfway presentable.

There's something about outward appearances that has always been important to me. I always thought I was so ugly. I mean, I really did. I remember being in L.A. at my mom's house as a little kid and just staring into the mirror for hours. It was like, if I looked long enough, maybe I'd finally be handsome. It never worked. I just got uglier and uglier. Nothing about me ever seemed good enough. And there was this sadness inside me—this hopelessness. Focusing on my physical appearance was at least easier than trying to address the internal shit. I could control the external—at least, to a point. I could buy different clothes, or cut my hair, or whatever. The pit opening up inside me was too frightening to even look at. But I could get a new pair of shoes and, here, I can make sure I'm clean shaven and have good skin.

It's so shallow and ridiculous and I see it, I do, but I'm powerless to change. I mean, I don't know how to change. All I can do is just shoot more goddamn drugs.

I decide that maybe I should try and apply for a part-time job at some coffee shop or something.

I drive to Clement Street—past the imported goods stores and stinking fish markets, the sidewalk dim sum stands and

Chinese bakeries. People are crowded together, talking loudly, walking fast. I go into the Goodwill and buy a forty-dollar Brooks Brothers suit and some nameless black shoes. After that I cross over to the Richmond Branch Library and sign up to use a computer. The wait is about two hours. The place is dingy and so full of bodies that the books and walls themselves smell of sweat. A slick, shining homeless man with layers and layers of clothes sleeps in the doorway. Old women with peroxide hair argue in Russian. A pregnant mother pushes her sleeping child in a blue-checked stroller—back and forth, back and forth.

I smoke cigarettes and wait and scribble in my notebook. I try to write out a resumé so I can type it up once it's my turn. Problem is, I can't really leave any references. My work history is solid and my jobs always start off great, but soon degenerate and end badly. Usually I just stop showing up for work one day. That's what happened at that rehab in Malibu. That's what happened with the six jobs before that. Actually, I've never seen a job all the way through to the end—not even in sobriety. I always get so overwhelmed trying to do everything perfectly. I can't do a job and not put everything I have into it. I need to be the best employee, the best coworker, the best whatever. I need everyone to like me and I just burn out bending over backward to make that happen. Having people be mad at me is my worst fear. I can't stand it. There is this crazy fear I have of being rejected by anyone—even people I don't really care about. It's always better to leave them first, cut all ties, and disappear. They can't hurt me that way—no one can. That's why I have no references. But, of course, there's always the hope that my new employer won't check them out.

After printing out about twenty copies of my resumé, I drive over to the different business districts. I drop the resumés off at all the coffee shops and restaurants I come across. No one seems real interested. A couple of places give me times to come back for interviews.

I drive through the financial district as I make my way down to the wharves. I park my car and look out on the white, beaten-down lighthouse of Alcatraz. The sky is quickly fading orange as the sun sets behind the horizon and a strong wind whips in across the bay. I pull on a jacket and sit drawing in my car for a while, until the light is gone completely. I sleep, curled up on the front seat as best I can. I sleep until my phone rings and I hear Lauren's voice.

"Come over, the back gate is open."

I listen to music really loud as I drive to Sea Cliff, hiding my car several blocks away from her house 'cause I'm paranoid all of a sudden. Plus when I try to push open the tall wooden gate, there's a brick holding it closed. I push harder and the thing gives, but the noise I figure probably wakes up the whole neighbor-hood. Still, I make it to the back door, which is unlocked, and into Lauren's room without her parents finding me. We kiss for a long time and speak in whispers. She's jonesing pretty bad, so I start cooking up a shot for us both.

"You ever done heroin?" I ask.

She shakes her head.

"You wanna try some?"

She nods. I add a good-size chunk of dope to the mix.

Lauren watches me closely. I soak it all up with some cotton and then draw a little bit into both needles. I'm kinda worried about giving her too much 'cause it's her first time and all. I pass her one of the loaded rigs and she digs around in her arm for a while with it, finally hitting.

She draws some blood up into the mix and then pushes it all into her arm. I watch it sweep over her. She goes slack, kind of—her breath rushing out. She puts her small white hand against her small white forehead and leans back, almost falling. She catches herself, straightens up—then starts almost falling again. I laugh, watching her.

I shoot myself up and we go over to the bed. There are pillows and comforters all over the place. The room is all dark, except for those Christmas lights, and I listen to Lauren's breath

coming through in short little gasps. Her pupils are like nothing—
pinned out. The blue overwhelms them and I am high, high, high.

"We gotta be quiet," she says. Her voice comes out slurred and deep.

I kiss her mouth and it's like I'm pouring into her—or like I'm absorbing her into me. Her tongue is my tongue, her lips my lips, her breath mine. She moans and I whisper, "Shhhhhh."

We kiss like that and then I have her clothes off fast, and mine—taking her nipples in my mouth, kissing her breasts roughly. We start to make love and it's, like, the most perfect, hard, pulsing, organic movement between us. We're so there and not there— drifting on sensations of color and beating hearts and the sweat coming down, down, down.

We go so long the bed is soaked through now with sweat— so much sweat. We're kissing and locked together and it just goes on. We're out of breath, but not. Every sensation is heightened. My hand holding hers is alive, sensual—hot. The bed is shaking and the walls are shaking and the ground and shelves and lamps and everything is shaking down around us and we just don't care—we just don't. I wanna stay like this forever—here with Lauren, high on meth and heroin. It seems like I've reached the pinnacle of my existence and I just don't want it to stop.

Three and a half hours go by. I pull out and see that there is blood all over me. My skin has been chafed away. Still, I can't feel it or anything.

Lauren lights a cigarette. We pass it back and forth between us. I wanna shoot up some more, so I stand and feel all light-headed, like I'm gonna pass out. I look down and I see my body and I'm amazed at how much weight I've already started to lose. My legs are starting to eat away at themselves, my hips are jutting out all dramatically. I teeter my way to the bathroom, piss, then hunt around for the rest of the dope and meth still in that cotton. That's when I hear the knocking.

Someone's knocking at Lauren's bedroom door and I feel this rush of panic. I lock myself in the bathroom and hold my breath. There are voices outside now and I figure, fuck, man, it's over. I see the jar with the cotton in it and a dirty rig. Since we're busted anyway I decide to suck up the rest of it and shoot it before getting thrown outta there—or thrown in jail. I sit on the toilet seat, as quietly as possible, hunting for a vein. I push off. There is a brief moment of, like, "Oh shit," as I fall forward, crashing into the solid glass shower door. I bounce off that, hit the floor, and then it's all black for some time.

DAY 6

Coming to, there's light flooding the bathroom and I'm lying on the tile, shivering. I stand and then my stomach seizes and I vomit into the toilet. I do it again. I choke and my throat burns and the tears and snot are wrenched outta my body. There's no noise outside the bathroom, so after drinking some water from the tap, I turn the lock and sort of crawl my way out into Lauren's room. No one's there. The lights are all out and the sun's coming in.

I put on my clothes and try to sneak out the same way I came in. I reach my hand in my pocket and there's a note there. The writing is scrawled hurriedly—frantic little marks on yellow lined paper.

> *Nic, if you're fucking dead in there, I'm gonna*
> *kill you. Call me IMMEDIATELY when you wake*
> *up. My parents are leaving tomorrow around*
> *one, so you can move your stuff in after that.*
> *Fuck, I hope you're not dead. CALL ME. Lauren.*

———

I wait till I'm well away from that house before dialing her number. Her voice is soft, like she's not supposed to be using her phone or something. The sky is blue, blue, but that San Francisco wind whips the hair around in front of my eyes.

"Nic?"

"Yeah."

"Jesus, what the hell happened to you last night?"

"Nothing. You know, when I heard your dad knocking, I hid in the bathroom. I guess I shot too much dope or something, 'cause I passed out. Didn't you guys hear me when I fell?"

"What are you talking about?"

"When your dad came downstairs."

"Nic, that never happened."

"But I heard it. I heard you talking to him."

"Uh, no, you didn't."

"Fuck."

"Nic, you can't do that again, okay?"

"Yeah, I'm sorry."

"Will you come over tonight?"

"Sure."

"Do you have any more of that . . . you know?"

"Yeah."

"All right, call me later."

I hang up.

It's around five thirty when Gack calls me. I spent most of the day just walking around the avenues, looking for ground scores—money, cigarettes, or whatever else might've been left on the ground. Once I found a black leather kit full of haircutting equipment that had five checks and almost two hundred dollars cash in it. I've found packs of cigarettes, bags of leftovers, even the occasional sack of weed, or coke, or something. Today, however, I find nothing but an Aiwa stereo system that I don't need. Actually, I see a plastic bag tied at the top in front of someone's doorway. I'm hungry and it looks like take-out maybe. I walk quickly past, circle back, then grab the bag and run off. When I round the corner I open it—hoping for some Chinese food, or Thai noodles, or anything really. The bag is full of dog shit—lots of dog shit. I drop the sack and my stomach convulses from the smell.

But, like I said, Gack calls at five thirty and tells me he thinks he's found a hookup for us. He says he can't go into details on the phone, but we agree to meet in the TL around eight. He says to bring three hundred dollars.

"Three hundred?" I say. "That's all?"

"For now, yeah."

I withdraw the money from my account. I've still got more than two thousand dollars, but just barely. My feet hurt from walking all day and I look down at the soles of my Jack Purcell sneakers—the left one has a hole starting to eat its way through the bottom. Still, I keep walking and I know that as soon as I do another shot, I won't feel the pain anymore. It's the same with my throat. As I start to come down a little bit, I can feel that I'm sick. My throat is sore and my nose is filled with snot. I must've gotten a cold somewhere. But crystal will take it all away.

The dark is settling in. The sky glows yellow—pale—anemic from the city lights. The Tenderloin at night is a real horror show. Every three feet someone is accosting you with a plea for a hand-out, or the offer of drugs or sex. The men and women wander the streets and alleys with a threatening, violent want. Takers looking to take, hustlers looking to hustle—all trying to satisfy a craving that is perpetually unsatisfiable. And tonight I'm one of them.

Gack is smoking a cigarette in front of a Carl's Jr. He's listening to music through some headphones. He's wearing the same clothes he always wears.

"What's up, man?" he says, doing some slap/snap hand-shake thing with me. His eyes are all over the place.

"You tell me."

He starts walking fast and I follow.

"All right, so there's this guy, Joe, right? Joe just got outta jail and he's movin' away to somewhere in, like, the deep South—Georgia, or some shit. Joe knows everybody and he says he's gonna hook us up with his connection, so we can start dealing directly from them. He's, like, passing on the torch, right?"

"Cool."

"So we'll just try these hookups out. We'll get three hundred dollars' worth of really good shit. We'll cut it and sell it—set aside maybe half for personal use."

"And you trust this guy?"

"Hell, yeah. I've known him for fucking ever."

"All right, man, so I'm gonna leave it up to you then."

"Word."

I haven't really been paying attention, but somehow we've ended up down this alley with nothing but one flickering light overhead. We stop at a rusted iron gate in front of an apartment complex. Gack pushes a button, says, "Yo, it's Gack," and we're buzzed in.

The hallway is cramped and smells of urine and mold. The carpet is bare, stained, burned. The walls are all uneven, giving the place the feeling of a rocking ship. I steady myself against the dirty brown banister.

A door opens maybe ten yards away. A long-haired man who looks Persian or something—with black, thick eyebrows—steps out into the hall.

"He's in here," he says.

We follow him inside a room the size of a small kitchen. There's a bed, a porno movie playing on the TV, and nothing else. A fat man—probably fifty-five, with a receding hairline—smokes speed from a long glass pipe. He exhales loudly and looks up at us. He shifts back to the far corner of the bed, settling in against the back wall.

"Gack, it's been a long time."

"Yeah, welcome back. This is Nic."

Joe reaches out and shakes my hand. His eyes are gray and glazed over. He has a scruffy beard covering his fleshy cheeks. His lips are wet and thick. He passes me the pipe and I take a hit without wiping it off or anything, even though I want to.

"So, Nic," he says, his voice trembling from the narcotics. "You wanna get into dealing this nasty shit, eh?"

I nod, sitting down on the floor next to the Persian man. Gack leans back on the bed with Joe.

"Gack and I are gonna work together," I say.

"All right, man, but I'd be careful. Anyway, let's get this started. You gotta phone I could borrow?"

I hand him my cell and he makes a few calls. I half listen to his conversation while Gack and I pass the pipe back and forth. The Persian man still says nothing. He doesn't hit the pipe when I offer it to him.

"So someone'll be by within the half hour," says Joe. "These are definitely some folks you wanna be down with. Gack, pay attention, man."

Gack is messing around with a portable CD player—taking it apart with some multi-tool key chain thing. He looks up briefly.

"Let me lay this shit down for y'all. If I'm gonna give you kids my connects, you gotta understand a few things first. Gack, you've always been real straight ahead and Nic, well, if Gack vouches for you, then you're all right with me."

He rambles on for maybe twenty minutes—talking about how you have to never let the other guy get up on you. Bottom line is it's all about money. Never trust anyone. Never do anything out of goodwill. It's all business. Never get sentimental. Never let anyone in. Start off selling small sacks, and as they get more dependent, keep making the sacks smaller. Always keep a weapon on you. The best is something discreet like a skateboard or a pair of drumsticks. Gack argues with him a little, stating that he's always found that being honest gets you further in the long run. Joe dismisses this entirely. He expounds on the virtues of coldhearted bloodthirstiness. I listen and just try and make him like me by nodding every once in a while as though I really get it.

The doorbell sounds and we buzz two large men into the building. One's white, the other looks Latino. The room is so full of bodies now, I'm sweating. The introductions are brief. Joe presents Gack as his successor, they shake hands, pass over a phone number, and that's it. I give them three hundred dollars for a rock of crystal about the size of a golf ball. It looks very pure. They leave and then it's just me and Joe and Gack and the Persian guy, who still hasn't said more than three and a half goddamn words.

I hand the sack to Gack along with two clean rigs, asking him to make us shots to try it out. As Gack is preparing it, Joe starts asking me questions. I tell him my story, maybe being a little too open—saying I got all this money I'm looking to invest. He stares so directly into my eyes while I'm talking, I have to keep looking at the floor.

He waits till Gack shoots me up before he says it. I cough so hard as the shit hits me. My ears just won't stop ringing. I think maybe I'll puke or something it's so strong—but I revel in the intensity. My whole body is paralyzed for a moment. I breathe out for a long time, light a cigarette, laugh. Gack's reaction is pretty much like mine. Shit's very pure, like I thought.

"You like that, huh?" asks Joe.

I nod.

"You know, I can get you some glass that's a whole lot better."

"Really?"

"Hell, yeah. I could do it tonight. How much money can you get?"

"I don't know. Two hundred's my limit, I think."

"Well, that'll be enough to start."

"Okay."

I look over at Gack, try to read his expression, but he's not paying attention. He's back with the damn CD player. The Persian man is leaning against the wall, asleep. Some guy is fucking some girl from behind on the small, grainy TV screen.

"Let me use your phone again."

I hand it over and Joe gets up off the bed. He's even fatter than he seemed sitting down. His stomach hangs way over his belt. He stomps outta the room, down the hall, and I wait. Gack says nothing. I take a notebook out of my bag and start to draw—faces coming out of faces with so many scratchy lines. Joe steps back through the door.

"All set. Let's go to an ATM."

"Cool."

"There's one down the street."

We walk.

Standing and moving after all the meth I've shot and smoked kicks everything screaming into hyperreality. As my blood starts to circulate more quickly, the drug crawls down the different pathways of my body. My nerves are shot. I can feel my toes moving compulsively in my shoes.

The Tres Amigos liquor store has an ATM in the back next to the ninety-nine-cent bags of chips. As I take my card out, Joe leans over and looks at it closely.

"Bank of America, huh? I used to work for them back in the day. They still use the same number sequence? Yup. I got a way with numbers."

"Not me," I say. "I'm horrible at that stuff." I insert the card and type my code in. Joe is standing almost on top of me and I can smell the sweat clinging to his black hooded sweatshirt. Two hundred dollars comes out.

We make our way back to the apartment and Joe is talking a lot. He's going on about the new life he's gonna have in Georgia, or some place like that. He's gonna leave all this behind him—thugging, meth—make a clean break, a fresh start.

I'm encouraging. I nod a lot.

He puts a hand on my shoulder. "You know, kid," he says. "You're all right. You're gonna do fine. Just remember, in this game, you can't trust anyone. You understand me?"

"Yeah," I say.

"Especially in the fucking TL."

———

We go inside and Joe asks to borrow my phone again. I pass it
over.

"This next connect is completely off the hook," he says. "You aren't gonna believe how good his shit is."

He tells me to get the money ready. "Put it on the dresser here."

I do.

Gack looks up suddenly. The Persian guy is still asleep. "Joe, what the hell is going on?"

"Nothing, G, I'm just settin' yer boy up with some more crystal."

"From who?"

"Dude, chill. Hold on a minute, I gotta make one more call." He walks outta the room.

"Something's weird," says Gack. "How much money you get?"

"Two hundred."

"Where is it?"

"There, on the dresser."

"Where?"

I look over. Of course it's gone.

"Fuck, wait here," yells Gack.

He runs off.

I'm just left staring. A sickness burrows into my insides. I wonder if I'll ever see Gack again—if it was all a setup. My phone is gone—all that money. I'm not sure what to do. I start cooking up a huge chunk of black tar heroin. The Persian man jerks awake suddenly.

"What's going on?"

"That guy Joe . . ."

"Yeah."

"You know him well?"

"Sort of."

"He just ripped me off."

"Oh."

"Gack went to go find him—maybe. I don't know. You mind if I shoot some heroin here?"

"No, no—whatever you need. That sucks, man. How much he get?"

I tell him.

"Fuck. I'm Ali, by the way."

"Nic."

He lies back as though trying to sleep against the wall again. I pump all the heroin into my vein. It maybe takes the edge off waiting. I focus on the ceiling fading in and out. Thirty minutes go by.

"All right," I say. "Ali, man, I'm leaving. This is bullshit."

"Yeah," he says, opening his eyes out of a half sleep. "You gotta be more careful, man."

I pack my bag up, sling it over my shoulder, and start outta there. Ali shakes my hand. I feel heat in my eyes—a stinging like maybe I'll cry. The hallway swells and shifts around me. The ripped-out feeling of my insides is overwhelming. But then Gack is calling out to me, just outside the gated stairway.

"Gack, man, fuck."

"Nic, I am so sorry."

"You weren't in on that?"

"No way, man. I fucking swear. Look, here's the deal—Joe took off. I just went home and my dad thinks he'd been there. He stole our computer—my dad is freaking out. He's skipped out now, man. No one knows where he is."

"When did he take the computer?"

"Just now, man; he had a key to our room."

"Gack, this is so not cool."

"I know, man. But look—I was talking to my dad. We're gonna figure this out. He gave me his phone. Already we got someone waitin' to buy a sack. We've gotta break that rock up and slang that shit. We'll make your money back quick."

"And?"

"And whatever extra we make we're gonna give to my dad, cool?"

"I don't know, man. Maybe I should just cut my losses."

"No way. This is gonna work out."

I light a cigarette and I don't offer one to Gack. We're still leaning against the white peeling walls of Ali's building.

"Gack, man, honestly, I'm not sure I can trust you anymore."

He's quiet a minute. "Yeah, I understand. I do. But you gotta believe me, that had nothing to do with me. I've known Joe since I was a kid. I'm telling you, man, he had a key to our place. We all trusted him and he fucked over a lot of people tonight. Everyone's lookin' for him. He's got nowhere to run. I bet we find him before morning—no joke."

"And you had no idea he was gonna rip me off?"

He's quiet again. "Look, at a certain point I, uh, sensed . . . something." He jams his hands in his pockets. "But what was I supposed to say? You just kept going along with everything. You're so open and nice—people are gonna tear you apart. They can sense it here, man. They feed on it. You gotta lot to learn if this is gonna work out."

Now it's my turn to be quiet awhile. "You're right," I say.

"Yeah, man, you gotta stay humble and you gotta watch me, man—you gotta pay attention. Watch what I do—how I act. I keep my mouth shut, man, and I never reveal more than I have to. Like if I have a pack of cigarettes, I never pull out the whole pack. I take out one cigarette and I keep it real discreet. If someone asks, I say I bummed it—even if I don't mind givin' 'em one. You never wanna let on that you have more than anyone else—you got it?"

I nod. Gack actually puts his hand on my shoulder. "Come on, man, let's move."

We do.

———

The first stop we make is at some cheap apartment complex south of Market. The streetlights are burned out and we turn down a back alley into almost total darkness.

There's a hooded figure leaning against the side of a corrugated metal garage door. The deep charcoal orange glow of a cigarette, smoked down to the butt, illuminates his scarred face.

"Excuse me, uh, could you guys spare any change?" he asks as we walk past.

"Bullet?" says Gack.

"Fuck, Gack, Nic, what's up?"

"Dude."

Bullet gets up off the ground and chucks the smoking filter out into the narrow street. He smells bad, like he hasn't changed his clothes in a week. His eyes are lined and creased—heavy, gray. We ask him what he's doing out here and he admits he was just trying to find a place to sleep.

"I'm so tired, man. You guys have any ups for me?"

I wanna say yes and give him speed and everything he wants, but I just shake my head.

"We gotta sell what we got."

Gack tells him the story of Joe ripping us off. Bullet doesn't seem that surprised, really.

"Well, you think I could sleep in your car?" he asks me. "I swear, I won't fuck with anything. I'll lock myself in, man."

I agree, but I won't give him my keys. Instead, I walk back where I parked and let him in. He lies down in the back and grabs one of my sweaters and is immediately asleep. The smell of him fills my car.

"It's pretty weird us running into him," I say to Gack, walking back toward the apartment.

"It's not weird," he says. "That's how it all works, or haven't you figured that out yet?"

I think maybe he's right.

Gack calls up on his dad's phone and a couple minutes later a man comes down and opens the door. We've already broken off what's supposed to be a gram but is obviously way smaller, and put it in the plastic wrapper from my pack of cigarettes. The guy is supposed to give us eighty bucks for it. He looks like he hasn't been outside in years. He has doughy, pale skin and bones protruding from his face. His dark hair is falling out, and he has a red alcoholic nose. His stomach is horribly swollen and he looks almost pregnant. His voice comes out curt and demanding— high-pitched, whiny. We all introduce each other, but I don't remember his name. He leads us through the shabby lobby—walls covered with rusted-out mailboxes—into a loud, clunking, dented elevator.

The doors open and we step inside. The space is cramped and I can smell something like baby powder on the man's pasty skin. He runs a meaty hand through his stringy hair, then reaches out and stops the elevator somewhere between the second and third floor. A light hums sickeningly overhead. Sweat collects on his forehead and runs down along his ears. My breath catches, waiting for something.

"What's up, man?" asks Gack.

"Let's see it," the man says.

Gack pulls out the sack, holding it tightly in his hand.

"Looks small," says the man.

"Whatever, this is fat."

The man stares at Gack. Gack looks right into the man's milky green eyes. The man looks away. He hands Gack a wad of cash.

"Take it, Nic."

I do—stuffing it in my pocket.

Gack passes the sack over and the man turns the elevator back on. It lurches up, bucks, and we struggle our way to the fourth floor.

"Good night, boys," the man says.

He walks out into the hallway and we take the elevator down. We're almost out the front door when I finally take the money out and count it.

"Gack, man, he's twenty short."

"What?"

I show him the three twenty-dollar bills.

"Fuck."

"What do we do?"

"Just, uh, hold on a second."

He dials the guy's number. There's no answer. I squat down and rock on the balls of my feet—holding my knees to my chest.

"Go get Bullet," he says. "Give him a shot, okay? I'll wait here and try and get my dad on the phone."

I walk out into the night, hiking up the collar of my jacket against the damp that's settled in over everything. The blood in my ears is loud, loud, loud and my hands shake. I think about Bullet's big bowie knife and the fat man, smelling of fine powder.

I tap on the window and Bullet starts up.

"What's going on?"

"Hey, unlock the door."

I slide into the front seat and immediately start making up two shots. I put some more heroin in both our rigs, explaining the situation to Bullet. He hoots loudly.

"All right, man, bring it on. We're gonna fuck that guy up."

I swallow something down in my throat.

"You packin' anything?" he asks me.

I laugh. "Bullet, come on, man, I've never even hit anyone before."

He can't figure that one out.

We shoot up and light cigarettes and get ready.

He hands me a screwdriver from his back pocket.

"Hold this," he says. "But if you have to swing it, use the handle side first, got it? We don't wanna actually kill this guy."

I don't think all the heroin in the world could make my stomach stop cramping up on me, but I do manage to lead Bullet back to the man's apartment complex. Gack is still talking on the phone to his dad, but he hangs up when we knock on the door and lets us in. The three of us pace the lobby, talking. Bullet's voice has dropped, like, three octaves since doing that H.

"So my dad says it was probably a mistake."

"Does your dad know which apartment is his?" I ask.

Gack shakes his head.

Bullet thinks for sure the guy was trying to rip us off. He goes on about all the shit he's gonna do to him. Gack and I both pretty much ignore this for now. We decide to go up to the fourth floor and check it out. Maybe we'll hear something. Meanwhile, Gack keeps dialing the man's number. There's never any answer.

The elevator carries us along slowly. We step out onto the dark splattered carpet and speak quietly to one another. There are potted plants lining the hallway. The numbers are nailed unevenly into the flimsy apartment doors—401, 402, 403. We listen at each one. None of us are really breathing at all. Everything is quiet.

I'm the one who hears the pounding first. It's faint and rhythmic—coming from the last apartment next to the window and fire escape.

"Over there."

A moan escapes the keyhole. Bullet pulls out the knife.

We all just listen.

Another moan and then the fat man's voice comes through—saying something like, "Hold still, hold still." He's repeating it over and over.

Gack nods and Bullet pounds on the door with his fist. The whole world is turned silent a moment. I back up and Gack puts a hand on my shoulder. He whispers in my ear, "It's all right."

Then the fat man's voice is right at the door.

"What is it?"

"Yo, it's Gack, Mike's son."

"What do you want?"

The door opens ever so slightly and all at once Bullet kicks the thing as hard as he can.

The fat man falls back on the floor. He's wearing white underwear and nothing else. His skin hangs down all over the place. When he falls his head whips back, smashing against the hard polished wood floor. He says, "Jesus Christ, Jesus Christ, Jesus Christ."

He keeps on saying it.

We all step in and I close the door behind us. I look away from the man crumpled on the floor.

"You shorted us twenty," says Gack. "It's eighty for a gram, last I checked."

"I gave you eighty, I swear."

"Nic?"

I take out the three twenty-dollar bills. Bullet grabs them from me—balling them up, throwing them at the man.

"Count it."

The man writhes around like a giant slug.

"I'm sorry. I swear, it was an accident. I'll get the money."

"Damn right," says Bullet.

Then suddenly, we hear something coming from the back room. It's like a grunting sound.

"What the fuck is that?"

Bullet has the knife all poised and everything and before I know what I'm doing, I have the screwdriver out and I'm clutching it tightly. We walk through the apartment, toward the back bedroom. Bullet pushes open the door just as the man on the floor yells, "Don't."

Inside there is a very hairy man tied so that he is stretched naked and facedown across the width of the bed. He is blindfolded and gagged. He seems to be choking a little or something, 'cause he makes this weird noise in his throat. Bullet says, "Awww, fuck" and then laughs and laughs.

"You have no right to treat people this way," the fat man says, walking with his head down into the small, immaculate kitchen. His pants are slung over a high-backed chair. He reaches his hand into the front pocket, pulling out a crumpled twenty and throwing it on the floor with the others. Gack gathers it up. He kind of nods at us and we all get the hell out of there.

I hear the man cursing behind us and I feel like I need to wash my hands.

Gack calls his dad from the cell phone once we're outside. Our next hookup is just three blocks away. His dad tells him that as far as everyone can figure, Joe is gonna be leaving on a Greyhound from the bus station sometime in the morning. We decide to stake the place out after we make some more deliveries. Actually, it's Bullet who seems the most enthusiastic about the whole idea. His loyalty is sweet, in a very not sweet sort of way. Anyway, he's going on and on about the best plan of attack, or whatever, when I start thinking about my ATM card.

The fog is so thick we can't even see the streetlights overhead, except for a dull, obscured glow. For some reason I can't get this image of Joe standing over me at the liquor store out of my head. He was staring at me—watching for what? My ATM code, of course.

"Oh shit," I say. "Yo, Gack, let me see that phone."

I pull out my card and dial the number on the back of it—hoping, hoping, hoping that I'm not too late. After what seems like forever, I get some guy on the line. He sounds fairly apathetic to my frantic pleas to put a hold on my account.

"Sir," he keeps saying, "even if your card was stolen, no one can access your account without your PIN number."

"Yeah, but I think this guy saw me enter my code."

"When was this?"

"I don't know, a couple hours ago. Just, uh, look, you gotta cancel that card, okay?"

"Yes, of course, sir."

I tear my card in half and throw it in a trash can. I think about retribution, maybe. I think about all the times I'd stolen my parents' credit cards. I think about the girl at my school whose Chevron card I used for about a month before they finally discovered it was missing. When I went to college in Massachusetts, I would wander the dorm halls, looking for open doors—dashing in quickly and stealing whatever money or cigarettes I found lying around. There was a pool and a gym there where I'd go through the lockers every couple of days. I never got very much cash, but it was enough to keep a steady supply of heroin in my arm.

I stole from girlfriends.

I stole from my grandparents.

I stole from aunts, uncles, friends.

I stole and justified it and stole more.

I feel sick being on the other side of it. I feel unsafe, violated, out of control. It's like the time in Amsterdam when I got beat up by an African guy at three in the morning. Even strung out and on the street, I had a feeling that I was protected somehow from the bad shit that went down—like it just couldn't happen to me. Walking through the twisted cobblestone streets of Holland, stoned out on Ecstasy and mushrooms, I was so surprised that the guy actually hit me. And for what? He'd asked me a question and I hadn't responded—that was it. It happened so fast—so abruptly.

An innocence I'd clung to was lost in that instant. Tonight with Joe, I have the same feeling. It is a dirty world and a dirty life. Everyone's out to fuck you over. Any illusions I have are dashed quickly to pieces. I feel just, you know, defeated.

But Gack doesn't see it that way. "This is just what we need," he says. "Motivation."

We walk quickly, making our deliveries. At a certain point we find out about some really cheap crystal a guy's selling farther south of Market. It's not great, but we buy a whole bunch of it and start slanging that instead. Already we've made almost two hundred dollars back. It feels so effortless. Mostly I just follow Gack—don't say much, just watch.

If dealing is this easy and profitable, I can't really see having any problems. There's no way I'm gonna fall into the life I had before—eating out of trash cans, hustling money from guys at gay bars, hanging out on the corner of Castro and 18th, where guys circle the block in fancy sports cars. It hurt so bad the first few times. I thought maybe I'd throw up—just praying for it to be over, for him to finish. They'd take me back to their apartments—or houses up near Twin Peaks. And, of course, there were the rough ones—the ones into violence, leather, different harnesses and things. You just try to shut it all out—getting as loaded as possible. But I'm determined not to do that again. There's a nausea that sweeps through me just thinking about it. Dealing has to work out for me. It has to. It took a miracle to get me outta that situation. I can't count on something like that happening again.

See, after I ended up stealing that money from my little brother and I got kicked out of the house, I didn't know what to do. I went to my friend Akira's apartment near the Presidio. He agreed to let me stay with him for a while. I had a little bit of money left over and I kept shooting meth and heroin, looking for work around the city. I finally got hired at a coffee shop near the Castro. I told the manager, a very clean-cut-looking, gym-toned gay guy in his late thirties, that I had been kicked out of my house by my tyrannical father after he discovered that I was sleeping with boys. The manager took pity on me and let me work for him, but it was only a couple shifts a week. My habit was growing and I needed money bad. Akira lived in a basement apartment beneath his mom's place. His mom had always hated me. At the time, you know, I didn't understand it. I thought she was just cruel and uptight. Now, of course, I can see that she was scared of me and worried about my influence on her son.

Anyway, I snuck upstairs one day while she was at work and found a checkbook hidden in her bedside table. I wrote a hundred dollars out to myself and cashed it at one of those check-cashing places in the Fillmore. I immediately spent the money on drugs, but the check place had called Akira's mom and she figured out that I had taken the money. Akira was upset and told me I had to leave. Our friendship was really never the same after that and I felt just so terrible about what I'd done.

I spent some time living in a youth hostel, and then when I couldn't afford that, I slept in a park. That was when I started turning tricks for the first time, really. I wasn't making a ton of money or anything, just enough to get high and not starve. The few friends I still had I never told what I was doing to get money. I ate maybe a candy bar a day—Snickers usually. I weighed very little. I walked all night long. I walked all day. I had nowhere to go.

One day I saw that an old friend of our family's was having

a retrospective of his work at the Castro movie theater. He is a director who is pretty famous and all. His son, JT, is an actor and they were both scheduled to be at the opening reception. I dragged myself over there, my clothes torn and stinking. I tried to get inside, but the doorway was being guarded. Thankfully, though, JT noticed me and came outside. He put his arms around me. The bulk of his frame crushed me. He offered me a cigarette.

"How did this happen to you?" JT asked, his voice so soft—gentle. He took off his glasses and rubbed his dark, narrow eyes.

"What happened to you?" It was more of a plea than a question. "I remember when you were a little kid, you were, like, the golden child or something. You were so happy . . . so . . . light. I'd play with you for hours and you'd never cry or anything. Do you remember that?"

"Sort of."

"Well, you were pretty young. But you were still, even then, so open and everything. And watching you grow up, I was always so proud of you."

"I looked up to you so much. All the music I listen to, all the books I read, they were all inspired by you."

"So what happened? Last time I saw you it was like, what, three years ago? You were lookin' at colleges in Manhattan. You were all excited about going to school—writing."

"Yeah. It's just crystal meth, man. I wish I'd never tried this shit, I swear."

"You wanna get off it?"

"I don't know. I need to."

"Well, look, I just broke up with my girlfriend and I'm moving back home for a couple months. Why don't you stay with me at our apartment? We'll get you a doctor, get you some medicine—you can just detox there and figure out your life, man. We gotta place in upstate New York you've never been to. We'll go up there, get you straightened out. We'll get my dad's masseuse working on you. We'll hook you up with an apartment, a good job. It'll be all good."

I agreed to meet him at the Four Seasons Hotel the next day. I went to my dealer's place in Oakland. I spent most of my money on speed and pills, then I went back to the park in Fort Mason. I stayed up for a long time, just shooting drugs. I had gotten my backpack full of clothes out of the locker at the youth hostel. I actually had two backpacks, and then I had the brilliant idea of cutting the packs up and sewing them together to make one, giant, SUPER backpack. By the time I finished cutting everything up, however, I got really tired and passed out. When I woke up I had no super backpack and no regular backpack, either. I put all my stuff in a laundry cart I'd stolen and pushed it from the park, down Columbus, to the Four Seasons on Market. There were two large doormen with earpieces and walkie-talkies. They weren't about to let me pass—all rags, a laundry cart full of clothes, an electric guitar, and a head full of so much heroin and meth I could barely talk. When they asked the names of the "guests" I was visiting, I just laughed.

"Look, you're not gonna believe me. Can you just call up and ask if anyone is expecting me. I was told my name would be left with the, uh, front desk, or whatever it's called. I'm Nic Sheff."

That didn't work. They wanted to know who I was there to see, so eventually I told them. Dropping my friends' names got me yelled at that I better get the hell outta there. They said they'd call the cops. When I refused to leave and kept insisting that they call up to make sure, they finally agreed. After that they apologized, like, a hundred times and brought us champagne and a fruit basket.

We flew out to New York on the red-eye that same night. I just remember talking to a flight attendant for most of the trip, sitting on the floor in the back where she was preparing the meals and things. I'd had to do the rest of the speed in the bathroom at the Four Seasons, about a gram at once, so I was pretty much in a blackout for the next week. I managed to stay off hard drugs for a couple months, but then I relapsed and I was worse than ever.

Gack and Bullet and I actually walk by that same Four

Seasons on our way back to my car. After all our deliveries and everything, we've made about three hundred dollars—plus we have a ton of the really good speed left. The morning fades in gray and cold. The streetlights extinguish one by one overhead. The wind picks up, leaving us all shivering slightly. Wet clings to the air, soaks through us—courses in our veins. We smoke cigarettes, but it doesn't warm us. I crank the heat up as we drive to the bus station. My jaw is so tight and it makes these popping noises as I open and close it.

Despite all the drugs and everything, I wanna sleep. There's a pounding in my head—the blood draining out.

I call Lauren from a pay phone and tell her what is going on with me. She agrees to leave the side door unlocked so I can go crash there after we find Joe and get my shit back. She sounds kind of annoyed with me for not having come over, but I don't care. Isn't that the greatest gift in the world—just not to care? I feel so grateful for it. That's nothing I ever knew sober.

The bus station is surrounded by a virtual shantytown of tents and cardboard houses. A girl I went to rehab with had lived there before getting checked into treatment. She'd lived in a tent with three guys, one of whom was her fiancé. The cops would raid these homeless settlements every couple months. They'd make a bunch of arrests, then leave 'em alone to rebuild or whatever. The place seems pretty full right now—young punk kids with ripped clothes and spiked hair looking angry and desperate, fighting over cigarettes and blankets and cans of beer.

Gack and Bullet and I decide to split up so we can each cover a different entrance. There's actually four ways to get into the station, so Bullet says he'll keep circling the main lobby. Honestly, I'm not sure what I'll do if I see Joe. I can't really imagine confronting him and kicking his ass or anything. Still, I try and psych myself up—my heart pounding like crazy every time someone comes through the electric sliding doors.

The station is almost empty. The sound of a few footsteps echoes in the tile corridors. A few of the torn-up black seats are occupied by sleeping men and women wearing layers of tattered rags. Two police officers are there trying to rouse one guy who's slid off onto the dirty linoleum floor. His skin is slick, like maybe it is covered in oil, and his long hair is matted together in one solid dreadlock. He has a long, long beard. The cops—male, with crew cuts and square jaws—are bent over him, shaking his shoulders. Both wear latex gloves. I go take a piss and when I get back all three of them are gone. Joe hasn't shown up yet either. I huddle myself into a corner and wait.

I blink a couple times. Pink and green geometric shapes form against the white walls. It's like a tower of flashing triangles is building itself up organically from the ground. I can't get rid of them. Not like it really bothers me that much. I'm used to hallucinations a lot worse than this. The bus station hums and flickers with pulsing brightness. It's all I can do to keep focused on the doors. I stand up and walk on over to Gack. He's asleep at his post. I nudge him.

"Uh, s-sorry man."

"Nah, dude, let's go."

"You sure?"

I nod. "He'll get his anyway," I say. "This is bullshit. If he needs the money that bad, he can have it. I gotta go sleep."

"Yeah," Gack agrees. "It'll end badly for Joe."

Bullet is still pacing the place like some tightly caged animal. It takes a little coercing to get him to let up. We get back in my car and I decide to buy them all breakfast.

"You can get four Home Run Pies for a dollar at Cala Foods," says Bullet.

"Whatever you guys want."

I drop them off in the TL and drive to Lauren's. We agree to meet up later. Bullet's got nowhere to stay, but neither Gack nor I offer any solutions. I want to help him, I do, but I can barely help myself. We leave him wandering and agree to meet up later. I smoke cigarettes in Lauren's white bed and wait to fall asleep.

DAY 9

Since Lauren's parents are gone, we've spent the last three days basically holed up in her house. Turns out her dad has a fantastic wine cellar that we've (or I've) been sampling from. Plus I'm a pretty good cook, so I've been raiding their pantry and things. I make coffee with a French press in the mornings, preparing pasta and salad and eggs—drinking Beaujolais, Bordeaux, pinots, and Chiantis.

I actually know something about food and wine. It was the summer before my senior year in high school that I went off to this study abroad program in Paris when I was sixteen. It was just for the summer and the thing was pretty structured and everything. You stayed in a hotel with all these other high school students— went to French classes during the day, then were supposed to eat together and go on these "excursions" at night. They'd go to the top of the Eiffel Tower or bowling or something. Drinking alcohol was grounds for immediate expulsion.

The first night I was there, I met up with this girl named Cappucine whose parents were friends with my stepmom. She was a few years older than me and had agreed to take me around the city. She lived just outside Paris in Saint-Cloud. We went to a bar that night and got very drunk—or at least, I did. We walked all over Montmartre—up the steps to the great church, the Sacré-Coeur. Looking down on the city with this girl and her friends, I felt so old—so mature—so cool. I was way into all those French New Wave movies like *Breathless*, *Bob Le Flambeur*, *The 400 Blows*, and *Elevator to the Gallows*. Walking around the city, a Gitane cigarette hanging perpetually from my mouth, I was Jean-Paul Belmondo, or Alain Delon, or one of those untouchable, unfeeling stars. I never went back to the hotel that night. I stayed with Cappucine. It wasn't long before I was drinking in the morning.

We went to visit her family in the south of France, drank rosé from vineyards in St. Tropez. I'd wake up and pour a glass of wine—or sometimes vodka—and drink that along with my coffee. I had my dad's credit card and I bought all new clothes for myself at Chevignon and Agnès B. I decided never to return to the United States.

Again, fix the outsides and maybe my insides won't be such a dark place.

Four months later, the credit cards were all canceled and I was finally convinced to come home and finish high school. Sitting in class back in the Bay Area, watching pep rallies and things, it was a little, er, strange. Here I'd been drinking ouzo and riding motorcycles around Montpelier—then suddenly I was dealing with curfews and the swim team. I wanted so desperately not to be a child anymore. I always thought once I was an adult, independent, whatever, these feelings of hopelessness and despair would go away. I could be like those characters in the movies. Drugs and alcohol gave me that feeling. Getting high, I was walking on the beach with Cappucine again, promising her a future and thinking that I meant it.

It strikes me how, being here with Lauren, it is more or less the same thing. Here I am, so old and yet so young. Stuck, suspended somewhere in between adulthood and a child's fantasy. But I keep all this to myself, shooting more and more heroin and crystal methamphetamine.

I leave Lauren to meet Gack a few times. I park my car at the Safeway at Church and Market. We just stand along the street and say stupid shit like, "Crystal, crystal," or, "You wanna stay up all night?"

The people who pass either just ignore us or express interest and we follow them around the corner and sell them a sack. It is that easy.

No one ever complains about how small what we sell them is.

We definitely aren't making a ton of money, but it's enough to at least use for free. Gack keeps trying to get me to buy walkie-talkies, but I don't really see the point. I guess he just thinks it'd be cool.

So I split the profits with Gack and take whatever money I can home to Lauren. The heroin's really working for her. She has this tendency to get all freaked out doing too much meth. We'll be making love or something, and all of a sudden she'll shush me—convinced there's someone in the house, upstairs. Granted, most of the time it does sound like there's someone up there. There'll be this banging around, or the noise of footsteps, or a door being shut. None of it ever turns out to be real. I keep saying something like, "Baby, look, I know it sounds like there's someone upstairs. It always sounds like there's someone upstairs. But we might as well just assume that there's no one up there because otherwise it's gonna drive us crazy. So what if there is someone up there? What are we gonna do about it anyway? Let's just keep telling ourselves it's all in our minds—'cause it is, you know?"

I'm pretty good about convincing myself that way, but she is more invested in her paranoia. The heroin calms her down nicely. So when we run out, she's all over me about calling Candy. It's around eight thirty and dark outside. Candy can't meet us for another couple hours, so I suggest we take a walk down by Fort Point. The gate is locked, so we park Lauren's car up on the cliffs and walk down the worn, wooden, creaking steps. We actually hold hands.

Listening to Lauren, I've been able to piece together most of her story since leaving high school. Basically, it's pretty similar to mine. She never quite reached the depth of depravity that I did, but she's still got time. At least, that's how I figure it. She went into her first rehab right out of high school, a dual diagnosis treatment center—one that dealt with both drug addiction and bulimia. Since then she's had a couple jobs temping at law firms around the city, but mostly she's just been in and out of different facilities and programs. Nothing ever took, obviously.

Fort Point stretches out to the pillars of the Golden Gate Bridge. The surf comes pounding in hard and fast against the rock jetty. Wind blows in from the mouth of the bay and the ocean is churning and spraying us as we walk. The lights from Marin reflect back across the channel and the abandoned military barracks—boarded up and covered in layers of graffiti—bend and shift under the weight of the salt air. I hold Lauren's hand and we talk about how beautiful everything is and how there really is no city like San Francisco, after all. At one point an official-looking truck comes our way, headlights blinding us as we look back. Lauren panics some.

"Should we run?" she asks.

"Definitely not."

The truck passes by without bothering us. My heart is maybe going a little bit.

"This is freakin' me out," she whines. "Maybe we should go back."

"It'll be fine."

"You don't worry at all, do you?"

I laugh. "If you only knew."

She asks about my plans for the future.

"I don't know. I mean, what else is there to do? People might say I'm wasting my life, but it's all relative. If I was a lawyer, I'd go to fucking law school—but I'm not. I'm a drug addict and so what do I do? Use, right? Use until the wheels fall off. We'll get by, Lauren."

I pull her in toward me and kiss her. "What more is there to life than this?" I ask. "Walking free through a city that we love—listening to the ocean—kissing each other—getting high. We're so alive, you and I."

She laughs now. "And when my parents get home—what then? We've got nowhere to go."

"I'll get a place."

"For us together."

"Sure."

"So are we boyfriend/girlfriend then?"

"If you want to be."

"Come on, Nic."

"Yeah, of course we are."

We kiss each other some more.

Getting into the car, Lauren realizes she forgot her scarf. It must've fallen off somewhere. I tell her to stay and I go running back the way we came. Tears well up in my eyes from the cold and I feel maybe like I'm flying—so grateful. Everything is working out perfectly. I even find her scarf, at the very end of the point. I run back and she's happy and we drive off to meet Candy and we listen to this old Tosca CD—smoking one cigarette after the other.

Candy has stitches all along her left cheekbone that weren't there before. It looks all swollen and glossy. She pushes her hair back behind her ears and asks me, "So what's the deal? How come it took you so long to call?"

"Well, I'm more of a tweakhead, you know. I just use this shit to level out the meth."

"It's good though, huh?"

I nod, looking at her. "Maybe you wanna come hang out sometime?" I say.

She turns her pinned, gray eyes on me. She's still wearing too much makeup, but the scar makes her markedly prettier. I'm kinda sick like that.

"Sure," she says. "But not tonight."

"I could take you out somewhere."

"Look, you're just a kid."

"In some ways."

She passes over the dope and I give her some money. She lights a Parliament Menthol.

"We'll see. Call me sooner next time, okay?"

"Sure."

I drive Lauren's car back to her house. Candy's look stays with me. I feel it wrapped serpentine around my spine. She reminds me of someone—the smell of her. And then I remember.

When that movie star's wife my dad had the affair with broke up with him, we moved to an apartment in the Mission. My mom had been forced to move to L.A. for work with an old boyfriend and I saw her only on holidays, like Christmas. My dad always treated me more like a friend than a son, really. I mean, especially back then. He took me everywhere with him—out to dinner, to parties. My godparents, a gay couple, lived across the street. We'd go over there for dinner and we'd all talk about politics and movies and things. They made me feel included, grown-up.

But, of course, then my dad started dating. He was single and young and it made sense that he'd go out and leave me with babysitters. I'm not sure where he met Audrey—at some gallery opening or something—but she was tattooed all over with long, long blond hair. She was maybe twenty-one or -two and smelled like incense all the time. She only babysat me like three times, but I'll never forget that smell of her. She looked so beautiful and ravaged at the same time. She would crawl into bed with me as I was falling asleep and hold me and I'd smell her and be so turned on. I'd try to hide my small erection. One night she rented *The Last Temptation of Christ* and we watched that together. I was eight years old.

But driving away from Candy, I think of Audrey and lying in bed with her. Candy has that smell—that same look. Something is tearing apart the lattice structure of my veins. I get home and go straight to Lauren's room. I fuck her hard and it goes on and on. We soak through her sheets and mattress and carpeted floor.

When it's over I cook up a bunch of heroin and go to pick out a bottle of white wine from the refrigerator. I take it up to the kitchen and pour a large glass for myself. I'm naked and standing at the full-length window, looking out on the street below—feeling powerful. I eat an apple and bring one down for Lauren. The room is very quiet and I call out to her, but there's no answer.

When I worked at the rehab in Malibu, they made me take a CPR class at the Red Cross. I thought it was bullshit at the time—some thick-necked EMT talking too fast and asking stupid rhetorical questions. The class was maybe three hours long and I guess I paid attention. I mean, I got the damn certificate.

Seeing Lauren on the floor, turning blue, my reaction is strange. I don't panic or anything. A calm sweeps through me. I remember the EMT. What'd he say to do first? You shake them and shout, "Are you okay?"

I do that.

Check for a heartbeat.

She's got one.

Check for breathing.

No on that.

All right, then open the air passage, tilt the head back, and start chest compressions.

I put my mouth to her cold, small lips.

Breathe.

One, two, three, four, five.

I feel her ribs and breastbone plate crack some under my weight as I push down. Her belly fills as I blow the air in. Her chest heaves.

I reach over and grab the phone, dialing 911.

Breathe.

One, two, three, four, five.

"911 emergency, how can I help you?"

"Yeah, my girlfriend just OD'ed on heroin. We need an ambulance now."

Breathe.

One, two, three, four, five.

"Do you know CPR?"

"I'm doing it."

"Where are you located?"

"I don't know the address. Sea Cliff. Trace the call, will you?"

Breathe.

One, two, three, four, five.

And now the panic sets in. Fuck, man, she can't die. Her skin is so transparent and the veins are blue, blue rising beneath the surface.

"An ambulance is on its way, sir."

I hang up.

Breathe.

One, two, three, four, five.

Check the heart.

Still going.

"God," I say aloud. "I don't believe in you, but now would be a good time to give us a goddamn miracle."

Breathe.

One, two, three, four, five.

And then, just like that, she gasps, gasps, gasps and jerks awake. She blinks twice and bursts into tears. I do the same thing, holding her.

When I hear the sirens outside I go out and tell the firemen and whoever that she's all right, but they come in anyway. They seem kinda pissed about the whole thing. Regulations say they gotta take her to the ER, but Lauren refuses. She's naked and we can't get her to put clothes on. She cries and cries—sounding like a sick cat or something. One of the bigger guys threatens to call the cops on us and that gets Lauren moving. She's still way out of it and nodding all over the place. She clings on to me and I basically have to carry her up to the ambulance. She kisses me, but at that point I'm just trying to get her outta there. They tell me to meet her at the UCSF Hospital. I hate fucking emergency rooms, but I agree anyway.

The only time I ever ended up in the ER was for a drug overdose, actually. I was living in New York, turning tricks. I'd been up for a couple days doing coke and crystal and drinking so much, I mean so fucking much. This very muscular guy whose name, I think, was Brian, had picked me up at this cheesy gay bar where they give you free drinks if you take your shirt off. They were his drugs. I had no money. I ended up back at my apartment in the middle of this orgy of guys. Vaguely I remember someone eating out my ass, while my dick refused to get hard. Then I just gave up and let whoever wanted to fuck me, fuck me.

At some point I noticed a vial of GHB on the bedside table. I drank about three-quarters of it down, figuring that would do the trick. I started to black out and I had this total sense of relief. Finally, I thought, it's over, and then I just fell out. Of course, I woke up at a nearby hospital, a tube down my throat, needles in my arms, a catheter in my dick, my ribs broken from the CPR. But the sick thing, the really fucking sick thing was my first thought when I came to. See, when I'd gone to the bathroom at my apartment, I'd managed to get alone with the bag of crystal and had hidden some of it in a bottle of Ambien I'd been prescribed. I knew it was still there.

I made some grunting noises for them to get the tube out, which they did, me gagging and retching all over the place. Then the nurse left and I started ripping all the needles out of my arms. The catheter in my dick was this plastic tubing connected to a bag I could piss into. I started to pull the thing out of the hole in the head of my cock and it burned, Jesus it fucking burned, but it wouldn't come out. Still, I just kept pulling until the pain got so bad that I begged the nurses to get the goddamn thing out of me, which they finally did. Then I got up, hospital gown and all, and started to walk out the front door. The security guard stopped me— physically dragging me back in. I kept trying to sneak out until they let me sign an AMA discharge form, 'cause I'd been such a pain in the ass. I ended up in my third rehab about a week later.

I think back to my night in the ER and I go downstairs and shoot a bunch of heroin before driving up to UCSF. They've already admitted Lauren by the time I get there, so they let me on in. She's sitting on a white cot in the middle of the cramped central areas. Doctors and nurses pass bits of paper back and forth, make jokes, enter information into computers. There don't seem to be any other patients around, but everyone seems rushed and frantic. A doctor with a mullet tied back in a ponytail and soft, squishy features is trying to get something coherent out of Lauren. I think he's trying to figure out whether she was trying to commit suicide or not—but he never just comes straight out with it. I step

in, saying she had only done heroin one or two other times and **71**
didn't know about the dosing. He talks to me as though I were
Lauren's concerned parent, the responsible one. He asks me all
these questions. What's her home life like? Does she need help
getting into treatment? I fight so hard not to nod out while he's
talking. I'm not sure how well I'm doing. I ask him if she can leave
and he says no. She has to be evaluated by the psychiatrist.

"I go to a psychiatrist," says Lauren. "Jules Bernabei. He
works at San Francisco General."

The doctor ignores her.

"Can't we leave AMA?" I ask.

"What?" the doctor asks.

"I was in the hospital once and I just asked to sign this AMA
form and they let me go. They had to. Come on, doctor, I'll take
care of her."

"No, no. I'm afraid not."

"Can you stop us?"

"Yes. We can involve the authorities if you wish."

———

Lauren hands me her purse and I kiss her and tell her we'll figure
this out. She keeps pleading to get her psychiatrist on the phone,
so they agree to page him.

I'm not sure what I'm feeling but I go out into the thick, wet
air and light a cigarette and pace. Maybe everybody is staring at
me. I pull out Lauren's cell phone. It's two thirty. For some reason
I call Zelda. Maybe hers is the only number I remember.

Zelda is singularly beautiful. The first time I saw her was
at some meeting in Hollywood. She identified herself as a
newcomer—wearing big, round sunglasses, her red hair hanging
down to the small of her back. I couldn't stop looking at her the
whole meeting—high cheekbones, a long, angular nose, chapped
parted lips. Her body was so tiny—jagged shoulders, sticking
out like angels' wings. She looks like an Egon Schiele painting.

I actually asked for her number that first day. I never do that. She gave it to me, but she was in this treatment program where she couldn't get calls for three months. I forgot all about her until I came back to my old Sober Living one night. I'd just turned twenty-one and was celebrating my birthday at the halfway house. She'd checked in about a week earlier.

We started talking and I felt so close to her immediately. It was like talking to myself. Of course, I later found out how much older she was than me—and, eventually, that she had a boyfriend. Plus she'd lived so much more than I had. She'd been married to that actor for seven years. All her boyfriends were famous in some way and her family was equally well known. She was humble about all this, but I was intimidated and never thought she could ever want me like I was increasingly wanting her. But we started spending more and more time together. I told her things I'd never told anyone.

One night we went to the Chateau Marmont on Sunset. We drank black tea and she smoked cigarettes while a little girl, maybe six or seven, played this haunting, real minimalist piano music. I mean, she was just some kid messing around, but it was fucking great. Someone even tipped her twenty bucks or something.

I'm not sure what we talked about, or why that night was any different from any other. She drove me home and we made out in her car and she cried the whole time. I fell ever more in love with her from that day forward. We kept trying to break it off, but would eventually end up seeing each other again.

How can I ever explain what it was about Zelda? Sure she was amazing to look at, but there was something more. There was a sadness there, mixed with wisdom, and a pained humor. Whatever it was, I felt like I could see right down to the moths struggling on their backs in the base of her silver, shimmering soul. I also felt like we were meant to be together—she, this ageless beauty, and I, this old man and tiny child. When we kissed and made love it was like nothing I'd never known before—and that was sober.

But she wouldn't leave Mike for me. I'm not sure why. Maybe

she didn't feel safe with me. Maybe I was really too young. It tore
me up—I mean, really.

So I call Zelda from Lauren's cell phone. She doesn't answer. I leave a rambling message. Even just hearing her voice on the machine brings back so much. It actually makes me kind of angry and I hang up and pace some more.

Eventually, I go back into the waiting room and try to sleep on two orange plastic chairs—no good. My legs keep twitching all over the place. The other thing is, I really have to take a piss, but the heroin has made all my muscles too relaxed or something, 'cause I can't figure out how to make that happen. There's a group of dark-skinned Hispanic women talking loudly now in the waiting area, their voices echoing off the linoleum. I decide to walk around the hospital some, since the woman at the front desk tells me the psychiatrist hasn't even arrived for Lauren yet.

I ride the elevator for a while, wondering if there are cameras in there—maybe I could stop it and shoot up right there. But, no, I'm too sketched out and I figure there're probably cameras. So I just go up and down. Even the elevator smells like a goddamn hospital. Kelly, the mother of a friend of mine, is a nurse at a hospital in Oakland. In order to graduate from high school, I had to do all this community service. Kelly agreed to take me with her for a couple days around the hospital. One of the things I remember most was this guy with a horribly fat stomach. He was very thin, but his stomach was huge. I sat with him while we waited for Kelly. He asked me questions about school and things. He was very sweet and polite and positive. Kelly came in and asked him to remove his shirt, so he did. What he had was a colostomy—his intestine had been rerouted out his stomach. Thing was, he had developed a lot of fluid swelling at the base of the wound. I excused myself to get some water, then nearly fainted in the hall. Kelly later told me he'd be dead in a few months.

The other thing I remember was this schizophrenic drug addict who'd tried to kill himself by jumping off a building. He broke his neck, but he didn't die—he was a quadriplegic.

"We're just going to look at this small wound on his bottom," Kelly said.

She pulled back the sheet and the guy literally had no left butt cheek. It had been rotted away by some flesh-eating disease. The place quickly filled with the smell of decaying flesh and shit. This time I passed out cold in the outside hall. The next day she had me follow a urologist around—putting catheters in old guys' dicks.

I get outta the elevator and go check on Lauren. They tell me she's sleeping and that they're giving her an IV of fluid to rehydrate her. I call Gack from Lauren's phone. His dad answers.

"Hey Mike, it's Nic, you guys up?"

"Always. You wanna talk to little Gack?"

"Sure. Fucking Lauren OD'ed. I'm at the UCSF ER."

"Is she all right?"

"Yeah. I had to do CPR and shit, but she's alive."

"Are you all right?"

"Yeah, I guess so, thanks, Mike."

He goes to get Gack. I'm struck by how sweet these fuckin' people are.

I tell Gack about the whole scene and ask if he can get me any herb.

"Dude, I got a little bit. It'll take me an hour to take the bus up there."

"I ain't going anywhere."

"Word."

We meet out front about two hours later. We shoot up some speed in Lauren's car, then smoke a joint. I feel stupidly high.

"So you saved her life," Gack says. "That's fucking intense." I swear the fool never changes his clothes. He's wearing the same bandanna around his head, Karate Kid style.

"Yeah," I say. "I was so weirdly calm about the whole thing."

"That's gonna be pretty heavy for her when she realizes what you did."

"Yeah, well, if it wasn't for me, she wouldn't have OD'ed in the first place."

"Nah, she was just lookin' for an excuse to start using again, **75** right? It would've happened eventually. You know, my girlfriend lives right around here."

"Your girlfriend?"

"Yeah, dude—Erin."

"Fuck, we gotta all go out sometime."

"She's only seventeen."

"So?"

He tells me about how he met her, trying to sell her a sack, actually. She lives with her mom—still goes to high school and all. Gack talks a lot and we walk around some. The UCSF hospital rests up in the dense forest and eucalyptus trees of the hills looking down on Golden Gate Park. The fog always wraps the place in a still wetness that is both eerie and idyllic.

"I love this city," I say.

"Yeah."

Lauren's phone rings twenty minutes later and I answer.

It's Lauren calling from the hospital.

"Nic, where are you?"

"Outside. Can we go?"

"Yeah, you gotta come fill out some paperwork."

"Me?"

"Yeah, why? What's wrong?"

"Nothing. I'll be right there."

I say bye to Gack and agree to meet him later. He says he's gonna go walk Erin to school. It's five a.m.

I walk into the hospital. I'm way too loaded for this shit.

Inside they make me promise to watch Lauren closely and make sure she gets some rest. I agree—again, the responsible one. Then I sign some papers and take her home.

I get whatever heroin's left out of the cotton and shoot us both up with it. We fuck as the sun rises and she says almost nothing the whole time. I notice how thin she's getting. Her bones cut into me. We pass out sometime around ten.

DAY 10

A few hours later the phones are ringing and ringing. The house phone and Lauren's cell phone—over and over. There's some light coming in the windows, so I can tell it's real late and sunny outside. The caller ID on Lauren's cell keeps showing DAD.

He just keeps calling. None of this wakes Lauren up ever, but I'm feeling kinda worried and restless, so I shake her awake.

"What? Fucking what?"

"Dude, your dad keeps calling. They must have heard something about last night."

"Fuck. I bet the fucking neighbors called them."

Her eyes are all swollen and her hair is everywhere. Her breasts are sagging strangely, suddenly too big for her shrinking frame.

"You want me to make some coffee?" I ask.

"Yeah. I'll sleep a little more, then figure out what to say."

"Okay."

"Nic?"

"Yeah."

"You saved my life."

"Nah, whatever."

"I'm falling in love with you."

"Yeah, me too, Lauren."

It feels like I mean it, but you can never be sure.

I go upstairs and it is bright and hot. I make coffee and an omelet with avocado and sautéed mushrooms. While it's all cooling, I set up a rig of meth. I hit a vein, but after I pull back the blood into the syringe, my hand moves and I feel a burning in my arm. I dig around some more. Maybe ten minutes go by of me just hunting and hunting and not finding any goddamn vein. Then suddenly I realize that the pressure has built up really high in the plunger, so

I pull out and try to press it down. The blood has coagulated in the head of the needle. I push and push, but nothing comes out. Finally I press the thing down as hard as I can and then it gives and blood sprays out all over the white kitchen wall. After that I try to find a vein again and eventually get the shot off, though I'm pretty sure I wasted the whole goddamn thing. I try to clean up the blood, but the shit has dried already and is a son of a bitch to get rid of. I eat the omelet with toast and drink the coffee with a whole bunch of sugar.

If Lauren's parents know she's relapsed, I figure I'm pretty much fucked. They're probably gonna come home early from their trip and then all this luxury living is over. I bring Lauren's coffee down to her and find myself kinda wishing I never called the goddamn ambulance in the first place. She would have been fine. But, of course, I had no way of knowing that.

I have trouble waking her up and when I do, she cries some.

"You gotta call 'em," I say.

"Yeah."

"You want me to leave you alone?"

"Just for a couple minutes. Hey . . . can you get me off?"

I do. I hit a vein on her wrist. It's the only one I can find.

After that I go outside and smoke cigarettes in the backyard. The wind blows patterns in the cypresses and across the long grass. There're three corgis out there that I've never noticed before. I wonder how long it's been since they've been fed. They all bark at me, but I ignore it. Somehow the warmth and the clear sky seem to be taunting me. I'm aware of how pale I'm becoming. Maybe I should go swimming, but I feel weak. Even the meth isn't getting me that high anymore.

I'm on my third cigarette when Lauren opens the back door. She's sobbing like crazy. Her face is all contorted and everything. "He wants to talk to you."

"Me?" I feel scared for some reason—my stomach drops out all at once.

"Please," she whines.

So I go in and see the phone is off the hook, lying on the bed. I pick the thing up and sit down, the words catching in my throat as I say, "Yeah, hello?"

The man's voice on the other end is broken with tears. He has a refined, sort of dignified Southern accent.

"You're Nic?" he says.

"Yeah."

"I remember meeting you before. You went to Lauren's high school?"

"Yes."

"Nic, Lauren tells me you saved her life last night. Son, I can't tell you how much that means to me. I love my daughter very much and I—well—I love you for saving her, you know?" He chokes on that one.

"I know you want what's best for her too," he continues. "That's why I'm asking you—begging you—to help me help Lauren, okay?" There's been a patronizing tone in his voice the whole time he's talking to me, like he's addressing a small child. Still, I play along.

"Yeah, of course."

He goes on to describe some of Lauren's history in treatment centers. He tells me that she's a drug addict and can't use like normal people and blah, blah, blah. I listen and don't say anything. He asks me to try and convince Lauren to go to her therapist's house in Santa Cruz for the week. He realizes she doesn't wanna go back to rehab, but surely that'd be a good compromise. I agree, telling him I'll do whatever I can. He says he knows he can trust me. I feel pretty sick inside.

"Okay, let me talk to Lauren again," he says.

I pass the phone over.

Lauren scratches at the back of her neck, says "okay" a bunch of times, then hangs up.

"Jules is coming over after work to take me down to Santa Cruz."

"That's your shrink, right?"

"Yeah."

"I said I'd make you go."

"I don't have to, you know?" She looks up at me. I see how glossy and red her eyes have become—like they are covered by a layer of wax paper.

"I'll pack my things right now," she says. "I'll go away with you."

I think about that. Honestly, I can't see Lauren cutting it living in my car with me. I need her to have this house and access to her parents' money. It's not that I don't care about her, but I'm just trying to be realistic. We gotta play things carefully—not throw away what we got working for us. I tell her this and she cries some. I drink the warm white wine from the night before, but she doesn't want any. We make love tiredly to pass the time. We take a shower and then she packs and I get whatever shit I have lying around. Just as I'm about to leave, Lauren stops me.

"Look," she says. "Why don't you stay here?"

"Here?"

She says she'll leave me her car and keys to the house. She says she'll go down to Jules's for one night—that'll appease everybody—then I can come pick her up.

"I love you," she says.

"I love you, too."

She makes me promise not to let anybody stay here while she's gone. Of course I agree.

Then I leave, not wanting her psychiatrist to see me here. I drive Lauren's car.

It's a funny thing about psychiatrists and therapists. I mean, I've been in therapy my whole goddamn life. It was sort of my dad's religion or something like that. After my mom moved away, they made me go to this shrink in the city. She was a large woman who wore big, flowing dresses and had a furry upper lip. Mostly I would just play with the dolls and toys in her office. She had a little wooden house that I would put the dolls in. I remember her asking me, in this very level voice, where each of the dolls lived. I pointed to the different rooms in the dollhouse.

"...his is where the daddy lives," I said, showing her one side ...house. "And this is where the mommy lives."

...gestured to the other side of the house.

"And what about that doll?" she asked, indicating the one still in my hand.

"Oh, that's the baby," I said. "The baby doesn't have anywhere to live—he sleeps outside."

She scribbled in her notepad.

Still, for all the therapy I had, none of it ever really fixed that feeling of torn-apartness inside of me. I learned how to express myself, that was all. And, for whatever reason, identifying the root cause of my problem—like fear of abandonment or something—didn't change a goddamn thing. I could see quite clearly why I acted a certain way, but that wouldn't make me any different. I sought out craziness. I was attracted to it. No therapy could take that away.

One of the first serious relationships I had was with this girl named Lyric. She was a year younger than me and—went to my rival high school. She was a virtuous, good-natured scholastic wonder who ended up going to Harvard. Thing was, she was also bulimic and would get so goddamn drunk with me. Even back then, I mean, when I was only sixteen, my drinking and drugging had already started controlling my life. She was nowhere near as bad as I was—though we would usually start drinking around midday and keep going from there.

This was the kind of girl I always ended up with. I have this strange magnetic pull or something that draws them toward me—and me to them. Knowing that it was all related to my childhood didn't do a goddamn thing.

So I leave Lauren's, driving her car to the TL, the keys to her parents' house in my pocket. I listen to music and feel so blessed—like the greatest hustler in the goddamn world. Not that it's all an act. I see a lot of myself in Lauren—the little child, the desperate self-destructiveness, the way she tries not to care.

I call Gack from a pay phone and we agree to meet in front

of his hotel. I'm actually getting kinda low on meth so we gotta re-up later. I go to the bank and withdraw a bunch of money. I have to go in and see the teller directly 'cause I had to throw away my card. Amazingly I managed to cancel my card before Joe was able to steal any money from me, but I still have only a little over a thousand dollars left. It's frightening how fast the money is going, but I figure Gack and I can up our dealing and make it back.

The sun is falling lower in the sky, but it's still clear and hot. It's almost six o'clock. There's a feeling, like, well, like fate is on my side. Any doubts are blotted out by drugs and the music in Lauren's car and blah, blah, blah. I've got the windows down and a cigarette in my mouth. I cry at how good my life is—or at least, that's what I think at the time.

Gack shows me that he's got new shoes on.

"My dad bought 'em for me," he says.

They're black skate shoes with thick laces.

"Cool, man."

"So how's Lauren?"

I tell him about her dad and the therapist in Santa Cruz and all.

"You got keys?" he says.

"Yeah. Hey, we should pick your girl up and bring her over. I'd like to meet her."

"Word."

"I need to buy some more shit, too."

"Cool. I got an idea."

We drive to Church and Market and cruise around there for a while. I try to get a little more of Gack's story out of him. I keep telling him that this whole thing will make a great book.

"My street education," I tell him.

"Yeah, man, you're doing pretty good. You got some crazy angels guiding you."

"You too, man. I mean, what a great thing it was to meet you. I'm gonna pitch it, man, maybe to the *SF Weekly* or something."

"Dude, I'll be famous."

"You deserve it."

Gack tells me about his foster parents, who live out in Napa. He ran away to the city when he was twelve. Until a little over a year ago, he'd been going back and forth between the streets and their trailer near Sonoma. He'd lived in different squats and abandoned houses throughout the city. He'd go home only when he ran out of options. Of course, once his real dad came back to find him, he moved in with him. His dad had a bad back and needed a lot of help getting around—plus he was on a shitload of pain meds. Gack doesn't know much about his dad's background.

Gack saw his mom from time to time. She lived up in Napa too. She had six years sober—going to twelve-step meetings and things. He guessed he liked her all right. He seems pretty okay with the whole situation—though maybe those tracks on his arm suggest otherwise.

Driving, I can't get Gack to say just exactly what we're looking for. He keeps repeating, "It'll reveal itself."

"What will?" I ask.

"We'll see."

We drive and drive. The bars are just starting to open and the early dining crowds are gathering around the different restaurants on Market. The street kids are sitting around the front of the Safeway—looking to get high with no money, somehow. I see some of the kids we've been dealing to—not that I know any of their names. Absently I wonder about their parents, families, childhoods, whatever. They all sort of dress the same—tight pants with a lot of zippers, boots, hooded sweatshirts—as much black as possible.

We circle the block a few more times.

"There," says Gack, pointing.

"What?"

"There. Pull over a second."

I wait while Gack goes running off down the street. I try to find just the right song on the CD player. I put that Talking Heads live album on track ten, "This Must Be the Place." Somehow I just seem to flip right to it.

It's funny 'cause this was the song my parents' friends Tim and Susan danced to at their wedding. They held the thing at our house in Point Reyes. Susan actually used to babysit me when I was little. But as I got older, I became really good friends with her boyfriend, Tim. Tim started surfing around the time I did and we'd go down to Santa Cruz together. We'd surf all day at Four Mile, or the Hook, or Steamers—floating in the cold, cold water, talking about music or whatever. We'd leave at, like, six in the morning and get coffee and muffins at the Beach Café. We'd stay out for hours, then go get burritos at El Toro—or Cole's BBQ, if we were in Santa Cruz. Tim would make mixes for me of all the new music he was constantly buying at Amoeba, this huge record store on Haight. He'd take me to clubs with his brother-in-law, Xi. We'd dance and play pool and stuff like that. Tim was a great dancer.

Xi introduced me to philosophy and the writings of Baudelaire, Rimbaud, and Camus. He is from China—born at the height of the Cultural Revolution. The two guys, Tim and Xi, were such heroes of mine. I benefited so much from hanging out with them.

At the wedding, a mariachi band played in our garden as Tim and Susan walked down the aisle. The DJ was this, like, six-foot-five, thug-lookin' dude from some bar south of Market. Tim and Susan danced to this Talking Heads song together. They held each other and danced. The lyrics go something like: "I'll love you till my heart stops—love you till I'm dead."

Listening to this song now, I think back to that night. I shucked oysters for the guests, helped set up speakers, helped build a shelter from the light rain over the dance floor. And, of course, I danced and talked and then woke up early the next morning to go surfing out at Drakes Estero.

And now Gack is coming up on the car with some older girl who's got this long, curling, natural red hair; white skin; and freckles, freckles, freckles. She gets into the back and Gack sits next to me and says, "This is Angela. She needs a ride back down Market. Can we do that for her?"

I introduce myself. She keeps telling me how nice my car is and I try to get her to understand that it's not mine—it's just some girl's and I'm like Gack, homeless and struggling. The only difference between us is this crazy stroke of luck, or God, or fate, or whatever—plus I saved up some money working while I was clean and blah, blah, blah.

Gack is giving me that look, like, shut the fuck up—or more like pity that I always feel the need to explain myself, obsessed with showing people who I am so they'll like me, or I don't know what. I need to chill out, shoot some dope, and change this fucking CD.

When we get to some alley off Market, Gack and Angela say they're gonna go up to her place a minute. I've calmed myself down by smoking cigarettes and just forcing myself to be quiet. Neither Gack nor Angela talked much in the car, which always makes me nervous—but I kept telling myself it was all right. So now they walk off down the alley, but then Gack runs back and leans in the window.

"Dude, I need your wallet."

"What?"

"She's gonna hook me up—but she needs to think it's my money."

"That girl?"

"Trust me."

I hand him my wallet.

I shoot a little heroin and nod, nod, nod waiting for them to come back. I'm actually in some weird dream/hallucination thing when he knocks on the side door and I jump ten miles.

He's giggling like a maniac.

"Dude, this shit is so good."

"How much you get?"

"Two teeners."

"Holy shit."

"So we gonna go divide this stuff up—cut it—slang it. Word?"

"You wanna go to Lauren's?"

"Hell yeah."

"How much should I put aside for us?"

"Half."

"Word."

We drive back to Lauren's. I order us a bunch of dim sum from this place on Geary and a six-pack of Tsingtao.

"You should tell your girl to come over," I say.

"Really?"

"Yeah."

"Hey, she's never shot meth before. You think I could borrow some to get her off with?"

"Dude, of course."

We eat pork buns and chow mein, drink beer, smoke cigarettes in the kitchen.

"There are so many rooms," says Gack.

"Yeah."

"I ain't ever been in no house like this before."

"Word."

"I'm gonna go get Erin."

"Take your time."

He leaves and I decide to check my e-mail on Lauren's stepmom's computer. As I'm walking up the carpeted stairs, though, I hear this strange yapping noise over and over. I walk down and open the back door. The three dogs are barking at the door. I let them in and hunt around for some dog food to give them. I guess I feel kinda bad about leaving 'em out there. It's wet and cold outside.

Lauren's stepmom's office is on the second floor and piled high with papers and photos of Lauren—but more of Lauren's half sister. She looks around my little brother's age, but with white-blond hair like I used to have. I log on and check my e-mail. There's not one. No one's written me. No one has even tried begging me to come home. There's nothing from my family—nothing from anyone. I wonder if I need to wait for Gack and his girl before trying that crystal. I decide I might as well wait—but in the meantime I can drink a bottle of red wine. I pick out a decent one and set about trying to write a story idea about Gack and Bullet and everyone. I figure I'll send it out to the *SF Weekly* or the *Guardian*. Writing usually comes so quickly to me, but I spend at least an hour obsessively trying to get the perfect words out. Even after all that, what remains on the page is virtually unintelligible.

Suddenly I'm scared. Writing has never been a struggle for me before. Somehow the idea of being this drug-fueled, outsider artist has always been really appealing to me. I remember this artist I knew in New York who was a recovering heroin addict and a big-time painter. He used to tell me that if being loaded helped him create better work, then he would definitely not have gotten sober. His work was better when he was off dope. After all, he said, art is the most important thing. I believed the same thing at the time.

The doorbell rings. I go down and let Gack and his girl in. The trio of dogs follow me to the front door.

Erin looks like she's maybe eleven or twelve. She's totally undeveloped—with a high soft voice and a tiny nose. Her blond hair is choppy and short. She has piercings all over. She wears an oversize hooded sweatshirt, jeans, and Converse tennis shoes. Her brown eyes are so wide open. She literally gasps stepping into the house. "This place is beautiful."

"Wine?" I offer her my glass and she drinks from it. "Let's go downstairs."

The girl is so nervous, she can't really talk. I put on some music—this old Amon Tobin CD—and Gack gets shots together for all of us.

"First time, huh?" I say, feeling ashamed of myself suddenly.

"Uh-huh."

"We're not gonna give her too much," he says. "She's got school tomorrow."

I watch Gack, noticing that his version of not too much is way fucking more than I would have wanted to shoot my first time—especially if this shit is as good as he says it is. Still, I don't say anything about it. Instead, I ask Erin about high school and her friends and things. She can't really answer with anything more than one syllable.

Gack holds the needle up to her and she pulls back her sweater. There are all these white scars up her arm.

"You a cutter, huh?" I ask.

"I was."

"That's kinda hot."

"No, it's not," says Gack, squeezing her bicep to get the veins to stand out. "She's never gonna do that again."

She rolls her eyes and makes a face.

When Gack hits and pushes it home, she starts gasping for air. "I gotta . . . I gotta . . ."

"In there," I say.

She runs into the bathroom and throws up in what I hope is the toilet. That's what it sounds like anyway.

"Girls always puke," says Gack.

"Well, you gave her a fucking truckload."

I hear her voice calling from the bathroom. "Gack, get me a cigarette."

He looks at me and I put my pack on the floor.

"Baby, you all right?"

"I think so. Damn, this feels pretty good, huh?"

I laugh at that. "You guys should go upstairs—check out some of the other rooms," I say.

"Yeah. Thanks, man."

Gack shoots me up and the shit is very good. I feel this surge of eroticism or something, all at once—maybe like an orgasm. Better than that, I'd say.

I hold my head in my hands.

"Good, right?"

"Yeah. Take that girl upstairs this instant."

I turn the music up really loud and they go to fuck, or whatever. I draw on a piece of cardboard with these oil pastels Lauren has. At least I still have that. Drawing you don't really have to think about anyway.

I swear it's only like ten minutes till Gack and his girl are back downstairs and she's kinda freaking out, saying, "Gack, come on, come on."

"We gotta go," he tells me. "I'll be back."

Erin doesn't say anything to me—she just pulls at Gack and looks spooked as hell.

He definitely gave her too much. I've really only had one experience with amphetamine psychosis. This drug dealer, Annika, who was my friend Tyler's girl, got really out there smoking speed. I came to her house in the Panhandle to buy a twenty bag, but when she came to the door, she immediately put her finger to her lips—telling me to get down, that the cops were outside. It was weird 'cause there was no reasoning with her. She kept saying, like, "I know what's going on. You think I'm fucking stupid. Well, I'm not. I know. I know."

Eventually I just left 'cause she started yelling at me more and more—plus she wouldn't sell me any speed. I had to go all the way to fucking Oakland to get it. I heard she was hospitalized that night.

So hopefully Erin's not gonna lose it. She's so fucking young.

I lock the door after they leave, then I go call Lauren. She answers, but sounds all stoned out.

"Nic?"

"Yeah."

"Baby, I'm sleeping."

"Okay."

"You gotta come get me tomorrow."

"You sure?"

"Yeah." She yawns. "I love you. Call me in the morning."

"Okay."

"I love you."

"You too."

We hang up and I draw and listen to music some more.

Gack doesn't show up again till, like, one thirty. He's all out of breath. "Let's get moving," he says.

"Get movin' how? Is Erin all right?"

"Yeah, I guess. She was hella paranoid—said she needed to just lie in bed for a while and sleep."

"Sleep? Dude, there's no way."

"Yeah, well, come on. We gotta cut that crystal. I got some vitamin B we can use to cook it with."

"Whatever you say, man."

We go to the kitchen and find a glass and pour a bunch of crystal in with the vitamin B powder. We add a tiny bit of water and start to melt it down over the stovetop flame. Once it forms a liquid, we lay it out on a cookie sheet and place that in the freezer. It's actually Gack who does it all. Five minutes later we pull out the sheet, and the vitamin B and crystal have fused together to make a layer of what looks like soap. He chips all the pieces out of the sheet and dumps it on the counter. It's sort of powdery and colored off-yellow.

"What the fuck is that supposed to be?"

"Don't worry," he says. "We just need to add more crystal."

I pull out both teeners—the one for us and the one we're cutting. Both of them look really small already.

"Jesus," I say. "We did a fucking lot."

"Yeah."

For the first time I notice that Gack's mouth is twitching. His eyes are wide and jumping. I look down at my hands. They're shaking bad.

"Fuck, man, you think we did too much?"

"No, it's cool," says Gack. "We just gotta focus. Give me the rest of that teener."

"You sure you know what you're doing?"

He asks if he's ever let me down before and I pass the shit over, shaking my head. He repeats the whole cooking down, cooling process. What comes out is, well, a little better than before—but still flaky and powdery and yellow.

"Dude, I would never buy that shit."

"It's cool," he says.

He tries a few more times—letting it cool longer, shorter, experimenting with cutting it different ways. Somehow, with each pass, it seems to be getting smaller.

"Fuck it," he finally says. "This is good enough."

"What?"

"We just gotta tell 'em this shit is raw—unprocessed. People'll buy it. Trust me. Look, it'll be better when I bag the shit up."

I go down and get my shoes and jacket and things. When I come up, all the "raw" meth has been separated into small plastic Baggies. Each one should, theoretically, sell for twenty bucks. I look at it skeptically, but don't say anything. I know Gack is trying his best.

"I'm sorry, man," he finally says. "We'll never use that cut again."

I laugh. "No shit."

"But come on, it'll work out."

It's late, like almost three, but the kids are still chilling around in front of the Church and Market Safeway.

I wait by the car while Gack goes and talks with a few of them. He comes back a couple minutes later.

"Fuck those guys, man, ain't never got no money. Let's cruise over to Castro."

So we walk fast down Market and there is no one around—I mean, no one. About a block away from the Safeway, though, some punk-lookin' dude with a bleached Mohawk and big lace-up boots yells out to us. We stop. He comes up and wants to buy a twenty bag. He's got sort of grizzly-looking facial hair and real spaced-out eyes.

He looks at the sack we hand him for a long time. "What the fuck is this?"

"Shit's raw, dude, hella pure and uncut."

"Nah, fuck that."

"Look, man, just try it. We'll roll back here in, like, twenty minutes."

"All right, but if this shit's no good, I'ma track y'all down."

"Don't worry."

The man hands Gack a crumpled twenty and we keep on moving down the street. There's some guy sleeping across the sidewalk—wrapped in a blanket like a corpse. We have to step over him.

Down Castro we manage to sell one sack to some gay couple in town from somewhere. Watching the men circle the block around 18th makes my stomach twist up. I actually think I recognize one of the guys—some Asian dude in a white Mustang. He just keeps circling, circling, circling. But, no, I'm sure it's not him.

As we walk back toward Safeway, we see that Mohawk kid coming toward us. He keeps playing with his nose.

"What's up?" asks Gack.

"Dude," he says, jerking around. "Something's weird about this shit."

"Nah, man, you're hella gacked out."

"Yeah, but something's weird. I want my money back."

"Don't we all," I say.

"Yeah, man, it's not gonna happen."

"Dude, you better not fuck with me—you can't sell bunk shit like that and get away with it."

His jaw's really going. I feel this surging in my head—or pounding—or whatever.

Gack keeps walking. "You know that shit's for real, man."

"There's speed in it, sure, but y'all did something."

"Whatever, man, yer trippin'."

"You can't get away with it."

He's so close to me, man, I can smell the sweat all over him. Gack keeps walking, walking—never stopping for a second.

"If you don't make things right, man, I'll tell everyone y'all are selling bunk shit."

Now Gack turns and squares off in front of the guy. "All right, that's enough. Fuck off . . . NOW." He jerks his body forward toward Mohawk kid and Mohawk kid flinches back. I get myself up tall next to Gack and clench my fists and the kid runs off, yelling, "You guys are fucking finished."

My heart is beating a little bit. Actually, it's kind of slamming against my chest and collarbone and whatever. "What was that?" I ask.

"Nothing. Let's get outta here."

We get back to my car, or, uh, Lauren's car. Gack keeps telling me not to worry. If I give him a bunch of the sacks to take with him, he'll sell 'em, no problem. Everything is working out, he keeps saying. For the first time, I'm not so sure. I think back to my life sober—working, getting up early to go on bike rides and shit, going to movies. I haven't looked at a newspaper in over two weeks. There could be a new war going on and I'd have no idea. But this is the life I want to live, right? I mean, I'm happier.

We drive around awhile and I feel like, there's nothing else to do but go shoot more drugs—or smoke more cigarettes. We go back to Lauren's and spend the rest of the night messing around in her room, not accomplishing anything. Gack manages to take apart a portable CD player of mine that was skipping, but he can't put it back together. We have to throw it away. I've pretty much finished all the heroin, leaving just a little bit for the morning—except, of course, it was morning long ago. The sun is up when we finally sleep some. I'm wondering if this is fucking worth it. We're kinda just goin' in circles. When I wake up, I puke for a while in the bathroom. I lie on the tile floor and, 'cause no one's looking, I cry a little. The feeling racks through me, but not a lot of tears come out. I'm sweating and shivering and I smell so bad. I take a shower, but the sour smell won't leave me. My skin is gray, scaly, broken out. My body is eating itself.

After shooting the rest of the dope and a bunch of crystal, I kinda blot out the doubts for a while. I call Lauren and she still wants me to come pick her up, so I try to focus on the directions she's giving me.

I drop Gack off in the TL, with his promise that he's gonna sell some of that whack, cut shit. Santa Cruz is only, like, two hours south of the city, but it feels like I'm going on this big road trip or something—freeing Lauren—staging a jailbreak.

The coast highway runs along Ocean Beach, through Pacifica, and up along Devil's Slide—a treacherous stretch of road with almost no barrier from the several-hundred-foot drop to the sea below—then winds down to the small coastal town of Santa Cruz. The cliffs are steep and unforgiving—the ocean surges, swells, slams against the rocks. Cypress trees and eucalyptus, pines and buckeyes, sway, sway in the heavy onshore winds. Everything is worn away from the salt and damp—the houses bleached out, faded and warped. I'm having fun taking the turns too fast and tight.

Lauren's shrink lives in some gated community where all the streets have "berry" names—Idleberry, Huckleberry, Boysenberry, etc. The guard at the front shows me where to find Jules's house. It looks like all the others. It's real big, but tasteless—boxy—tan, generic, nothing paint. I pull into the driveway and sit there for a minute, breathing.

The front door opens while I'm trying to figure out my next move. Smoking a cigarette is the best I can come up with, but I stamp it out nervously as I see this woman coming out to greet me—or at least, I hope that's what she's doing. She has short curly hair, dyed to disguise the gray. She's a little overweight and heavily made-up—her clothes conservative and not at all stylish. I get outta the car.

"You must be Nic," she says, way too sweetly.

"Yeah."

"I'm Ruth-Anne."

I shake her hand and meet her eyes with mine. I smile.

"Come in," she says, and I follow behind her.

The house looks out on a golf course and the ocean. Two teenage girls are eating bowls of ice cream at this long glass table. Lauren and a balding, very white man in a dress shirt are talking outside on two cushioned metal chairs. I assume that must be Jules.

"Do you want some juice?" asks Ruth-Anne, her voice still way too cheery.

"Uh, okay."

"Apple or grape?"

"Apple, please. Thank you."

She pours me a glass.

"Should I go out there?"

"Yes," she says.

I walk outside into the windswept afternoon and the man stands instantly to shake my hand.

"Nic, I'm Jules," he says. His voice is very soft and soothing, like someone talking on one of those goddamn guided meditation tapes we had to listen to in rehab.

Lauren lights a cigarette, so I do too. I pull a chair over next to her and put my hand on her thigh. She leans her head against my shoulder.

Jules tells me, as kindly as possible, what a bad idea it is for Lauren to return to the city with me. He crosses and uncrosses his legs. He wraps his fingers around one another—long and pale with polished nails. He tells me that if I truly love Lauren, I'll leave her alone to clean up for a while. I look in his eyes. They are striking blue. I say I want to help Lauren, but it's ultimately her choice. Besides, we kind of have to see this run we're on out to the end. We'll bottom out soon enough.

He tries to reason with me. He asks me if OD'ing on heroin isn't bottom enough. I keep repeating that it's Lauren's decision and she says she wants to go home. She assures Jules she won't use.

He obviously doesn't believe her, but it's not like he can stop us or anything. For a while he drills me about my history. I answer honestly. I don't hide anything.

"Yeah, I'm definitely a drug addict—but, uh, it's kinda working for me right now. I mean, I know it's gonna end badly—but I gotta see this through."

"You don't have to," he says. "You want to."

He offers to see me for a free visit sometime—maybe get me on some medication. I thank him all over the place. Jules more or less says nothing the whole time. Lauren looks real out of it—tired—and I realize she hasn't had any speed for over twenty-four hours. The depression, the painful crashing need to sleep, is sweeping through her. I actually have to support her with my arm as we walk outta there.

"You're making a mistake," says Jules.

"Probably."

As soon as we get down the block, we pull over and I watch for patrol cars while Lauren gets off with what's left of the good crystal. I'm definitely using more than I'm selling, which is bad, obviously.

I try not to think about money and how, at this rate, shit won't last another week. Between the meth and heroin, Gack and me and Lauren are using over two hundred dollars a day. If you add food and cigarettes and eventually having to find another place to live other than Lauren's parents' house, well, I can feel the top of the ladder getting closer. I try not to think about it, but you know how that goes.

"Better, baby?" I ask.

She tells me she loves me and I drive us home. "We do gotta cut back," she says.

I agree, taking hold of her hand. "Yeah, plus Gack fucked up a whole teener. Shit's unsellable. We gotta be really careful with what's left."

She tells me that Jules said he would have to call her parents if she left his house. I ask what that means.

"They're gonna come home and try and talk me into getting help."

"What?"

She tells me not to worry. We'll go live in my car together—it'll be all right. We'll find a place eventually. Maybe we'll get sober. If we get sober, her parents will support us.

"We can have a baby," she says.

I just squeeze her hand. "How much time before they come back?"

"It'll probably be by tomorrow night."

"Fuck."

She keeps trying to calm me down, but I can't really see her living in my car. I can't really see getting sober, either. I kinda wish I'd left her in fucking Santa Cruz. We call Candy on our way back into town and I drop another eighty bucks on some heroin.

We shoot most of the cut meth at Lauren's. The cut makes both of us kinda sick, but we still make love like we do. There's always that, isn't there? I feel her moving on top of me on the whiteness of her bed. I feel the pillows and quilts. I feel all this luxury that is about to be gone—so quick, too. We soak the room with our sweat and I can't feel anything, but I keep on fucking her 'cause I don't know what else to do. My mind is going, going, going and even this isn't stopping it, but it helps. When I was a little boy I used to masturbate like this. I was too young to come—but I had all this sexuality inside me and I'd play with myself for hours to escape, or whatever. Hell, maybe it just felt good. There were a few friends I had when I was little who would masturbate with me. It was when I was like nine or ten—maybe younger. We were all too little to have anything happen. I remember telling sexual stories to my friends—making shit up that would turn us all on. I would talk while we were doing it. It's funny 'cause lying here with Lauren, I'm doing the same thing—making love to her in a whisper with my words and my body. That must mean something, right? I guess I'm still that confused little boy, or is that too simple?

DAY 16

Lauren's fucking scared about facing her parents. We do the rest of that nasty cut shit and I can't believe it's all gone. Gack may have sold some, but it's not real likely. I make breakfast and help clean up. She talked to her parents early this morning. They should be in at, like, six. Still, I'm not taking any chances having to meet them like this—so I leave early. Lauren says if I don't call her many times this evening, she'll fucking kill me. I try to look at her objectively.

Over two weeks and she looks completely changed. She's lost so much weight her small head looks enormous on her withering neck. Her cheekbones are standing out against the hollowness of her face and eyes. Her arms are bruised, bloody—brown splotches—white scars—swollen in some places, horribly shrunken in others. Her lips are washed out—white—cracked. I kiss them and taste her dry nicotine tongue.

"We'll be all right," she says.

I take my stuff and walk out to where I parked my car. There's leaves and shit all over it. There are four parking tickets under the windshield wipers. The back tire is flat and I got no spare.

Back to Lauren's.

I use her phone to call a tow truck. When we get to the gas station, the attendant—an aging, lined white guy with long hair slicked back—tries to sell me new tires all around. I tell him I just need it to be drivable.

"These other ones are gonna go," he says, his voice all thick and hoarse.

"I'll take my chances."

"Yer chances ain't good."

I thank him.

While his boys are fixing the tire, I go call Gack. Between the tow truck and the tire, well, that's a little under two hundred bucks. I worry about how fast my money is disappearing. I'm on, like, the corner of Geary and 21st and the early afternoon streets are mostly empty. Gack said he sold three sacks and used the other. That's sixty dollars he got, at least.

When I pick him up, he's all excited 'cause he found a pair of pants behind some church. They have all these pockets, which he thinks is just fucking great. They're, like, army style—dark, olive green—torn at both knees. I see his pale knees sticking through.

"How's Erin?"

"Oh, dude," he says, his voice cracking some. "She fucking lost it. Shit weren't cool. She called me all wanting me to take her to the hospital and shit. Poor thing had to go to school like that in the morning."

"But she's all right?"

"Sure."

We go cop behind some donut place near the Bay Bridge. Gack goes in like always and I wait in the car. I'm tired, man. All the speed in the world can't seem to get me up. I watch some black dude with a thick beard and a thicker parka asking for money on the street corner. I've tried it before. Really, there's no feeling worse. Not even hustling is as bad. At least with that, there's a sense of being a commodity of some value. Asking for money is a proclamation of your own unfitness for survival. It's saying, "I am the weak one of the herd." Or worse, a parasite that feeds on society. Trying to meet a person's eyes, begging them for scraps—it is humbling in a way that few things are. And sitting here, I keep thinking that I'm about to have no other option. Tricking or begging—that's what's gonna be left for me. Plus I'm so goddamn worn out.

When I was on the streets before, I had so much drive. I remember when I was living at Akira's, he let me stay in this storage space in his garage. I had to clear all the shit out that was in there, but keep it secret from his mom—so I just piled it all up in the rafters and put a mattress under it all. One night I was sleeping and it all came crashing down—splitting my head. There was blood everywhere. In the morning, I woke up with this huge scab on my forehead. I put on a shirt and this apron I had from a job I'd gotten at this Italian restaurant. They gave me the shirt and apron, but I never went back. So I put that shit on and got this bag of ice and started walking up Park Presidio, Clement, and Geary. I picked the scab off and the blood was coming down. I went up to people and was, like, "Please help, I just got in this accident at work. I need money to get a taxi back home."

I made around fifteen bucks in about half an hour, but then this Russian woman with very platinum hair stopped me.

"What you say doesn't make sense," she said. "If you got hurt at work, why didn't they help you?"

My eyes widened. "Good question."

That was the end of that scheme. I guess it was pretty stupid to begin with. But doing that shit now—I just can't see it. Plus, back then, fifteen bucks would get me through a day of shooting speed. I've moved far beyond that point now—but we know that already.

When Gack comes back he's all freaked out. He tells me to drive—quick. Walking through the alley, some guy approached him and told him to empty his pockets. He had to throw his skate at the guy and run. I screech outta the parking lot. Gack is breathing hard.

"What the fuck is happening to us?" I ask. "Doors are closing."

"Nah," Gack assures me. "It's all good."

Driving toward Church and Market, I ask Gack to get me a shot ready. "Do you need one?" I ask.

He shrugs.

"All right, fuck it. Make 'em big, man. I'm not even getting high no more."

"Word."

We shoot up in the Safeway parking lot. I actually feel it, which is good, and I cough and all. Gack bags the shit up just like it is 'cause I ain't fucking cutting shit anymore. I'll sell small sacks, but I don't wanna deal with all that again. He goes off to try and make some sales on twenty bags. I try writing in my notebook—Daisy's notebook. My thoughts are scattered. It's all bullshit. I draw instead, looking up every once in a while to watch the couple in the car next to me. The guy is real haggard-looking, but young—late twenties. The girl is sort of pudgy, with a bob haircut, dyed black. The car is full of crap. It's a boxy red nothing, like mine. After a while, I realize they're both shooting up—or, uh, the guy is shooting them both up. I get outta the car and lean against the hood, lighting a cigarette. I watch them both get off, then the guy looks up and notices me staring at them.

"Yeah?" he asks, rolling the window down.

"Nothing, don't trip. I just didn't know if y'all wanted a little up for later."

"What?"

"I got this really good crystal I'm selling if y'all are interested. I ain't no cop or nothing."

He turns to his girl.

"What do you think, baby, you want some crystal?"

"Crystal?"

"Is it good?" she asks.

"Kid says it is."

"Is it good, kid?" she asks, laughing.

"You can try some if you want."

"No shit?"

I tell them again it's good. I tell them it's what I'm on. We're talking like old friends. They agree to buy forty dollars' worth and I'm so grateful that I actually hook them up really fat. I even give them Lauren's number. If they want more they can just call. They thank me and I thank them. I feel this power inside—a renewed faith. Maybe things'll work out after all.

But then I see Gack coming up and he's talking to himself and clenching his fists.

"Let's go," he says.

"What?"

"We're fucking closed out here."

"What do you—"

"That fucking guy, he talked a lot of shit."

"Mohawk kid?"

"Yeah. He said I was selling bunk shit. No one'll buy from me. I'm gonna find him and beat the shit outta him. We gotta go down to Haight."

"Haight?"

"Yeah, they say he'll be down there."

I do what he says. Somehow Gack thinks that beating up the Mohawk guy will prove he's been straight ahead with everyone. When I tell him about hooking the couple up, he sighs like I'm so fucking stupid.

"Come on, man, you can't be doing that. These people ain't ever gonna call you. Just 'cause you are cool with someone and hook 'em up don't mean they're gonna have any loyalty to you. People don't give a fuck."

"But—"

"I'm different. There are a few of us who are. Hey, pull over a second, I think I see one."

"One what?"

"One of us."

So I pull over. We're in the Panhandle—actually right near my old drug dealer Annika's place. There's nothing here but row after row of Victorians—maybe a liquor store or whatever. The pavement is all cracked with blades of grass growing through. There's dog shit everywhere. The street stinks of it.

I see Gack go up to this guy who is short and hunched. He has a scruffy beard, a beanie, a black jacket. He's drinking from a brown paper bag and smoking a hand-rolled cigarette, or I guess it's a joint. They talk for a second and then they're back to my car.

"Nic, this is Ben. Ben's all right."

He gets into the backseat. The weed he's smoking fills the

car with this sweetness. I take a long pull from the wet roach and pass it to Gack.

"Ben, you wanna help us find this kid who's been dissin' us? We gonna kick his fucking ass."

"Yeah, all right. I gotta parole board meeting at four in Daly City."

"Dude," I say. "I'll drive you."

"What about that punk-ass motherfucker? We gotta take care of that shit, Nic."

"Whatever," I say. "Fuck that kid. We'll see him around sometime. Why waste our energy looking for him? That's like giving him power and shit."

"Word," says Gack. "Maybe you're right."

"Yeah."

So we all drive out along the beach to Daly City. At one point, way down the avenues at, like, Judah and 30-somethingth, Gack wants me to stop. We're right near his girl's place and he wants to call her—see if she can hang out awhile. He goes to find a pay phone and I sit with Ben. Ben doesn't say much—except that he just got outta jail. He mentions some letter he's waiting for. Apparently there was some guy he shared a cell with who promised to give him the deed to a big piece of property in England. By some coincidence they turned out to be related or something. The whole thing sounds like bullshit to me, but I don't tell him that.

I look out on all the Chinese and Korean markets. I'm thirsty as hell, but I don't wanna buy any more shit. I just filled up my tank with gas and bought hella cigarettes and shit, so I'm pretty fucking worried about the fact that I got only five hundred dollars left. That'll be gone in a week—and that's if I try real hard to conserve it. Basically, I can't be buying food anymore.

I have this empty water bottle in the back of my car, so I go into a dry cleaning place. Now, I'm pretty used to having people look at me and not trust me and whatever. No one in the city ever lets you use their bathroom or anything. And, in general, folks on the avenues are real suspicious and cold. I'm nervous about walking into this place, but, like I said, I'm thirsty and can't afford to throw any more money away. So I go inside and the woman leaning on the counter scowls at me behind thick glasses. She speaks in not great English—asking what I want.

"Nothing. I just, uh, I need some water."

"Water?"

"Yes, please. I'm so thirsty. Could you fill this bottle up with water for me—or show me where I can fill it up?"

"You want water for drinking?"

"Please."

"No, you go buy."

"Please, I just want some tap water."

"No, you go."

She points a long, thin finger toward the street.

"Go." I meet her eyes for a second, then turn and walk silently out. The sun seems very far away.

I shove my hands into the pocket of my sweatshirt, but then I hear a voice calling after me.

"Boy. Boy."

Turning, I see the woman from the dry cleaner's running after me. She has a small bottle of water in her hand.

"You take this."

"What? Why?"

"You take."

I thank her. She just turns and walks back into her store. I guess I feel like crying. I'm not sure why.

Gack comes back and I tell him the story and he doesn't really seem to care. He can't find Erin, so he decides to just come with us down to Daly City. Ben's meeting takes about five seconds. He basically just has to show up. The building is this big institutional-looking green block slab. My car is kinda jerkin' and being weird and shit. When we park, the engine lets off this steam or something. I mean it's kind of hissing and smoking. I lift up the hood and stare at the insides—not like I know shit about cars. I suppose it's only a matter of time before the car gives out. I'm just gonna have to drive it till it stops running completely. It can't be long.

Ben says he's really hungry as we drive back to the city.

"If we get to Glide by five then we can get in the dinner line," he says.

"Glide?"

"Sure."

I know Glide Memorial Church from when I was little. In grade school, we used to take trips down there to help work in the soup kitchen. We all hated it, of course. Mostly we just served punch, or whatever—helped clear away trays. We were too young to chop anything or handle serving the hot food. I remember distributing bread to the line of men and women—none of 'em looking at one another or at me. Mostly they weren't too scary or anything. Sometimes they'd ask for an extra piece of bread, or more juice. We weren't supposed to give it to them, but I always did.

I can't say what I thought about seeing those people having to be fed like that. I mean, I'm not sure if I really thought about why they were in that position. Obviously, growing up in the city, I was used to seeing the homeless. I know I felt sorry for them—men and women wrapped in blankets lying on the hard concrete. I guess I thought they were sick or something. No, I don't remember what conclusions I drew.

But one thing was for sure—I never in my life imagined being one of them.

Yet here I am, standing in line with a little yellow ticket in my hand—the sun blocked out by the dry-rot buildings. I'm standing in line with all these other men and women, mostly older than me, huddled together—but never touching, never looking up, never talking. I stare at a piece of gum turned black, stamped into the sidewalk. I'm suddenly real paranoid about someone I know from when I was a kid driving by—a teacher, or even my parents. I'm hoping we can just get inside, you know?

The church stretches up, up, up, with dirt caked into the worn-away bricks. A stained-glass window reflects no light and purple flags hang from the steeple. We're let in through a side door, down these bare carpeted stairs. There are a lot of pictures of Jesus on the walls and signs posting times for substance abuse counseling groups and AIDS testing and whatever. I follow Ben and Gack follows me. We don't say one thing. The whole room of people is weighted with shame.

I grab a tray. Two young black women and an older white man with a tie-dye T-shirt serve beans, coleslaw, white rice, and stale bread. I ask for everything on my plate and thank them. We go sit down at one of the long plastic tables. We eat fast. We're below the street and the only light comes from some fluorescent pale bulbs along the ceiling. The food actually tastes great. I eat it all.

Lauren sounds terrible when she finally answers her phone. She's crying hysterically and chokes and gasps for breath. Her parents are kicking her out if she doesn't agree to go into rehab. She has about a week to decide—that's when they're all going to meet with Jules about her options for treatment. They want me to come to the meeting.

"Me? Why?"

"Because I love you and we want to help you."

"Oh, Lauren, I don't know."

"It'll be fine, we'll do it together."

"I'm not going back to rehab."

"Just come," she says, sniffling loudly. "Maybe they'll figure something else out."

"And until then?"

She says she has to stay home. She can go out to some appointments and things. Maybe she can meet me then. Otherwise we just have to wait and see.

I hang up the phone. Suddenly I don't feel like hanging out anymore. I tell Gack and Ben that I've gotta go. We agree to meet up tomorrow. Ben gives me a number of some hotel where

I can leave a message for him. I get in my car and start driving back toward the parking lot on 15th and Lake—figuring I'll maybe walk around the Presidio some, see if there's any old abandoned army housing that I can sneak into. I've always had this fantasy of squatting in one of those places. They're all single-story brick or white wood houses—boarded up—doors fastened shut with heavy padlocks.

Driving over there, the heat gauge is, like, busting through the glass. I can hear this hissing noise and there's a bunch of gray-black smoke. The car stalls out right at the base of the lot and I manage to coast it into one of the parking spaces.

Fuck, fuck, fuck.

I put some stuff in a shoulder bag—a screwdriver, a note-book, pens, three CDs, a portable CD player, and these big studio headphones. I play this Fantômas record. It's sort of arty death metal with all these sudden starts and stops—strange vocalizations over hardcore compositions. I set out through the Presidio—the trees hanging down and the streetlights all glowing orange. The roads wind through the dense forest. The shadows are dramatic and startling. I keep feeling like someone is coming up behind me and I look back, nervous. It reminds me of this time outside my old drug dealer's place in Oakland.

I mean, downtown Oakland's pretty safe and all, but the little suburbs are just totally fucked up. No one even knows they're there, so you could basically just go in and never come out and no one would ever know. I remember walking through there and I was listening to this John Coltrane CD. It was the Impulse stuff after he kicked heroin and started talking to God through his music. It's really out there and I was listening to one of those CDs, walking through this neighborhood. It seemed like everyone was staring at me and it was really just a matter of time before this big car, a Cadillac or something, crept up slow next to me. I was just pretending not to notice and all, so I walked on. But the car sped up, then pulled this fat U-turn and stopped. These three big-ass dudes with fucking bandannas and football jerseys got out and they were just mobbing straight toward me. You know that walk? When they stick their chests out and sort of waddle, but it looks tough, you know, a tough waddle. Basically, I thought I was fucked. I had this goddamn backpack full of CDs and drugs and money, all of which I figured I was about to part ways with. I didn't know what to do. They got closer and I turned and started to run. They actually fucking chased me. Somehow, tweaked out, listening to Coltrane, running from these big guys, about to get jacked, it all seemed so funny and I started laughing. I mean, I was really fucking laughing so I couldn't stop. But I was still trying to run, which made me laugh even more. They just stopped and, like, looked at me all puzzled and shit and then they started laughing. They were laughing and I was laughing and I just kept running till I was outta there.

But here in the Presidio, there's absolutely no one around. I can't really understand it. With all the homeless folk in SF, the fact that these woods remain unmolested is sort of a mystery. I remember talking to this strung-out older man camped out somewhere near the Steps of Rome Caffe on Columbus. I was like, "Dude, why are you sleeping on this concrete, man? For one dollar you take a bus twenty minutes and are in this national park."

The guy turned his head toward me and asked, confused, "There's a national park around here?"

"Yeah, man, the fucking Presidio."

"How do I get there?"

I told him, but the next day I saw him back on Columbus—trying to sleep in the same goddamn spot.

So I walk along the trails and small paved roads. There are large abandoned houses all around—but I keep feeling like someone's watching me or something.

In a way it's like too serene or whatever—too empty. I feel that familiar feeling of being a dark smudge on this otherwise pristine white canvas. There's just no way to blend in out here. And then, walking along the street, I feel these headlights behind me. I turn quickly—just glancing back and, sure enough, there's a car comin' up slow. I pick up my pace some, but then back off—not wanting to look suspicious. I turn my head again. A wave of nausea sweeps through me and my blood drains as I see the roof of the car—a police cruiser. It's right alongside me and staying there. I try to remember if there're any drugs in my bag. I'm pretty sure there aren't—but there is that screwdriver—plus my arms are so completely covered in tracks. I wonder if they can arrest you for that. It seems like they can pretty much arrest you for anything.

I lower my headphones and look over at the car. They've got one of those sidelight things out the passenger window and it is mad shining at me—white and glaring. I stop walking and just stare it down, my arms dangling—not making any sudden movements. The cruiser slows to almost nothing. I can't see anything but the light. I wait—my heart going, going, going.

And then they drive off.

Just like that.

They don't say anything.

I'm shaking all over.

I walk back to my car and try to sleep in the backseat. Every twenty minutes or so, I wake up—sure that some cop is banging on my window. When morning comes I have to throw up three times. A shot of heroin calms my stomach, but can't take away the fear.

DAY 23

It's Sunday morning, five a.m., cold before the sun is up. I'm shivering, shivering, shivering. Gack and Bullet and I are outside the Fairmont Hotel. We've been waiting all night and I'm not really sure how we ended up here. It's been five days of basically nothing but shooting drugs, selling bags of crystal here and there, sleeping in my car—if at all—eating at Glide, or stealing sandwiches from Starbucks. One day we find half a box of pizza on the ground, another day there's a plate of rice and fish leftovers wrapped up on top of a garbage can in the Marina. Everyone seems to have forgotten about that Mohawk kid, but the crystal's still hard to move—plus we're using so much. I've only seen Lauren a couple times, mostly just to drop off a sack for her.

The meeting with her shrink and all is tomorrow morning. I'm nervous about it, but I agree to show up. Honestly, I'm not sure how much longer I can keep doing this. It's like there are seven candles lit in my stomach. One, two, three, four, five, six, seven. Seven candles burning and smoking—lit—seven flames of doubt, fear, sorrow, pain, waste, hopelessness, despair. They turn my insides black with soot and ash. There is something at the back of my eyes—a pressure building, building, building—hot like the flames of seven candles, which no amount of breath can extinguish.

I imagine drinking glasses of water. One, two, three, four, five, six, seven. I dive into the clearest pool. I drown myself in the coarse, dry sand. I swallow handfuls of crushed white salt, but the flames burn higher still—brighter, hotter, deeper. Sweat runs in delicate patterns down my back, over my crooked spine and jutting hips. I scratch at the wounds these last weeks have left, but I can't break free of them. The flies gather and vultures circle overhead. The fire eats away my flesh. The fire spreads. The fire runs through my veins. The fire courses beneath my muscles—my tendons—the marrow of my bones.

I sit rocking on the street corner. No, I can't keep doing this. I just can't.

Bullet shoots the last of the heroin. He found out his mom died this morning from her lymphatic cancer and I couldn't say no. I give him a lot of cigarettes. He doesn't cry, but he keeps breaking shit. He kicked this newspaper stand to pieces. He's mumbling about being taken to the park by her as a child. His words are all slurred over the heroin nods. Gack tries to comfort him but Bullet just yells at him. I mostly say nothing. I haven't changed clothes in three days. I can't even smell myself anymore. The money is going. My veins are already collapsing so it's getting hard as hell to hit. I've started having to dig around, like Lauren. I've even started trying to shoot up in my hands and legs and feet. Gack tells me not to fuck with my legs, 'cause if you miss you can't walk without being in, like, so much pain. I don't listen to him.

Anyway, Bullet keeps going on about going to a park with his mom—or that he wants to go to a park—I can't really tell. But we've hiked up California Street past the Fairmont 'cause we are trying to find some sort of park to hang out at so Bullet will shut up about it. I seem to remember a playground up here. It was this huge place with a big orange slide and tunnels and monkey bars. Before we get there, though, Gack and I are gonna do some more speed and we're trying to decide whether to go into the Fairmont bathroom or not. It's gonna be impossible to go in there at five a.m. without drawing a lot of attention to ourselves. Bullet shot up on a doorstep down the street, so Gack and I end up going back down there.

Bullet plays watch guard while we shoot up. That's the end of our speed.

Gack is able to hit somewhere on my forearm and the rush hits me and I'm satisfied for about a minute—then it dies out. I know I'm high, I just don't feel it. The sun begins to lighten the sky and everything turns clear and crisp and pale—cold. There's a layer of pink sky on the rooftops. We walk up the hill toward the playground. My legs are sore—my body is giving out.

We walk to the playground and it is so much smaller than I remembered. After all, I was just a child when I was last here. The park is actually filled with people, mostly Asian, wearing sweat suits and moving slow, slow, slow. Arms outstretched, then in. Legs up, out, down—moving like they're underwater, or weighed down with lead. The three of us stop and stare.

"Tai chi," I say.

Then suddenly, cars begin pulling up all around us—limousines, town cars, BMWs, Mercedes. Men and women, young and old, dressed in fine suits, tuxedos, long flowing dresses with flowers and expensive purses—they're swarming around us, going up the steps to . . . what? Grace Cathedral.

"What the hell is going on?" I ask.

"Fuck if I know."

Gack runs off to ask somebody. He approaches a young lady in a pink ruffled dress. She looks kindly enough, but freezes when she sees Gack. Still, he gets her to talk to him.

"It's Easter," he yells back at us.

"No way," says Bullet. "Fucking Easter. I gotta go to church."

"What?" I say. "Bullet, there's no way."

"Yeah, don't you see—that must be why we came here."

"Maybe, but I don't think you can go in there like you are."

"What do you mean by that?"

I leave that one alone.

Gack comes back over and Bullet tells him all about needing to go to church.

"Do what you want," says Gack. "But there's no fucking way I'm going in there."

Bullet asks us maybe ten times what the chances are—us being up here on Easter and all.

"It's gotta be a sign."

"Yeah," says Gack. "A sign that if you go in there, they'll call the cops on your ass. Look how those fools are dressed. You wanna go to church? Well, then let's go back down to the TL."

But Bullet insists and so we watch him disappear into the crowd.

I laugh.

I laugh and fucking laugh and Gack does too.

"This is all so pathetic," I say. "We can't go on like this."

"What else is there?"

"Should we wait for him?"

"Nah, fuck it."

We walk back through the playground and back down the hill and the sun is up and the sky is clear.

"I love this city," I say.

"Yeah," agrees Gack.

"But it's gonna fucking kill us."

"Yeah."

"You ever think of getting out?"

"No."

My feet hurt so bad—there're blisters everywhere from walking so much. I tell Gack all about Lauren and having to meet with her family tomorrow. I tell him I'm thinking about getting clean again. He tells me it's a waste of time.

"What is life for, if not for living?"

"Is this living?"

"We're so free."

"Sort of."

Back in the TL the streets are already crowded with people looking to eat, or get well, or whatever. There's no sign of Easter here. I smoke cigarettes while Gack goes up to his room to get some shit. I wanna try to take a shower and change clothes maybe before seeing Lauren—maintain some semblance of looking like I've got it together. Gack isn't allowed visitors in his hotel anymore—so we've gotta find somewhere else around here to take a shower. Most of the apartments have communal showers, so it's just a question of getting through the front gate.

Gack thinks he knows someone a couple blocks down who'll buzz us in. He brings down a Snickers bar for my breakfast.

The apartment house is maybe five or six stories—white peeling paint, warped siding, a white painted gate blocking the stairs from the street. Gack pushes one of the buttons on the call box, but it just rings through. I smoke another cigarette and wish I had some water. After trying a few more buttons, we still can't get inside. We walk around the back of the building. Gack thinks maybe he can climb one of the drainpipes up to an open window, but there're cameras back here and the whole thing just seems sketchy as hell. The back door is just as impenetrable as the front. The alley smells like beer, or piss, or both. It dead-ends at a big concrete wall circled with barbed wire.

After discussing our options for a while, we see a very voluptuous-looking black woman with long extensions click-clacking in high heels up toward the rear entrance. She stops there in front of it and tilts her head back. She's wearing a lot of makeup.

"Hey, Kevin, man—gimme the fucking key!" She yells that up at the building. "Yo, motherfucker—the key!"

A bald man sticks his head out the window and tells her to be quiet, then lets a key chain fall down several stories next to her. She picks it up delicately with her pink acrylic nails.

She gets the door open and starts to walk in and Gack runs up to grab the door. She turns and lowers her eyes at him. "Nuh-uh. I don't think so."

"My cousin lives in there," says Gack.

"Then yo cousin can let yo ass in. Step back."

Gack does and the door is closed in his face.

We go around to the front again.

"Come on," I say. "Let's forget it."

But just then, as the sun clears the top of the building and the street is washed with noonday light, an old Asian woman—stooped, with silver hair and thick glasses—exits the building with a metal cart and several bags. I rush up to hold the door for her—ever the chivalrous one—and Gack does the same. We watch her leave, then go into the building. It looks the same as all the other cheap fucking run-down places around here—smoky, stained carpeting and uneven hallways.

"The showers are in there," says Gack. "Here, I got you a towel."

He pulls this crumpled damp shredded rag outta his bag and I thank him. He's also got a bottle of some shampoo. I take the stuff and try the door to the bathroom, but it's locked.

"Fuck, you think someone's in there?"

"Not likely."

He knocks and there's no response.

"Let's try the next floor."

We turn to find the stairs, but then there's this man standing there behind us. He's tall, with a paunchy belly and a red Mohawk—though he must be in his late thirties. His eyes are bugged somewhat and his lips jut out—as though he had puckered up to kiss somebody and his mouth just froze like that. He's wearing an Asian print silk robe that doesn't conceal very much. His chest and legs are thick with hair.

"Oh, yes," he says. "They started locking the showers so kids would stop coming in off the street to use them." His voice sounds very, uh, lazy—tired, or bored, or something. He speaks like he sees everything that is going on and it is very tiresome indeed. I guess you could say he sounds haughty. Yeah, that's it.

"You gotta key?" asks Gack.

"Yes, but you may as well come along and use mine. I have a bathtub with soaps and whatnot. I'm sure you would find that preferable."

"Sure, thanks," says Gack.

There're eels slithering through my belly, turning and flicking their tails. But Gack doesn't seem worried, so I follow them up several flights of stairs.

"You'll have to excuse the place," the man says. "I just moved into this room from a smaller one and I haven't unpacked yet. Also, an ex-boyfriend is asleep in the kitchen—well, passed out really. I'm sure you understand, boys."

True enough, there's stuff all over the room—boxes and blankets and clothes and trash and shit. In the small kitchen, a younger-looking boy is out cold, naked on a pile of clothes and magazines and things. I have to step over him to get to the shower. The bathroom is cluttered with lots of soaps and shampoos and things. There's a wood-handled scrub brush and razors and lotion and whatever. There's no showerhead, but an extendable nozzle that comes from the faucet. I have to sort of crouch down, balancing on the balls of my feet. It reminds me of all the showers in Europe. There's a small window letting in shafts of light. I do the whole bathing thing.

Around the time I'm washing the shampoo out of my hair, the door opens and I kind of freeze a little. The man with the robe comes in and says, "Don't mind me," then goes over and takes a piss in the toilet. His cock is very big and the veins are sticking out grotesquely. I try not to notice that he's staring at me. I keep going with the shower. The guy stares and stares. Finally, he walks out.

I breathe a little more easily.

So I finish and dress and go back into the main room. That one guy is still passed out in the kitchen. I step over him again.

Gack is on the floor messing with this little radio or something.

"You ready?" I ask.

"Sure, sure, sure."

We start to leave and then the man has his hand on mine— gently pulling me back. "If you should ever need a place to stay sometime, I'm sure I could make it worth your while. Here's my phone number. My name's Daryl, by the way." He hands me a little piece of paper and I stuff it in my pocket.

"Yeah, thanks."

We get outta there and I feel this nausea in my throat.

"What a fucking creep," says Gack.

"Yeah, word." But my options are running out. Soon fucking guys like Daryl is gonna be all I got. Not that I can say anything about that to Gack.

The two of us take a bus down to where my car is abandoned and I change clothes and shoot the rest of the heroin. Gack thinks we should re-up on speed to try and make some money, but I'm so broke I think I'm gonna wait till tomorrow.

Still, he convinces me to at least hook up a gram to get us through the night. We walk up to Haight Street and there're people everywhere—shopping and whatever. I feel actually fairly normal, even though I can tell I'm nodding a little as we walk. I've already dropped my cigarette, like, ten times. Anyway, Gack goes and scouts around for some crystal and I head into Amoeba.

It's a little overwhelming, all the CDs and people and everything. I go to the "just released" section. There're tons of albums I see that I normally would buy—or would have anticipated buying. The Secret Chiefs 3 have a new album out—as well as Trevor Dunn and Eyvind Kang. Obviously I can't buy them now. I realize I have no idea what movies have been released or anything. I'm so isolated—insulated in this world of scrounging to get money so I can buy drugs, to get high, then start all over again.

But Gack manages to get us a gram for fifty bucks from some kid in the park. The kid is wearing a thick, dirty jacket with safety pins all over it. He has a red-orange beard and wide, paranoid eyes. The stuff he's got doesn't look really good but there's a lot there. It definitely isn't short.

So we buy the drugs and I have only a couple hundred bucks left. Gack and I go and shoot up in the bathroom of a taqueria off Clayton. Shit gets me high—that's what I can say for it. The emptiness in my stomach—the well digging down—the nausea—the aching won't leave me. It's profound—consuming. I feel like curling up, serpentine on the floor, crying. I need a thousand pounds of heroin. I need to drown myself in methamphetamine. I need pills, weed, vials of liquid acid.

Or maybe—maybe—I just need to get sober.

My head keeps going around like this.

Gack asks me what's wrong and I tell him I think I gotta be alone a minute—take a walk or whatever. He says that's all cool and to call him. I leave like that. Sea Cliff is miles away, but I walk over there. I walk down Stanyan, down Park Presidio—then on down Clement. I listen to music—Miles Davis's *Live-Evil*. My heart is beating, beating, beating.

I think about Jasper and Daisy. I think about my dad and stepmom. I think about Spencer and my friends in the program. I think about my mom and her husband and their two dogs. I think about my job at that rehab. I'd started taking some classes **117** at Santa Monica College. I'd had a life. Suddenly I can't even remember why I started using again in the first place. I wanna throw up, I think. I'm sweating from everywhere. I'm sweating from everywhere, but I'm real cold, too.

The avenues are deserted as always, but I feel like people are watching me from their windows as I pass. I know that's not the most sane thought in the world. I call Lauren from a pay phone and she answers right away.

"Lauren," I say, my voice cracking some. "I need help. I think I'm ready to get help."

"Oh, baby," she says. "Where are you?"

"Right near your house?"

"Then come over."

"Are you sure?"

"Yeah, no one's home."

So I walk over to Lauren's house and already the sun is going. When she opens the door, I hold her and then I cry and cry. I sob so hard. All those damn corgis are all over—whining and trying to lick me and I just cry, cry, cry. I don't know when I've ever cried like this before. It's been a long time. I smell the soap in Lauren's hair as she wraps herself around me. I can't stop.

"It'll be all right, baby." She just repeats that over and over.

Eventually we make it down to her room and I'm still crying but we make love and all. A crack in the floor breaks open and we tumble in—swallowed by the eroticism of sex and our closeness to death. Our bones stick together and the joints pop, pop. I'm blind, or disoriented, or not really sure what. The blankness of white nothing pulls me out of myself for a moment and I feel very far away—disconnected. Somehow I fall asleep like that. I don't dream.

I wake up with my jaw tight as hell from clenching it so hard.

Lauren's shaking me. "Come on," she says. "We gotta go— my parents are home."

"I can't stay here?"

"Candy called." Lauren's all dressed and everything. "She's got some really good heroin in. She's gonna cut us a deal, er, uh, something."

"Baby, I ain't got any money left really."

"I have a little," she says, all but pulling me out of bed. "We'll get clean right after this—I promise."

"Okay," I say. "Yeah, I know this cool old hotel off Grant. We can hole up there till we're done with the heroin."

"Then we'll come back here and my parents'll help us."

"I love you," I say.

"Yeah, I love you, too."

And so fast, fast, fast we're outta there. It makes sense to me. We'll just go on one more run—blow it all out till the end. I know it's gonna be all right now. We shoot most of the crystal in her car down the block from her house. She hasn't used much in a couple days, so she gets real high. I drive.

———

The San Remo Hotel is, like, fifty bucks a night—but nice. Dark wood paneling, strange potted ferns and things, thick carpeting. The place feels like a ship—warped, uneven, sinking.

We hook up a bunch of tar heroin from Candy and pack some stuff up to take to our small room. There are two twin beds. I look out the window at the clear sky—streaked white and blue. The sun is still warm, though falling—shattering the leaves, littering the ground with bright yellow and shadows. I watch the branches sway, sway—weeds growing up through cracks in the parched concrete—vines twisting up the brick walls across the street—green turning red and brown. It is all so, uh, lovely—but then I pull the shades down and turn to Lauren.

"This is it," I say. "You ready?"

"Yeah, baby—let's do it."

I cook up the heroin so it is thick, syrupy black and add whatever's left of the meth. Lauren actually hits real easy, but I gotta dig for fucking ever. I swear all the veins in my arm are straight collapsed. I finally find one in the back of my hand.

The bed is soaking and stinking—but as night turns to day, turns to night, turns to day, we don't leave. The cleaning staff knocks but we tell them to go away. Maybe they're talking about us, maybe they're not.

I smoke cigarettes out the window and throw up several times. The only food we eat is candy from a vending machine down the hall. We drink water from the tap. Four days go by. Lauren's phone rings and rings, but we never answer until all the heroin is gone and most all the money, too.

"Dad," she slurs into the mouthpiece. "Dad, I'm ready. I'm ready to get help."

He tells her to come home.

"What about Nic?"

He wants me to wait till the morning for the meeting with her therapist, but Lauren insists he let me stay the night.

He relents.

We get our stuff and leave quickly. I have to throw up a bunch more on the way to Lauren's car. The world's just going around and around and I'm blacking out. Clouds filled with gray, gray rain make ready to drop their heavy load on the streets below. It's so cold that my teeth chatter and my stomach is tight, tight, tight.

Lauren has to drive. We're both crying some now, as we get closer. I put my hand on her thigh.

Pulling up to the house, her dad comes running out to the car. He's short and sort of round—with a tiny head and a dyed brown comb-over. He cries some as he hugs Lauren to him. He shakes my hand awkwardly and I try not to throw up all over him.

"Dad, please," says Lauren. "We need to go sleep."

"Okay, sweetie, Jules will be here soon with some medicine for you."

Lauren has to support most of my weight as we walk. I'm actually sicker than she is. Those dogs bark at me all over the place and the smell of them makes me cringe. I'm blacking out. I lie in Lauren's white bed and try to just focus on my breath going in and out—the way my lungs expand and contract like they do. I'm hyperventilating some and I try to calm myself, but it doesn't really work. Lauren holds me, but the feel of her skin on me is suddenly repulsive.

"Please—please—I just need to lie here." That's all I can say. I maybe pass out for a moment, waking up only to take some pill Jules is shoving in my face.

"Thank you," I say, but I throw up whatever it is he gives me. I roll out of the bed onto the floor and vomit into a blue plastic trash can.

I sleep like that on the carpet.

DAY 26

Waking up, the sickness has passed some. My clothes are soaked through with sweat. I pull on one of Lauren's sweatshirts and stagger up the stairs into the living room. It's raining outside and I can feel the damp underneath my skin. Lauren, Jules, Lauren's dad, and some woman are sitting around the living-room table. Lauren is so pale and sunken in. They offer me coffee and I take it. I add lots of sugar. I also eat a piece of toast, but I feel them all staring at me with each bite I take. It seems like the noise of me chewing is, like, the loudest thing ever.

"We were just discussing treatment options for the both of you," says Jules, in this voice that sounds like it should be from a guided meditation tape—soothing and serene. "Please, sit down."

"Thanks."

I'm introduced to Kathy, Lauren's stepmom. She is definitely less than thrilled to meet me. She has a creased, overtanned face with blond highlights and a lot of makeup. Her lips are thin, lined, and painted bright red. She mostly says nothing.

Jules explains that he wants to get Lauren and me into our own place—a furnished monthly hotel off Van Ness. He knows the owner and he will certainly keep an eye on us. As well, we will be randomly drug-tested throughout the week. We will have to go to seven twelve-step meetings a week and meet with Jules twice a week—separately. Both Lauren and I will have to get jobs and Lauren is no longer allowed to work for her mother. Her parents will pay for food and rent.

I just nod my head. It sounds perfect, you know? I'll be taken care of. I won't have to worry about money and whatever.

"What if we test dirty?" asks Lauren.

Jules looks at Lauren's father.

"Then all deals are off," Jules says. "You'll either have to go back into a residential treatment program, or you're on your own."

"I don't know," says Lauren. She starts talking about why what they're saying isn't fair and now I'm trying to talk her into taking it. Her dad and Jules seem grateful that I'm so enthusiastic. We are all trying to convince her now.

And so it's decided. They're gonna take care of us while we get back on our feet. We all shake hands and then Lauren's dad asks if he can talk to me privately. He puts a hand on my shoulder and leads me into this study area. There are books all over the shelves and a white stuffed tiger-head rug on the floor.

"Nic," he says, "I appreciate everything you're trying to do. I know you care about Lauren very much and that means a lot to me. But I have to ask you one favor—I need you to stay away for a few nights. Just till we get your place set up. I want to have Lauren here, alone. We have to talk over some things and I'd just feel safer that way."

"Yeah, I understand."

"You do? Excellent. Thank you."

He shakes my hand again firmly and I try to meet his eyes. They are distant blue, like Lauren's.

When we tell her I'm leaving, she kinda throws a tantrum. I'm just trying to keep on her dad's good side, you know? I mean, what a fucking opportunity, right? I wanna do whatever he says at this point. Plus, the sickness is coming back and I figure I should at least say good-bye to Gack and maybe Candy, too—maybe get high one more time—just one more time. I've still got a little money anyway.

So I call Gack and we agree to meet back at Church and Market. The rain's stopped, so I'm able to walk to the bus stop without much trouble and ride down there. I sit toward the back, looking at some graffiti drawn on the seat in front of mine. As we sway and stutter down Geary, I think about the possibility of me staying clean in this city. It feels impossible again. Not that I don't want to—but it's just so easy to get on a bus, call Gack—justify it to myself. I guess it's that way in every city—I just know this one so intimately. The thought scares me some.

Gack shows up with a bag of a few clean needles and he goes off with twenty dollars of mine while I wait for Candy. I'm leaning my back against this video store and watching all the street kids trying out whatever hustle they got on those who pass. Some of 'em are just straight-up begging—ain't got no hustle at all. I've got that cold sweating again from the heroin withdrawal and I ache, ache, ache all over.

Candy pulls up some minutes later and I get in the passenger door. Her skin's broken out and her mascara is starting to run down, but she's still fucking striking as hell.

"You only getting half a gram today?"

"Yeah," I say. "This is it. I'm getting clean."

She sighs, lighting a Parliament Menthol cigarette.

"You goin' away then?"

"No, I'm stayin' around."

"All right, then, don't throw away my number."

"No, we're done."

"We'll see." She hands over the wax paper ball and tells me she's gotta get going.

"You ever think about stopping?" I ask.

She puts on a pair of big sunglasses before turning toward

me. "Honey, we've all tried. I'll see you around. You're a good kid."
I leave.

Gack's reaction is basically the same as Candy's. We hike up to Dolores Park and shoot the speed (and heroin for me) in someone's doorway. Everything is all cleared out in my head suddenly. I feel a surge of power and find myself thinking, thinking, thinking back to what Candy said.

"Yeah," says Gack, walking down to the still wet playground. "I went to some twelve-step meetings and shit. I didn't really get it. They say the average life expectancy of tweakers like us is around three years. I've been going for at least twice that and I'm doin' all right. I wouldn't worry about it."

"But I just feel like I'm not even getting that high anymore—and I'm outta money, you know?"

"There's always money. We'll figure it out."

"Maybe you're right."

"Trust me," he says. "You only get to live this life once. I'd rather be blissed out for a short time than fucking bored and miserable till I'm like ninety or something."

"Yeah, I've thought about that too."

We're quiet awhile after that—or at least, I am. Gack is kinda rambling like he does, but I'm not paying attention. I try to remember—was I happy before all this? The fucking tweak won't let me think. It tries to tell me I wasn't. Maybe that's the truth.

"This is life," says Gack, shaking me. "This is living. Every day is an adventure."

"I don't know," I say after a moment. "Every day is the same thing. Gack, I love you for everything you've done for me—but I don't think I can go on like this. Maybe you could get help too."

"No thanks," he says, smiling. "But, yeah, I love you too. And we'll see each other soon. It'll do you good to clean up for a while—especially get off that fucking junk. That's some nasty-ass shit."

"Word."

"Word."

We walk together down Valencia, talking shit—just keeping it light, you know?

We walk all the way to the TL and it's dark and starting to rain again some. I say good-bye to Gack, then call Lauren. She begs me to sneak into the house and spend the night. I figure since it's raining, that's the best option I got. Her dad'll either understand, or he won't. I don't care. I shoot the rest of the dope and it's all I can do to get on the bus again. My hands shake so bad that I can't get the dollar into the little machine. I have to hand it to the bus driver and get him to do it. He looks bored, or annoyed, or both.

Lauren doesn't even bother trying to hide the fact that I'm there. She lets me in through the front door, dragging my loaded ass down the stairs. When she sees how fucking high I am she tries to get me to give her whatever's left of the drugs—but I don't have any. She pretends to be less pissed off than she is. My world fades out into an opiated fantasy.

DAY 27

I have been throwing up all night.

Sleeping and then jerking awake, dry-heaving into that plastic trash can. I lie on the floor, on the bare carpet. Lauren keeps trying to get me to come up in bed with her, but moving makes my stomach turn, so I lie still. Plus there is the smell of her and the smell of that house, those dogs, cigarettes, Gatorade, and leftover Chinese food. The stench is overpowering. I retch over and over. Everything is heightened, but sickeningly so. At one point Jules is there, standing over me and giving me a tablet of methadone. I throw that up too.

Lauren is whining, crying for me to hold her, and I just want her to shut up.

"You don't care about me," she says. "You don't love me."

My skin itches and the top of my head itches and I scratch until I'm bloody. "Lauren, man, I'm sick."

I am so tired—this painful, aching tired. I just want to sleep and be left alone—or maybe just to die there. I can't take it. I drift in and out of hallucinations. At one point I think I'm walking around with Gack, or that he is there at the house. I can't tell what is real and what isn't. My spine digs into the floor, but I can't move, I just can't.

I have to get out of there—I have to. Please, I mean, please, I'm ready to do anything.

After sleeping some more, I wake up and it is night. Lauren has gone somewhere. I pull myself up on the tattered couch, pushing aside all the clothes and things that are scattered everywhere. The room is all dark and I'm sweating. My breathing is strained. For some reason my shirt is off, my ribs sticking through the skin—tracks up and down both arms. From where I'd missed the vein while shooting up, my arms are swollen and aching. I'm broken out all over and thin, so goddamn thin.

I close my eyes, tears streaming down suddenly. I don't know what to do. I think back on all the stories I've heard at twelve-step meetings. I think back to what my sponsor said. Broken down, defeated, they'd all asked for help from a power that they called God. And so that's what I do—I pray. I pray from somewhere deep inside me. I pray out loud to a God that I don't even believe in. The words just start coming out.

Spencer used to talk to me about God. He talked a lot about God, but I always dismissed it. I was a militant atheist. I thought the belief in God was totally backward, delusional, and ignorant. Spencer would talk to me about prayer and meditation, but I basically avoided ever experimenting with it. I just couldn't believe, there was no way. But Spencer sure did talk about it a lot.

Tonight I pray. Maybe it isn't the first time, but it is the first time I pray with sincerity. I am desperate. And so I cry and ask God for help.

"God," I say. "Look, I don't believe in you or anything, but if you're there, I need your help. I can't do this anymore. I'll do anything. PLEASE."

Nothing happens. No flash of light, no burning bush, nothing.

What I do is, I call home.

My dad answers on the third ring. "Hello?"

That voice—my dad's sweet voice.

I cry so hard. "Dad . . . I . . ."

"Jesus, Nic. What are you doing calling here?"

"I need help."

"I can't help you, Nic, we're done."

"Dad, please."

"I'm sorry. Maybe Spencer will be willing to talk to you, but I can't. I'm through." He hangs up.

"God," I say aloud, folding in on myself, my body shaking from crying. "Please help me. What do I do?" My hand trembles all over the place, but I dial Spencer's cell phone. He picks up right away.

"Spencer?"

"Nic," he says, actually laughing into the phone. "It's about goddamn time you called me. You had enough?"

"Yeah. Please, what do I do?"

"Come home, man, we're waiting for you."

"Back to L.A.?"

"Sure. Eric still hasn't rented out your room. Something told us you'd be back before long."

"I'm so sick."

He laughs. "Come home, you rotten little snot. I'm fat 'cause there's been no one to ride bikes with me."

"I don't think I can ride any bike, Spencer. I can barely stand up."

"What are you comin' off of, meth?"

"And heroin."

"Lovely. Come on, Nic, it's time to come home. You don't have to prove anything anymore. So what do you say?"

"My car's dead."

"Get on a plane."

"Right now?"

"Yeah, right now. I'll pick you up."

"No, you don't have to . . ."

"No shit. But what can I say? I missed you, man. I might've even been a little worried. Now, let's go. You've had all the good times you're gonna have out there. It just gets worse from here."

"Worse?"

"Yeah, man, you've peaked." He laughs again.

"Spencer," I say between sobs. "I'm gonna go to the airport right now."

"Damn right you are."

"And Spencer . . ."

"What?"

"Thank you."

"Yeah, yeah, just get going."

"Okay."

"Call me when you know what flight you're comin' in on."

"Yeah." I put the phone down and then cry some more.

I call a taxi.

I try to stand up, but all the blood rushes to my head and I fall back down again. I decide crawling is the way to go. I find my shirt stuffed under the bed. I put it on and it smells so strong that I gag, but nothing comes out. Somehow I manage to get my suitcase and things together. There are a bunch of clothes and CDs and things still in my burned-out car, but I don't really care anymore. I just want to go home.

One of my shoes is gone, a black Jack Purcell sneaker. Between walking outta there with one shoe and no shoes, I figure maybe if I wear some dark-colored socks, no one will notice. So I pull my bag over my shoulder, grab my backpack, and hobble my way up the stairs. I have three hundred dollars cash in my wallet. That is all that is left. If I need more, well, I don't know what to do then. Throughout all this I'm praying. It is like the voice in my head, the running monologue; it has switched over to thoughts of prayer. Please help me—be with me. I just keep repeating it over and over—up the stairs.

Walking out into the living room, I see Lauren. She is just coming back down to her room and she sees me with all my bags and everything. She drops to the floor, curling fetal-like, and now she is crying.

"You're leaving me, aren't you?"

"I'm . . . yeah. I'm going back to L.A. I can't . . . I can't do this anymore."

"But you promised you'd stay with me."

"Did I?"

"Yes, goddamn it, you did."

"Lauren, please. You and I both know that we'll never stay sober if we stay here together."

"Fuck you. You think you're so much better than me. I wish I'd never met you. You've ruined my life."

"I . . . I'm sorry."

"Don't go." She springs up off the floor and tries to kiss me and I think I'll be sick if I touch her, so I pull away.

"I have to," I say, and I walk outta there, leaving her screaming and crying behind me.

The outside air is so cold, the wind blowing straight off the water. I tuck my arms into my T-shirt and shiver. But still, it is cleansing, that air. The night is clear and I look up at the starless sky and feel the sweat seeping out under my skin. The taxi finally gets there and I get in, collapsing on the clean-smelling nylon seats.

"The Oakland Airport," I say.

The man asks how I'm feeling and I admit that I've been better. Mostly I can't think at all. I just pray, like I said, over and over. I watch the poison city sweep by as we drive out to the Bay Bridge. The lights blur out. I maybe sleep or something, 'cause the guy has to yell, "Hey, kid" a few times when we get there.

That is sixty dollars gone.

I walk, or more accurately, stagger into the United terminal

of the Oakland Airport. The patterned carpet makes me sick and
dizzy and I hope so bad I won't have to throw up again. The
fluorescent bulbs shine violently overhead, the flickering nearly
unbearable.

I stagger over to the ticket counter and I'm still not wearing
any shoes.

"Welcome to United, can I help you?"

The woman is wrinkled, with dyed purple hair, too much
lipstick, and a smile that quickly disappears when she sees me
step closer.

"I need to go to L.A.," I say.

"Okay, uh, sir. Let's see." Her fingernails click, click on her
little keyboard.

"There's a flight at nine fifteen that has a few seats available.
Would you like that?"

"Sure."

"Round trip?"

"No."

It costs me two hundred dollars.

She prints out my ticket and then tells me to take my bags
over to the security checkpoint. It is only after I hand my suitcase
over to one of the two uniformed baggage handlers that I begin to
panic. I hadn't thought to check for Baggies, or needles, or dope,
or whatever other paraphernalia might be left in there. The woman
puts latex gloves on both hands and begins rooting around in my
bag. Her hair is braided back in tight rows against her scalp and
she looks at me with open disdain. She searches and searches
and I say nothing, still praying maybe.

And then she is done.

"Thank you, sir, have a nice day."

"Yeah."

She puts my suitcase on that conveyer belt thing and I watch
it disappear. When I get to the metal detectors, the passengers
are all taking off their belts and shoes, putting them through to be
x-rayed. At least I am saved that trouble.

I go and call Spencer and he agrees to come get me around ten. I buy a piece of sweet potato pie from Your Black Muslim Bakery, but can't really get it down. Mostly I just try not to be noticed by anyone. The wait is long.

On the plane I sleep, thank God, and when I wake up there is drool all over my shirt. That's how I greet Spencer. Actually, as soon as I see him, I start crying and can't look at him.

"Come on, asshole," he says, but sweetly. He puts his arm around me and even carries my bag. He's grown a goatee since the last time I saw him, but otherwise looks just the same. He wears a black leather jacket over a black pullover sweater. We get into his BMW and drive off through the Los Angeles night. It is warm. L.A. is always so goddamn warm.

We don't talk much. He drives me home and tells me to sleep and asks if I want any food.

I shake my head. "Can I see you tomorrow?" I ask.

"Sure," he says. "Maybe we can go to a meeting at noon."

"A meeting?"

"Yeah, brother."

"Fuck."

"There's no other way."

"Yeah," I say. "I know." And so I go upstairs into my old apartment, using my same old key. And there it is, exactly as I left it.

PART TWO

DAY 32

I detox on the floor of the apartment. Spencer doesn't think I need to go to the hospital. According to him, well, I should rely on my Higher Power to get me through this. I am so weak and shaking—throwing up—not able to sleep. I try renting some movies, but I can't focus on the screen. All I can do is shiver in bed, staring at the ceiling and struggling not to pull my skin off.

These are the worst withdrawals I've ever had. I'm alone. I have no medication, nothing to ease the suffering. The only things I have are the twelve steps and Spencer.

I know I have to stay close to him.

I have to do whatever he says.

That's the only chance I have.

If Spencer tells me God can get me through my detox, then I will trust him. I feel so desperate right now. I am ashamed and terrified of everything I've just gone through. Spencer is the one person I can trust. I've tried doing it without him, without the twelve steps—it has never worked.

It's still very hard for me to believe in God, but I'm just too beaten up to fight it anymore. That's always been my problem with the twelve-step program. There's all this God talk, or Higher Power talk. I could never get past the third step, "Made a decision to turn our will and our lives over to the care of God, as we understood him." It just seemed like some religious cult or something. But I just can't afford to question it anymore. I have to go to meetings. I have to work the steps with Spencer. I've been told in all the different rehabs I've gone to that the only way to stay sober is to be an active member of a twelve-step program. I have to believe that is true.

While I'm still detoxing I actually go with Spencer to a couple of twelve-step meetings, but I can't really focus enough yet to hear anything. It is like someone came in with a vacuum cleaner and sucked out my brain—removing any trace of joy or excitement, leaving me with nothing but this overpowering hopelessness. The world turns bleak, dull, and oppressive. I have grown so weak and pale. I look in the mirror at my sunken-in eyes and coarse skin—scaly, gray, almost reptilian. My legs are bruised and sinewy. I lie staring at the ceiling. I lie there like that until around two in the afternoon when my phone rings and I see Spencer's number come up.

"Hey . . ."

"What's up, brother?" His voice is irritatingly joyful.

"Dude, I'm dying."

"Uh-huh. You know, it's a beautiful day out."

"Is it?" All the shades are drawn on the windows and my apartment is bare and dark.

"Yeah, it is. So, you wanna go on a bike ride?"

"Are you serious?"

"Yeah, man, I'm way outta shape, we gotta start riding again."

"I can barely move."

He laughs. "Come on, man, we'll go slow."

"Look, I don't know, uh . . ."

"Nic, I'm already on my way."

"What?"

"That's right. I'll be there in twenty minutes."

"Uh . . . okay."

"See you downstairs."

I hang up, pulling myself out of bed and feeling all dizzy, or like I'm gonna faint or something. I curse and go over to my dresser. The bottom drawer is filled with old bike clothes. I'd left them here, sure I would never need them again. Those nights I'd slept in my car outside the Presidio, I'd watched the groups of cyclists climbing up the forest road. It was hard to believe that I had once been like that, pulling away on a sprint, spending five or six hours at a time on the bike. I looked at those riders and I told myself that I **133** was better off sitting in the car, loaded outta my mind. But the thing was I had experienced some of the good life that the twelve steps had to offer. I remembered riding my bike with Spencer through the Marina as the sun rose over the Hollywood hills. I remembered him telling me how much he loved his life, and in those moments, I felt the same way. I just hadn't been willing to fight through the difficult moments with the faith that it would get better—that maybe, one day, I could have what Spencer had—a beautiful life.

That seems a long way off, but what is there left to do but try?

I take off my clothes and I smell terrible. I put on some bike shorts and a jersey. I feel naked and exposed—embarrassed by my white, strung-out body. All the definition has been eaten away from my muscles and I try to avoid the mirror that is leaning against the wall. My Raleigh is there in the corner, a fifteen-hundred-dollar road bike that I'd saved up for and bought with my own money. It was the first thing ever that I had really done that with.

I put some air in the tires, sweating and out of breath from the exertion. This is definitely not a good idea. But I put on some socks and my cycling shoes and fill up a plastic water bottle. Spencer calls from outside and I go down to meet him. He's driven his wife's Blazer over, but he's already all dressed in his cycling gear.

"Lookin' good," he says.

"Yeah, yeah."

The sun is out and the sky is still and blue and perfect.

"It's so warm out here."

"Yep," he says.

I click into my pedals and spin my legs a few times, cruising up the block. Everything aches and is tight and I feel sick. I figure I'll just tell him I can't do it, but then he is pedaling up next to me and smiling, so I hang on a little longer. It is very foreign—steering, the feel of sitting on the bike, turning my legs, standing out of the saddle. It is foreign, but at the same time not.

"God," I say quietly. "Please, if you're there, could you help me. Please. I know you allowed me to come back to L.A. and get sober. Now help me to ride this bike." We pedal faster and then the wind is cooling my sweating body and Spencer says, "How does it feel?"

And I start to cry. I close my eyes and the tears run down and I sit up tall and let the handlebars go and just drift like that, down California Street, toward the calm, pulsing ocean.

"I forgot about this," I say.

"No you didn't, otherwise you wouldn't be back."

"Is it too late? Will I ever be where I was?"

"You'll be far beyond that."

"But—"

"Look. Let's make a list."

"What?"

"A list."

We turn left along the Santa Monica cliffs, the palm trees stretching up, bent forward from the onshore winds. The street is cracked and I stand to avoid the impact of a manhole cover. I am breathing pretty hard.

"Just think about it for now," says Spencer. "But I have a guarantee for you. We're gonna make a list of all the things you want out of life, okay? Not anything too dramatic, but just the stuff you think you need in order to be happy. Put it on paper—write it down. In one year from today, one year, if you follow this program to the best of your ability, you will have everything you wanted and more. Your life will be inexplicably transformed. Just think of it as an experiment. Give it a year and see what happens."

"But," I say, "I had a year."

"Give it a year where you actually commit to this thing—where you, like they say, grab hold of spiritual principles with all the fervor with which a drowning man seizes a life preserver. You've got nothing else, man."

"I know. I know I don't."

"So what have you got to lose?"

"Nothing, I guess."

"You guess?"

"Nothing."

We make it down to the bike path and I look out at all the joggers and bladers and cyclists participating in their lives. Men and women walk dogs or hold each other's hands. A group of boys play hand drums in the coarse sand.

"So what do you want?"

"Uh . . . I don't know."

"Come on, come on."

"All right, well, I'd like to be healthy again. I'd like to be able to ride like I used to."

"How 'bout a car?"

"Yeah, I'd like a car again."

"And a career?"

"Sure, I'd like to be a self-supporting writer."

"What else?"

"A relationship. A meaningful relationship."

"All right."

"I'd like friends and, uh, to have my family forgive me."

"Write it down, man. I'm telling you, either you'll get exactly what you want, or you'll find that you've been given infinitely more."

"No way."

"Either you're gonna trust me or you're not, man, it's your choice."

"I trust you."

"Well then . . ."

We ride on in silence, around the Marina. I watch the boats rocking in the harbor and I pray—I just keep praying.

Spencer is in front of me most of the time, but I try my best to keep up. We circle back around. He talks to me about the last movie he produced. There are problems with the director and cast, but the editing is coming together. He asks if I'll come out with him to the sound guy's studio tomorrow. I agree. He talks about closing his corporate video company—moving his business back home. He wants to me to help him pack the office up in a week or so. I agree to that, too. When we get back to my house, we change and he drives me to get some groceries.

"Thank you," I say.

"Hey, man, helping you is how I stay alive. Never forget that."

I hug him and go upstairs. I write a list of all the things we talked about. I put it on paper, thinking there's no way I can get these things—there's just no way.

DAY 59

Spencer's lent me a bunch of money and now he wants me to help him move out of his office—which is annoying. Still, I can't tell him no. I've written up a resumé and started passing it out around local coffee shops and things, but no one is real responsive. I'm probably terrible at making the damn things. Sounding professional has never been my strong point. Plus the big chunks of missing time are hard to explain. Other than my road bike, I have this old beater that used to be my mom's. I ride that around, though I'm still weak as hell. It's hard to look anyone in the eye. I feel, well, like I'm completely transparent or something—like everyone can see exactly what's going on with me.

Spencer picks me up around one. It's almost May and it's hot outside. Just walking from my apartment to his car has my T-shirt sticking to my back. My long hair is all matted and everything.

We drive east to Thousand Oaks, where Spencer owns a little corporate video production company. He's shutting it down to concentrate exclusively on making his horror movies.

I ask a lot of questions about recovery and the twelve steps, trying my best to listen. We both agree I should call my dad and stepmom, just to let them know I'm safe and all. I'm nervous about calling them. I feel embarrassed, but also kind of angry

or something. I mean, what I do with my life should be up to me,
right? I say as much to Spencer.

"So you think you should just be able to kill yourself and no one should care?" he asks. "You don't think your actions are gonna affect other people—the people who love you?"

"No, I mean, I know it's gonna affect them. I just . . ." I stare out at the canyon walls, dry earth broken out with thorned, crawling vines; snarled brush, prickling cacti. The sea air gives way to hot, stifling desert wind as we climb over the Santa Monica Mountains, over Kanan-Dume Road toward the valley.

"You just wanna be able to do whatever you want, whenever you want. That's all it is." Spencer smiles. "If you're gonna kill yourself you might as well just jump into those bushes there and roll around till you get thousands of little cuts all over your body and you bleed to death. I'll tell you what, that's gonna be a lot more fun than what you've got to look forward to if you go back out there. And that way we all won't have to worry about when you're gonna break into our house, or steal our car, or run someone over."

I nod.

"No, I know . . ."

"What does that mean, you know? What do you know?"

"I know that going out again is not an option."

"It's not an option. You've had all the good times you're ever gonna have with meth, heroin, or any of that stuff. It just gets worse from here on out. But there is another way. I was no different, man. I was just like you. But today, man, I love my life. I love my life." He grins with his big block teeth and steers the car fast around the steep mountain curves.

I feel like maybe he means it.

"So how do I get that?" I ask. "How do I start to love my life?"

"By committing yourself to the program. By doin' what I did—going to meetings, working the steps, and by helping other alcoholics and drug addicts so we don't have to be thinking about ourselves all the time."

"But I tried all that before."

"Did you?"

"I think so."

He smiles and I can see my reflection in his wraparound black sunglasses.

"Did you work the steps? Did you commit to this thing with your whole life?"

"Sort of."

"There is no sort of."

I drink from the coffee that Spencer bought me.

At the studio we pack everything into boxes. It's mostly just extension cords and whatever—computers, cameras, things like that. There're a couple big tables and filing cabinets. I'm tired and frustrated, but at the same time, grateful to just have something to do. Plus Spencer has already done so much for me. I figure this is some sort of payback or something.

When we get to his house, his wife, Michelle, cooks us all dinner. They have a little girl named Lucy. She is four, with short black hair and eyes that are wide and green. She has a very round face and she hides from me as I sit at the table. We eat pasta and salad and Michelle is quiet, but warm to me. She doesn't ask a lot of questions. She lets me be. Mostly she and Spencer just talk about business and school stuff and Lucy keeps hiding.

It's strange, you know, being around Lucy. It reminds me so much of being with Jasper and Daisy. Growing up, I always wanted to take care of them, teach them things, help them along. We were so close at times. I remember coming home from high school and not doing my homework 'cause I just wanted to hang out with them. I loved being able to babysit them at night, or take them on walks in the garden. In some ways it felt like, well, since I'd sort of missed my own childhood, I was getting a chance to experience it all over again with them. Or, more importantly, to help give them the childhood I never had.

It's not like my childhood was that awful or anything. I just grew up very quickly. I remember going to see *The Crying Game* in a theater with my dad when I was around nine. It's a movie about a man in the IRA who falls in love with a transsexual. I went with my dad everywhere, to parties and concerts and whatever—everyone drinking and getting high. I felt like I was one of the adults and it was very exciting, though I missed out on just innocent playing and all that a lot of kids get.

And it was confusing for me to see my dad dating different women. I remember waking up one morning and running to my dad's room like I always did. I climbed under the sheets with him, but the familiar smell of him was tainted with a new smell—perfume and sweat and I didn't know what. I heard a high-pitched giggling. There was a naked woman in the bed with us. This was in the late eighties, the height of the AIDS scare in San Francisco. I was worried my dad would be infected because I knew he was having sex. He showed me with a condom and a carrot how he protected himself. I went to my first-grade class that day and told about it during show-and-tell time. My teacher sent me to the principal's office. My dad used to tell that story to his friends like it was really funny and cool.

Plus my mom moved to L.A. when I was five, though I would visit her on holidays and over the summer. During these visits my mom would be working all the time at her magazine job, while my stepdad was laid off from his job producing TV. My stepdad would work on writing most of the day while I watched TV and movies and things. Sometimes we'd go run errands together—or play baseball, or basketball, or football. He was always trying to teach me stuff. But it wasn't as if we just played these games and had fun—he was constantly criticizing me and telling me how I needed to stand, or toughen up, or whatever.

Todd would tell me stories about his childhood or young adulthood and all the great things he'd done. There was the time he scored the winning basket right at the buzzer. There was the time he convinced these two lesbians to fuck him because he said he had a bag full of cocaine, but it was really just Ajax. In fact, he told me a lot of stories about the women he used to fuck. I'd sit next to him in his silver Buick and stare out the window, trying not to meet his eyes.

I remember glancing over at his hands, seeing his thick fingers covered with bleeding sores—each thumb picked raw. He chewed Nicorette gum and his teeth, even then, were yellow and discolored. His breath stank. I guess I was terrified of him.

When Jasper and Daisy were born, I got to sort of regress with them, while also trying to protect them. I wanted to treat them differently than I'd been treated. Of course, once I started using that all was destroyed. I feel a strangling in my throat when I think about how I've thrown my relationship with Jasper and Daisy away. I look at Lucy and already I have a sort of longing to be a part of her life.

"Lucy," says Michelle, trying to sound—what—authoritative? "You come eat your pasta or you get no dessert. I mean it."

"Moooommmm," she squeals in her little high-pitched voice.

"It's pretty good," I say.

Lucy stops and stares, stares, stares.

"Really—I mean, you might like it."

She shakes her head—her eyes so big. I'm not sure if maybe she's gonna burst into tears, or what. "Look, I'll eat it." I lean over and take a small bite of her pasta.

"Mmmmmm," I say. "That's the best thing I ever tasted. I'm gonna eat it all. You can't."

"Mooommm," screams Lucy. "That's mine."

"Oh, all right. Here . . ." I hand the bowl to her and she takes it, tasting the pasta cautiously.

"Thanks," says Michelle.

"Sure. I have a little brother and sister and all sorts of little cousins and things."

"Well, we're always looking for babysitters."

"Yeah," says Spencer. "But only if they can stay sober." He whacks me playfully on the back of the head and I stare down at my plate.

"Spencer, be nice," Michelle says, kissing his cheek. "What

we do need is a receptionist to work at my salon a couple days a week. You ever think you might be interested in that?"

"Yeah," I say, brightening. "I need a job."

"He sure does," says Spencer.

"I'll have to talk to my business partner about it, but that could be perfect for everyone."

"Sure. But, I mean—don't feel obligated or anything."

"I don't. Call us tomorrow at the shop."

I do the dishes while Lucy talks to me. She tells me her age and that she likes horses and things like that. I goof around with her some—talking in funny voices and whatever. Michelle keeps saying I don't need to wash the dishes, but I do.

Spencer drives me home.

"Everything I have in my life," he says, speeding through a yellow light on Lincoln. "Everything I have in my life is a result of working the twelve steps. My wife, my child, my career, my house—everything. As long as I put my recovery first, I can never lose. Even when it seems like something terrible is happening, I always find that, if I apply the steps in my life, it is ultimately for the best."

"That's not just some platitude or something—some Pollyanna bullshit?"

"Not in my experience. It's like that story of the father whose son breaks his leg. The villagers come up and say, 'Your son broke his leg, what bad luck.' But the father replies, 'Good luck, bad luck, who knows?' Then there's a war and all the young men in the village must fight. There is a terrible battle and most everyone is killed—except for the man's son who couldn't fight because he broke his leg. So the villagers come up to him and say, 'What good luck, your son didn't have to fight and now he is alive.' But the father replies, 'Good luck, bad luck, who knows?'"

Spencer goes on to give some more examples.

"Yeah, yeah," I say. "I get it."

"I'm just saying," he continues. "You relapsing seems like the most devastating thing now, but you may look back at this as absolutely essential. Nothing happens in God's world by mistake."

"Yeah, except I don't believe in God."

"Then how do you think you got back here? What pulled you out of San Francisco?"

He leaves me with that one.

I go upstairs and try to sleep, but end up watching some movie I rented till real late. In the morning I ride my bike down to Palos Verdes—still trying to answer his question maybe.

DAY 92

Recovery is strange, you know? I mean, it is so easy in a way and yet, well, so difficult. The woman who ran my Sober Living in L.A., the place I checked into after moving here from New York, describes addiction as a disease of amnesia. I think that pretty much sums it up. It's not hard to stay sober at first. Sure, it's hard as hell to *get* sober—to pull yourself out of the cycle of getting high every day and going through the horrors of detox. But, honestly, once the drugs are out of my system it isn't too difficult to genuinely feel like I never want to go through that shit again. Staying sober right after coming back from a relapse is no struggle. Every time I've come out of detox, the last thing I ever want to do is get high. This time is no different.

But the thing is, as the months go by, I always seem to forget why I needed to get sober in the first place. The bad shit starts to not seem really that bad. I start blaming other people, thinking they're all just overreacting and whatever. I tell myself that I wasn't really that out of control. At least, that's my rationale.

I swear, every time I've relapsed has been the same story. And, each time, I get a little closer to being dead. Things fall apart more quickly. I hurt more and more people.

I cannot let that happen again. I cannot.

Somehow I have to make this different. But how do I accomplish this?

One thing I do is I stick close to Spencer. He gives me hope, and at the same time, he reminds me of where I came from—how bad I got. But, well, the thing is, I can't help but feeling kind of like a loser living the way I am—so simply. I mean, I just hang out with Spencer and a few people in twelve-step meetings. I have no girlfriend. I live by myself. I'm sort of embarrassed by who I am.

All my heroes, Kurt Cobain, Iceberg Slim, Donald Goines, Charles Bukowski, Henry Miller, Jean-Michel Basquiat, they all lived these crazy lives. None of them ever had to go to these cheeseball twelve-step meetings and talk about all this corny twelve-step crap. Not that I don't completely appreciate everything Spencer is doing for me. I am so grateful to him. But I can't help feeling like I'm just not cool anymore. I guess that's stupid, but it's true.

When I talk to Spencer about it, he asks me how cool I was when I was prostituting and stealing. I understand his point, but, you know, I still feel hopelessly inadequate about myself and my life. I don't want to live like some goddamn Pollyanna, yet I'm terrified to use again. I wonder to myself if maybe there is something chemically wrong with me. I feel so completely crazy sometimes. I don't know which way I'm facing. All I can do is just shove all this shit to the side and try to move forward.

Spencer has me going to twelve-step meetings every day, which helps. The meetings aren't like the stereotype at all—you know, old men in trench coats sitting in a circle complaining about how much they wish they could be drinking Long Island Iced Teas or something. There're a ton of young people at the meetings and, because it's L.A., a lot of industry people—like actors and musicians, or whatever. It's almost, like, hip to be in recovery here. And despite the fact that I'm embarrassed about going to them, the meetings are really inspiring to me. Listening to the people who share about their experiences and how they've turned their lives around is amazing. They are brutally honest and introspective—not like most people you meet in the real world, outside of recovery. And everyone, it seems, agrees that if you go to these meetings and work the steps, you will stay sober. So I go to a meeting every day and I'm working the steps with Spencer.

Spencer encourages me to go through the steps very slowly, although the first step, "We admitted that we were powerless over our addictions—that our lives had become unmanageable," seems pretty simple to me. I have no problem admitting that I am powerless over my addictions and my life is completely unmanageable. But the second step, "Came to believe that a power greater than ourselves could restore us to sanity," well, that's a lot harder for me. Sure I've experimented with prayer, and Spencer is always pointing out to me how the Power is working in my life. He tells me that each day I'm able to stay sober is only by the grace of God. I admit that I do feel very blessed, or lucky, at times and prayer does help me clear my head and all, but my rational mind always tells me that these are only coincidences. No matter how much I want to, I can't actually believe that there is a power guiding me. It just doesn't make sense to me on a deep, visceral level. I don't believe in God—not really.

Honestly, that scares me. I'm worried I won't be able to work the twelve-step program. Spencer tells me to be patient. The longer I experiment with relying on God, the more I will come to believe. So I try it. I ask God for help in every aspect of my life, even if I don't really believe it.

Anyway, for some reason this old girlfriend of mine, Emily, wrote me an e-mail yesterday. She was just checking in with me, but it made me think back to my time in western Massachusetts with her. Right when I started going to school there, well, I pretty much relapsed that first week. It was kind of ridiculous to think I could stay sober making that transition. I mean, I'd only been out of rehab less than a month. Of course, it just started with me smoking pot and then drinking and then taking acid and ketamine and cocaine. I was living in the dorms and I didn't know anybody and no one knew me. I was grateful for the anonymity. There was no one there to express concern or whatever. There was no one there before I met Emily.

How we met was I brought this Bukowski poem to our beginning poetry class and she liked Bukowski and we started talking. Eventually I told her I'd had a problem with crystal and I'd been in two rehabs over the past year. She seemed to understand. Her best friend had just gotten out of rehab. She started getting on my case about using and she was worried because I wasn't sober. She said she wouldn't hang out with me if I didn't stop, but we still ended up making out one time.

Back then, there were these two girls, Jessica and Anna, that I partied with all the time. They were sweet, but lost and very, you know, insecure—like me. We ended up taking acid and eating some Adderall this one night and getting really drunk. We all went to my room and got into bed. Neither one of them was very attractive to me, but I guess I'm not very attractive either, so we all had sex together pretty much all night. When I woke up both girls were in my bed still and I looked in the mirror and I just saw the most horrible vacantness in my eyes. I don't think I've ever hated myself as much as I did at that moment.

Later that day I found Emily and asked if she would mind taking me to a twelve-step meeting since she had a car. She agreed. I had barely gone to any classes since going to school there and I really just wanted to pull things together.

So I actually got sober. Emily and I started dating and I fell totally in love with her. She brought me home for Christmas at her mom's house and I got along great with her family. I went to meetings and I spent every day with Emily, basically living in her dorm room. And we had fun, you know? Sometimes I'd dress up in drag and wear this pink wig and we'd go to the movies, or wherever, laughing at everyone who gave us strange looks. We'd rent tons of movies and play old-school Nintendo and go to coffee shops and the library and bookstores. We went into Manhattan a couple times, once to this protest and another time to see her sister in some performance art thing off of Union Square.

We were both doing really well in school and I couldn't imagine ever being away from her. Even today, I'm not sure what happened. I guess it was the same old story. I stopped going to meetings and working a program. I was really just trying to do it on my own. Relapsing came up on me and it was such a goddamn surprise. Emily and I went home to her mom's house for the weekend. I had to use the bathroom in her mom's room and there was a bottle of Percocet on the counter. I had a headache and what harm could one Percocet do? It was that simple. I just forgot for a second how bad things had been. A disease of amnesia, right?

By the end of the weekend I'd cleaned out quite a bit of her mom's medication, plus I stole some packs of insulin syringes from her mom's drawer. I'd never shot drugs before, but the needles had just presented themselves to me. When we got back to school, I taught myself how to shoot heroin. I lied to Emily and my family and somehow managed to keep up the act of being seminormal. It lasted until I went home that summer and ended up stealing the money from Jasper.

Using is such a fucking ridiculous little circle of monotony. The more I use, the more I need to kill the pain, so the more I need to keep using. Pretty soon it seems like going back, facing all my shit, well, it's just too goddamn overwhelming. I'd rather die than go through it. But for whatever reason—some tiny bit of hope or just pure stupidity—I go through the hell of detox and start trying to stay sober one more time.

And now Emily has contacted me.

"Just checking in," her e-mail says.

It reminds me of all the craziness I keep trying to forget. I wonder how I can ever make the past up to her. How can I make it up to anyone? How can I make it up to everyone?

Spencer tells me to be patient, something I've never been very good at. He tells me I'll have a chance to formally make things right with her when I complete the eighth step, which is "Made a list of all persons we had harmed and became willing to make amends to them all."

So I write back three lines to Emily.

"I'm doing all right. I'm so sorry about everything. I'm so goddamn sorry."

I know how meaningless these words must sound. I want to say much more to her, to everyone. I feel so powerless and, well, that's what I am. I am powerless. I guess that really is the first step in recovery.

I stare at the computer screen. My message has been sent. I want to buy out a billboard over Sunset Boulevard. I want to take out ads in all the big papers. I want to write my message in the sky. I want to tell them all, "I'm sorry. I'm so goddamn sorry."

Spencer just keeps telling me to take it day by day. He suggests I call my mom and my dad, just to open up the conversation between us. I'm terrified about calling both of them, but I know I have to do it. I decide to start with my mom because she lives here in L.A. My hand shakes like crazy as I pick up the phone.

My relationship with my mom has never been very mother-and-son-like. I mean, she was pretty removed from my life when I was little. My dad had custody of me, and I only saw her on holidays and over the summers. After I moved here from New York, however, we became pretty good friends. She helped get me into Sober Living and we began spending more time together than we ever had before. We'd go running, or to movies, or out to dinner. I still wasn't close to her husband and avoided going to their house, but I talked to my mom at least once a day over the year that I was sober and living in L.A. Of course, I left to go relapse without telling her anything. I haven't spoken to her since.

So, hand shaking, I dial her number. She answers the phone right away and I'm not sure at all what to say. I stumble over my words.

"Mom, uh, I'm, uh, back."

"Nic? Thank God. Are you all right?"

"I think so."

"Can you meet me for lunch?"

"Okay."

I ride my bike up La Cienega to the high-rise office building where my mom works. It's been in the same place for the last twenty years—tall, tall wood-colored paneling and glass. As a little boy I would spend hours drawing quietly on the gray vacuumed carpet beneath her desk—waiting, waiting, waiting for her to get off work.

The place we're meeting for lunch is a little café down the street from the office, where I've eaten probably a hundred times. The place is very L.A., right? It's all egg-white omelets, vegetable drinks, and vitamin elixirs. There was a redheaded girl I asked out here a while ago. The idea of even hitting on anyone is totally inconceivable to me now. I have just nothing to offer. I feel so drained, pathetic—an emptied-out container of nothing. I wait, drawing on a napkin, and when my mom walks in I can't meet her eyes. She looks the same as ever—pretty, small-boned—wearing jeans and a shawl draped over her shoulders.

Standing awkwardly, I let her reach over and hug me. Her arms are shaking and she cries and I do too. She puts some sunglasses on and sits down across from me.

"All you had to do was call." That's the first thing she says. She chokes on the words.

I try and say something. "Mom . . ."

"No, damn it, just a call—just to say you're all right. We thought you were dead—or'd been kidnapped—or God only knows what."

"Mom, I was afraid. I was afraid and ashamed. I couldn't face you guys like that." I cross my legs and arms and make myself as small as possible.

She keeps her hands clasped in front of her. "I know, sweet boy. You just don't understand what it's like to be a parent. I felt like there was a knife sticking into my side every minute of every day you were gone. I was so worried. I couldn't sleep, or eat. I just **149** lay on the kitchen floor and cried. Days I spent like that."

"Mom, please . . ."

"I mean it. How was I supposed to go to work, or take the dogs on a walk, when all I could think about was you out there on the streets? It's not fair, Nic. It's not, not fair."

I apologize, knowing how meaningless my words must sound. I try to explain how sorry I am and she does seem understanding. She just wants to help, after all. She kisses my forehead three times, short—longer—longest. She tells me I can use her car to go meet with Michelle at the hair salon. She gives me some cash. I thank her—feeling just, like, nonexistent. We walk together back to her office and she hands me the car keys.

"I'll be back in an hour," I say. "Maybe two."

"Okay, sweetheart. I love you. I thank God you're back."

I nod and drive off.

The hair salon is right near the Venice pier—on a strip of sidewalk that is lined with small shops and businesses. I've been told to park in the garage, so I do, walking into the back entrance to the salon.

The place is sparely furnished—a small space decorated only with hanging Japanese lanterns and long red curtains that look like something out of a David Lynch movie. There are two floor-to-ceiling windows that look out on the street and there're mirrors everywhere. There are four women cutting hair, or applying color foil. A young girl is answering the phone behind the counter. I don't know what to do with myself, but then I see Michelle coming in the front door with an armful of official-looking papers. Her business partner, a tall blond woman with dark green eyes, comes over and introduces herself. We sit in the garage, the three of us, and they ask me questions about my experiences and what I'm willing to commit to. It's only part-time work, but I am very grateful. We all agree to try it out. Fawn, the blond woman, has been sober a number of years and one other stylist is a recovering alcoholic. They promise me it'll be a safe working environment and I promise to show up on time and work hard and I really mean it. They introduce me to Raquel, the receptionist. She takes me around and starts showing me the basic aspects of the job—answering the phone, making appointments, doing laundry, cleaning a little bit, and all that. I feel so blessed to have this opportunity.

I drive to my mom's office, drop off her car, then ride my old bike back home.

DAY 124

It's been a hard week. I ride my bike, go to work, go to a meeting, then go to sleep. Every day it's the same thing. I am lonely and bored. I miss the excitement of my life using. I know how terrible things got and all, but still, there is a part of me that just wants to go back to that.

It's not that I don't appreciate my life sober. I appreciate Spencer, Michelle, my family, my job, but it's like there are two different people battling inside me. I want to be good, do good, be a worker among workers, a friend among friends. But there's also this part of me that is so dissatisfied with everything. If I'm not living on the verge of death, I feel like I'm not really living. I've even been thinking about Lauren a little bit. I know she had problems, but at least I had a girlfriend. So far I haven't met anyone that I could possibly have a relationship with. That is a big thing for me. I've always felt sort of worthless if I didn't have a girlfriend.

When I was five I remember playing Sleeping Beauty with a girl from my kindergarten, pretending to be the prince—kissing her to wake her from her spell. I was twelve when I had my first serious girlfriend, a girl named Savannah. She was a year older than me and her father was this famous director. I remember him being passed out on the couch the whole weekend I'd stay over there. He was shooting heroin at the time. His girlfriend would take Savannah and me to the video store to rent horror movies. Savannah and I would lie in bed watching the slasher films and clinging to each other. This led to my first real sexual experience.

After Savannah, I continued pretty much going from one crush or girlfriend to the next. If I wasn't dating someone, I was searching for someone to date. It made me feel more complete. By myself I felt like I was nothing. I guess I still feel that way. Right now I have nobody. And, ironically, sometimes twelve-step meetings just make me feel worse. They remind me what a loser I am.

The days that I don't work are even harder. All this free time makes me go crazy. I have all this anxious energy in me that I just can't release. This morning I got up and rode my bike for eighty miles. I pedaled up the PCH to Trancas Canyon. It takes over an hour to ride out there, then the climb to the top is another hour, then I have to ride back. As I stood in the shower after the long ride, I felt a rare clarity in my head. It was like my thoughts had finally turned off; I was literally too tired to think. But now I've drunk a cup of coffee and eaten some cereal and my mind is just going again.

My mom has asked me to check on her dogs today after my ride. Todd is working and she can't get away. My mom has two standard poodles, Andy and Warhol, and I swear she treats those dogs better than most people. Before I relapsed this last time, I remember going over to dinner at my mom's when Todd was working nights. My mom would cook hamburgers for the dogs, grate parmesan cheese and carrots into their bowls, then top off their meals with flaxseed oil. We used to take them running out at the beach or on hikes around the Santa Monica Mountains and I actually grew pretty fond of those dogs.

Anyway, I pedal my bike up to my mom's work. She's really busy closing a story, but she gives me her keys and asks me just to make sure the dogs have water and to maybe take them on a short walk.

Driving down Wilshire the air is thick with fog and I can barely see the brake lights of the car in front of me. It reminds me of San Francisco. I miss the weather there. L.A. is usually so hot and clear. San Francisco's weather has a lot more personality, even right now, in the middle of summer. I wonder what I'm doing in Los Angeles anyway. I mean, it's not like I'd have to start using again if I moved back to San Francisco. I could live with Lauren. At least I'd have a girlfriend.

I think about it while I play with my phone. I try to remember Lauren's number. It takes me a few tries but I finally get it right. She answers. Her voice sounds like a stranger's. I have absolutely no memory of it. I wonder for a moment if I really even know who she is. After all, I never spent one second with her when I was sober. Still, I tell her it's me and she gasps. "Nic, Jesus, what are you doing?"

"Uh, nothing." I'm really just trying to breathe. I feel very nervous all of a sudden.

"Nic, I've missed you so much."

"I've missed you, too. I think I might come back to San Francisco."

"Oh, yes, please. I have an apartment, you can stay with me."

"Okay. Yeah, I'd like that."

"Are you serious? Are you coming?"

"Uhmm, yeah. Let me figure it out and I'll call you back."

"I love you."

"Me too."

I hang up. I'm shaking and sweating now. What the fuck am I doing? It's like I'm running on automatic pilot or something. It feels like I have my foot on the gas and I'm going fast and out of control, but I just can't stop. I try to focus on the road. I'm turning in at my mom's house. It looks the same as ever.

Beyond everything, it is just hard being back here. I step out into the fog and walk through the white trellised arch that leads to the front yard. The dogs are barking at the door, and as soon as I open it, they burst out, climbing all over me—licking me and whining. For a moment I feel intense jealousy toward these dogs.

They get to just live here with my mom while being completely taken care of. They don't have to struggle with trying to build their own lives, going to work, building relationships. They have no obligations other than to be loved.

"Come on dogs, inside."

We rush into the living room all together. It is the same—deep brown wood floors and ceiling, full of my stepfather's little knick-knacks and sports pennants. There's the same worn-out sofa covered in blankets that they've had since I can remember. My stepfather has all these stuffed animal toys, which he displays everywhere. There's a furry multicolored crab and a spider with a red top hat. My stepfather named the thing "Spidey." I look at the photos on the walls. There's one of me with long blond hair down to my shoulders, a long Batman T-shirt, tights, and cowboy boots. I was probably around five. The background is a sloping-down hill of golden-colored grass. I ask myself, what the hell is wrong with me? I have so much and I always want to throw it away. Why am I this way? John Lennon says that "living is easy with eyes closed." I want to close my eyes. I want to close my eyes so badly.

I know I'm going to go get high now. I want to. It doesn't seem like there's any real reason to live. I'm going to go be with Lauren and use until it kills me and then, well, that'll be a relief, won't it?

The impulse seems to have hit me fairly abruptly, but I know I'm going to follow it. My stepfather was always freaked out about terrorists after 9/11 and I know he has hidden supplies around the house—extra water, canned goods, flashlights, batteries, and emergency cash. I'll bet the money is either in the kitchen or the garage. Maybe it's in his closet. I'll find it. I almost felt like crying a minute ago, but now things seem all right again. I have some purpose suddenly—get money, get high.

A piece of me thinks about calling Spencer. In twelve-step programs they tell you to pick up the phone if you feel like using. But what'll Spencer tell me? He'll probably say I should ask God for help. I'm just so sick of that crap.

I open the kitchen closet and begin moving the stacks of

grocery bags from Gelson's Market. There's all sorts of cans and things, but no envelope full of money.

Andy and Warhol are right on top of me, trying to get me to pet them. I look at Andy.

"What the hell am I doing?" I ask him.

He doesn't answer.

I look up at the ceiling. It is stained with something that looks like coffee and it's cracking in places.

"All right, fuck. God, please, if you are there, then, well, could you help me? I don't even know what's happening."

God doesn't answer either.

I get down on the floor with the dogs. I lie on my back and they start licking my face. I laugh.

"What do I do?"

They keep licking me. I pull the phone out of my pocket and dial Spencer's number. I don't press send. I just stare at the screen. The dogs are whimpering like they need to be let outside. Fuck. I call Spencer.

He picks up after a second. I hear his voice and I start crying. The dogs are licking my tears.

"Spencer, I want to die. I mean, really, I just want to go back to San Francisco and use and then die. I'm sick of trying. It's just too hard."

I hear Spencer laugh.

"Congratulations," he says. "Welcome to the real world. I'm glad you made it."

"But I don't want to live in the real world."

"Yes you do. You do. You called me, didn't you?"

"Yeah."

"Well then, you want to live. Look, I know how hard it is. When you've got nothing it seems like you'll never pull yourself out. Give it time, Nic. You have such a beautiful future ahead of you. Just stay sober."

I don't believe him. I don't believe I have a beautiful future ahead of me. I want to believe him, but I don't.

"Spencer, it's just no use. I know I'm gonna fail."

"Bullshit. That's your disease talking, man. That's your disease wanting you to get high again. Your disease wants to isolate you, to get you all alone so it can kill you. That's what it wants, but that's not what you want."

"Spencer, I don't have a disease. This is not like fucking cancer. This is my choice."

"You're right," he says. "Right now, what you do is up to you. Once you get high, though, then you've got no more choices. You get high and you lose everything. But you have a real shot at building a great life for yourself and your family. Look, if you fail in ten, twenty years, whatever, then deal with it then. But if you stay sober, I guarantee that you will learn to love your life and you will not fail. I believe in you, Nic. I really do."

I cry harder at that. Who is this man? How has he come into my life?

"Anyway," he continues. "We're having steaks tonight if you want to come over. I know Lucy would love to see you."

"Thank you, Spencer, I'd like that."

"So what are you gonna do now?"

I tell him I'm gonna take the dogs on a walk and then come straight over. He tells me to call him if I need anything in the meantime. We say good-bye.

I clean up the kitchen and get the dogs' leashes. We walk together through the neighborhood. Actually, it's more like the dogs are pulling me the whole way. The eucalyptus trees are enshrouded in fog and I pull my coat tight around me. There are little purple stocks, like maybe lavender or something in the yard of the house on the corner. I feel exhausted, like I just fought a goddamn war or something. I let the dogs drag me.

When I get back to the house I call Lauren.

"Look, uh, I think I'm gonna stick it out here," I tell her.

"Good," she says. "You know I want you to be safe. That's the most important thing."

"You too."

"Well, call me sometime."

I tell her I will.

Spencer gives me a hug when I see him.

"It's all right, Nic. This is all part of the process. There are no mistakes in God's world."

I try to just feel him hugging me.

"It's crazy how fast my moods change," I say. "It's like from moment to moment I never know what I'm gonna feel. I just wanted to die, you know, but now I feel so grateful to be alive. I'm so grateful for you, Spencer. Thank you for helping me."

He tells me not to worry about it. I help him make dinner, then clean the dishes. We all watch TV together, Spencer, Michelle, Lucy, and me. It feels almost like we're a family sitting here. I wish I never had to leave.

DAY 167

I worked all day at the salon. Mostly I just have to answer the phones and book appointments. The girls and I talk a lot about whatever—celebrities and things. They have a huge stack of magazines, like *Vogue* and *People* and *Interview*. I read through them 'cause I've got nothing else to do. I write some. I'm trying to work on a children's book and a screenplay about zombies that take over a drug rehab. These writing projects usually go nowhere, but it feels like I always have to be working on something. Writing gives me a purpose. I think in some ways it has helped keep me alive. Without it I'm not sure I would ever have enough hope to get sober—to make that decision to live.

I remember when I was younger I read *Nausea* by Jean-Paul Sartre. The main character is this man, struggling with his existence. He can't find any reason for living and he is sort of horrified by humanity. Finally he decides that the reason life is worth living is for art—to chronicle his struggle. That gives him enough purpose to keep going every day. I can really relate to that. Of course, Spencer would tell me that the only reason for living is helping other people. That's what gives his life meaning. I really do want so badly to get to that point. It's not like I enjoy being so selfish and self-absorbed.

And that's the other thing I've been really practicing at work, experimenting with Spencer's idea of how to work the second step, which is "Came to believe that a Power greater than ourselves can restore us to sanity." Spencer has told me that I need to experiment with asking the Higher Power for guidance throughout the day. That way, he says, like a scientist doing research, I will collect examples of how my life changes once I start developing a relationship with God. Spencer tells me that I need to find my own interpretation of a Higher Power. He says that there is no right or wrong way to think about the Power. He says he uses the name God because it is just simpler that way—though his God has nothing to do with any religion. Spencer thinks that should make coming to believe easier for me, but I still have a hard time with it. I still don't really believe in any of this spiritual stuff. But I trust Spencer. And I have no options.

So at work each day I ask God to be with me as I fold the towels, or answer the phones, or even just talk with the girls. Spencer has told me to always pray in the affirmative, as though the prayer has already been answered. I should say, "Thank you, God, for helping me be kind and patient." As opposed to, "Please, God, help me be patient." Affirmative prayer reinforces that you have already received the guidance, therefore you are able to focus on the solution. Saying that I need help just reinforces the problem—helping me wallow in it.

I try what Spencer says. I practice and practice.

"God, thank you for being with me as I wash these brushes. Thank you, God, for the perfection of my life."

They're like positive affirmations. And, really, they do seem to work. My head clears some and I don't obsess as much about the past or the future. It keeps me very in the moment, but it is a struggle to keep focusing on the prayers—driving out all other thoughts. My head sort of hurts physically from the battle going on in there.

The girls at the salon are all incredibly nice to me. They have become like my family here. They look out for me and I try to look out for them. I share everything with them and I listen as best I can. Besides Fawn and Michelle, there are four other stylists. Ayuha is the wife of this wannabe rock star; she has Bettie Page black hair and giant fake breasts. Simone is blond, and when she's not doing hair, she cooks macrobiotic food for cancer patients. She's in recovery and has a weakness for cowboys. Gertrude is a little sexpot from outside of Boston. She's sort of the most hated among the women because she complains so much about her love life. Nikki is very light-skinned black—born and raised in L.A. She's Christian and always talks about church groups. She's very sweet and it's fascinating to watch her do all these weaves— literally sewing other people's hair to her client's heads.

It really is a great job for me and I am very fortunate. I feel very safe there.

Spencer and I are going to a twelve-step meeting tonight and he is picking me up in about ten minutes. It's warm outside, even though it is almost night. The sun is still up, though just barely. People say it's the smog that makes the sunsets so vibrant here. Tonight the sky is bright purple, fading into a deep red and orange on the horizon. I go wait for Spencer outside.

When I get into Spencer's BMW he has a coffee waiting for me. I thank him and drink it down.

"How was your day?" he asks.

I tell him it went all right.

"You know," I say, "I think I'm starting to get this talking to God thing. But I swear, man, my head hurts from trying to control my thoughts all day."

Spencer laughs.

"It shouldn't hurt, Nic. Just let go, it'll come naturally. It really does become effortless."

I nod. Spencer's been really urging me to call my dad and check in with him now that I'm sober. So far I just haven't had the courage, but Spencer brings it up again.

"You know, Nic, I'm not telling you what to do or anything, but if I were you I would just call him. He is someone you want a relationship with and I bet it's pretty hard having this weight on you."

"I'm just so embarrassed," I tell him.

It's true. Every time I've gotten sober in the past my dad has reemerged as one of my closest friends. I have always shared everything with him. When I was a little boy my father was absolutely my hero. I loved just hanging out with him. We went everywhere together and he introduced me to so many amazing people because he worked for all the great magazines doing interviews. I got to paint on a mural with Keith Haring with him. We went to plays and avant-garde art shows. I remember marching in protests with him against the first Gulf War. The rallies started down the block from us, in Dolores Park. I had a set of bongo drums I'd tie around my neck and I'd beat rhythms along with the antiwar chants. My dad introduced me to the writings of everyone from Henry Miller to Herman Hesse to Milan Kundera to political essays on socialism and class wars. He instilled in me a sense of deep caring for people and their struggles.

When I was a junior in high school, my dad encouraged me to attend a vigil outside San Quentin the night a prisoner was set to be executed. The prisoner was Native American, and men and women played ceremonial drums outside as they counted down the minutes to his death. We held candles and listened quietly. I cried so hard when they announced the inmate's death. It was as though I could actually feel that his life had been extinguished from the Earth. It was this visceral sorrow. I shared that with my father and we cried together. It was incredibly painful, but also an absolutely beautiful experience.

My father took me on trips to Paris and Italy and London. He took me to rock shows when I wanted to go—Michael Jackson,

Nirvana, Guns n' Roses, Primus, Hole, Tom Waits. He always supported me and expressed genuine interest in the things I liked. Our life together was definitely not conventional. I mean, I've had therapists in the past denounce how overexposed I was as a child. But, honestly, I wouldn't trade it for anything. I am proud of the way my dad raised me and I love him for it.

But then I started doing crystal meth and we just grew further and further apart. I'm not sure whether my father will ever forgive me for the direction my life has taken. I'm not sure if he ever should. I am a disappointment. I have let him down so many times. I guess that's another reason I don't want to call my dad. I'm scared of taking on the responsibility of having a relationship with him. I never want to hurt him again by building up his hopes and then smashing them all to pieces. I've done that so many times.

"Just ask your Higher Power to walk you through this," Spencer tells me.

I agree to make the call later, after the meeting. I know it is the right thing to do.

We park in a lot on 18th and Olympic. The meeting is in a school classroom. They have coffee and cookies inside. As I walk in, I realize that all these people from the rehab I went to in L.A. are there. A bunch of them are friends of mine from before the relapse. I've been scared to run into them, just 'cause I'm so embarrassed.

But here they all are, standing out front smoking cigarettes. There's Josh—a skinny kid from Beverly Hills who knows everything you could ever want to know about movies and, oddly enough, the Civil War. He was smoking heroin until a little over a year ago. There's Karen, an alcoholic about my age who's blond with big, big blue eyes and a degree in sociology from UCLA. There's Trace and Angelina, a couple who actually started hooking up in the rehab we all lived in. That was completely against the rules—but somehow they managed to get away with it. There are a couple of other old friends of mine who I see.

Josh comes up to me first. "Holy shit, Nic, I thought maybe you died or something."

I hug him. This is my friend, I think to myself. This is a real friend. I remember going to movies and to dinner with him. I remember talking with him for hours when I was going through my affair with Zelda. He listened and tried to help, though he told me I was crazy for sleeping with a woman who had a boyfriend. I've missed Josh and I hug him more and then I'm almost crying 'cause I'm so grateful to be back here.

I talk with some of the other kids I haven't seen in so long. Then the meeting starts and we all take our seats. We listen to a man's story about his crack addiction and then we all take turns sharing about our own struggles. I ask God to be with me, to help me hear. I repeat that over and over. It does seem to help, really.

After the meeting Josh and Karen are going out to eat and want me to come. They agree to drop me at my apartment. At first I want to tell them I can't make it. I'm worried because I have to get up early to ride my bike before work. I get up at six a.m. every day to exercise and I feel really crazy and anxious if I miss it. It's like I need to kill my body with exercise in order to be calm enough to function throughout the rest of the day.

Anyway, besides that excuse, I also have incredible anxiety socializing with people. I mean, if I'm at work, or I'm high, then that's okay. But sober, going out with people my age, I am just really uncomfortable. I'm not sure what it is that scares me. Maybe I just don't know what to say and I'm constantly worried about what they think about me.

But I know that I need to try and reach out to people in the program. And I am incredibly lonely. So I agree to go with them and Spencer seems happy for me. He tells me to call him tomorrow.

Karen and Josh and I drive together in Josh's old Volkswagen. We go to this diner on Santa Monica Boulevard. It's kind of a fifties throwback place. I don't eat anything, really, 'cause I don't wanna feel sick on the ride tomorrow morning. I drink tea and Josh makes fun of me. He gets a burger and fries.

They tell me all this gossip about what everyone we went to rehab with is doing. One guy, Evan, OD'ed and is dead. They all went to the funeral. Evan was an amazing guitarist and toured professionally. I always thought a passion like that could keep you sober. I guess that's stupid. What about Hendrix, or Janis Joplin, or Kurt Cobain? Each one either OD'ed or killed themselves. I'm sad thinking about Evan and I feel really terrible about not being here for the funeral. It makes me wonder what my life would be like if I hadn't relapsed. Things had been good. I had good friends who I cared about. I feel like an idiot.

When we finish dinner they tell me how good it is to see me. It feels so good to hear that. I hug them when they drop me off, agreeing to call both of them tomorrow.

Upstairs I know that I have to call my father now. I don't want to, but I know I have to.

"God," I say. "Thank you for walking me through this. Thank you for letting me be there for my dad. Thank you for letting me hear him and treat him with humility and kindness. Please guide me, God. I mean, I really need help."

I dial my dad's number, lying on the bed and staring at nothing. I guess he recognizes my number, because he picks up, saying, "Nic, I'm glad you called. What's going on with you?"

I tell him as best I can about my job and going to meetings and everything. It feels like he's weighing every word, just trying to feel out if he should trust me or not. I guess that could all be in my head, though.

"Well, I'm happy you're safe," he tells me. "I love you, Nic. I was really worried."

"I know. I'm so sorry. I'm gonna figure things out. Things are gonna be different this time."

"Oh, Nic. I've heard that so many times."

I know he's right. Someday I will make this up to him. I have to. I tell him I love him and we get off the phone pretty quick. I guess it just felt really awkward for both of us. I didn't really know **163** what to say. I tried asking for God's guidance during the conversation, but I was too nervous.

Out the window from my apartment there are a bunch of different buildings and I watch a couple arguing in their living room. They are around my age and the girl actually looks a lot like Lauren. I close the blinds and lie back down. I try to sleep. My mind is going round and round. I think about my dad, my little brother and sister, my stepmom. I think about Lauren. This image keeps repeating itself in my head—an image of sticking a needle in my arm. I see it so vividly. I see an image of Lauren and me making love. It makes me feel sick to my stomach. I see an image of Gack and I just want my mind to stop—to become completely empty. I try redirecting my thoughts to thoughts of God. It doesn't work. I lie on my bed for over an hour. My thoughts are just obsessing on everything—my past—my fear of the future. I can't turn them off. I lie there like that till I fall asleep.

DAY 229

So I've been riding my bike like a fucking maniac.

Almost every morning I'm out at six thirty with this group of riders who take different routes around West L.A. It's a big pack, maybe fifty or sixty guys. The pace is intense and it's taken me a while to keep up, but I'm getting stronger—faster and stronger.

Work is going well. The girls at the shop are all very nice and patient. It's almost like I can do no wrong—like even the mistakes I make are the cutest things ever. I've become a sort of mascot for the place. Spencer and I talk every day and we spend a lot of time together and he's helped me just so much.

Anyway, Spencer and Michelle are coming back from a trip up to Calistoga. It's October, so they went to some harvest festival up there. They actually had me house-sit and watch their little brown dachshund, Tom. How they ever trusted me with all this responsibility, I have no idea. Still, they're coming home tonight and Tom is still alive—though I have wanted to kill him a couple of times. He has this habit of getting all excited when I come in and turning on his back and peeing all over me—plus he stole a really nice piece of meat off my plate last night.

It's early evening when their taxi pulls up in front of the house. Lucy comes running out and Tom jumps all over her and then she hugs me. She's wearing a pink ballerina skirt, a thick wool sweater with bumblebee patches sewn on the front, and a pair of knee-high, red plastic rain boots.

"Nicky," she screams, wrapping her arms around me.

"Hey, girl."

Michelle gets out next and her face is drained of all color. She walks over and hugs me, but then takes me aside and puts a hand on my forearm.

"Nic," she says in a whisper. "Nic, Spencer is very sick."

"What do you mean?"

"He needs to go to the hospital."

Her eyes blur and tears come down.

"Something's wrong, Nic. Please . . . we . . . we need your help."

"Of course."

"I'm sorry," she says. "I hate asking you."

"No, are you kidding? You guys have done so much for me. I'll help any way I can. What's wrong with him?"

"He has a fever—he can't stop shaking—he's soaked through with sweat—he has this pain in his head."

"Jesus, well, I'm sure he'll be fine."

"Yes, of course. But do you think you could stay with Lucy tonight? You'll need to make dinner, then get her ready for school in the morning. Here, I'll go in and write you a list."

"Okay, and Michelle . . ."

"Yeah?" she asks, wiping away the mascara that's running down her cheeks.

"Don't worry. It's my pleasure to help you guys."

She goes into the house with Lucy and I help Spencer out of the taxi. Sure enough, he's dripping wet and shivering and just out of it. I tell him it'll be okay and then get their bags. We go inside and Lucy seems unconcerned; she has the TV on and is watching *SpongeBob SquarePants*. Spencer lies down for a moment. Michelle shows me the pasta and stuff and how to make it just right—butter and parmesan cheese and nothing else. She says I should try and get Lucy to take a bath, but I don't have to wash her hair. Otherwise, she just has to be at school by nine. Then they leave—off to the hospital on Robertson. Lucy kisses them good-bye and we eat buttery noodles and watch TV. I'm sure Spencer's gonna be fine—I'm just sure of it.

After dinner she takes a bath and then we go play in her room a little bit. There're toys and stuffed animals all over the place. I walk around, looking at the same photographs mounted on the same walls I've looked at a hundred times before. I stop at one where Spencer is holding a naked baby Lucy stretched out, no bigger than his forearm. I smile at the photograph. Spencer kinda took me in his arms like that, giving my stray, hungering dog self a place to rest—when no one else would take him in. Spencer had held on to me. I stare at the photograph, the image grainy, processed on cheap photo paper. I stare until Lucy pulls at my pant leg.

"Tell me another story."

So we lie together on the small bed, overcrowded with stuffed animals and pillows. It is hot and the air hangs thick and still. I tell her a story about a frog and a caterpillar. When I finish I just wait, not sure what to do next.

"Nic?"

"Yes?"

"Will you sing to me and rub my back?"

"Sing?"

"Yeah," she says.

"Sing what?"

"Whatever you want."

She yawns and turns away from me. She wears a thick yellow nightgown. I put my hand against it, rubbing her back and trying to think of what to sing. Surely I must know many songs, yet suddenly I can't remember any. I try "The Itsy Bitsy Spider," then "Twinkle, Twinkle, Little Star." And then it comes to me. Without really meaning to, I start singing an old John Lennon song, "Beautiful Boy (Darling Boy)," but I change the words, of course, to "Beautiful Girl." I sing it over and over, at first absently, not really connected to what I'm doing.

> *"Close your eyes*
> *Have no fear*
> *The monster's gone*
> *He's on the run and your daddy's here."*

Something catches in my throat as I sing this last part. I can see myself, suddenly, a little boy, my dad singing that same song. It was right after my mom left. We were on some cheap futon in an apartment in San Francisco. I think of my dad, that smell of him—the sweetness, and sweat. Him rubbing my back with that calloused hand of his. Me curled up like I always was—my stomach all tight and fluttery.

> *"Beautiful, beautiful, beautiful*
> *Beautiful (girl)*
> *Darling, Darling, Darling*
> *Darling (Lucy)."*

I press my hand against her back and sing—softly, almost whispering the words. And then there are the hot, salty tears streaming down.

"Are you crying?" asks Lucy.

"No. Shhhh, go to sleep."

But I want to keep singing for some reason and I choke on the words.

"Before you cross the street, take my hand,
Life is what happens to you
While you're busy making other plans . . ."

And that feeling is there, inside me—being small, with all
the confusion and worry and longing—but also the peace and
safety—being wrapped in a blanket with my dad rubbing my back
like that, singing. And now I'm here, giving that feeling to Lucy.
She is an angel—light and sweet and delicate and lovely. That is
so there in her. But it's also in Spencer, in my dad lying with me
as a child on the futon. It's even in me. Sure, I buried it. I buried
it and buried it and turned away from everything light and sweet
and delicate and lovely and became so scared and scarred and
burdened and fucked up. But that goodness is there, inside—it
must be.

"Every day, in every way,
It's getting better and better . . ."

I let those words fall, wanting—wanting so bad to believe
them.

DAY 230

I sleep on the leather sofa in the living room. Lucy is standing right
in front of me looking out from under her bangs. She's tugging at
her yellow Powerpuff Girls nightgown with small, clumsy hands.
She's startled me and I jump some, which makes her giggle.
The freckles splayed out over her nose and cheeks are more
pronounced this morning somehow. She smiles, showing me her
tiny, straight teeth.

"Good morning," I say.

She curls up on herself, shyly.

"What's the matter?" I continue. "Did you have good dreams?"

"Yeah," she says.

"Really? What about?"

She pauses for a moment before rolling her eyes up to the ceiling and twirling a lock of hair around her finger.

"I forget."

"You forget? Lucy, I'm very disappointed in you. What do we have for breakfast?"

She skips over to the kitchen chanting, "Waffles, waffles, waffles."

As I put some Eggos in the toaster, the phone rings shrilly and I answer.

It's Michelle on the phone. She sounds like she's been crying. Spencer has been admitted to Cedars-Sinai Medical Center in Beverly Hills. They had to do a spinal tap on him last night. He's been diagnosed with meningitis. The doctors aren't sure whether it's viral or bacterial. I don't know what the difference is anyway. Michelle spent the night on a cot in the hospital and is exhausted. They finally gave Spencer a morphine injection, so he's fallen asleep. Michelle wants to come home and change clothes and shower. I agree to go sit with Spencer for the afternoon while Lucy's at school. Michelle says she doesn't know how to thank me enough.

"Please," I say. "I'm just grateful to be able to do something for you guys for a change."

"I love you, Nic. You'll always be a part of our family."

That makes the tears burn hot in my eyes. "I love you, too," I say. "You know, I wouldn't be alive right now if it wasn't for you guys. You're the only ones who've stood by me."

"Well, we always will. Thank you, Nic. I'll see you when you get to the hospital."

We say good-bye.

I have to drop Lucy off at her preschool by nine, so I'm pretty busy getting everything ready—making lunch, trying to persuade Lucy to make up her mind about what clothes to wear. She's having a minor fashion crisis—pulling out every piece of clothing in the drawer. It's funny 'cause I remember hearing stories about my parents' having to wait forever while I struggled to find just the right outfit. I watch as Lucy looks in the mirror, scrutinizing her tiny features. She pushes out her belly and rubs it with her hand, frowning.

"You want me to pick something out for you?" I ask.

"No! I can do it myself!"

"You're right, I'm sorry."

I walk out of the room and go drink some coffee.

It's strange, but not being able to exercise these last couple days, I feel really crazy in my head. It's like my thoughts race so fast and I have this underlying anxiety and feeling of hopelessness. It is very acute and I'm not sure what to do but go ride my bike or run ten miles or something. It's this obsessive-compulsive feeling that never goes away. Even being here with Lucy, I can't help but be somewhat distracted. I just can't control my spiraling thoughts.

Anyway, Lucy comes out about ten minutes later wearing the same thing she had on yesterday. I kiss her forehead. We watch TV together until it's time to walk to school.

The neighborhood is all single-story homes with manicured lawns and wooden fences. We play that game where you try not to step on the cracks 'cause you don't want to break your mother's back. Lucy seems pretty calm about Spencer and Michelle being gone. She arches her back, holds her head up, and won't let me hold her hand. I guess she's being a big girl.

When I get to the hospital Michelle meets me in the waiting room. Her eyes are all swollen and ringed with red. She hugs me for a long, long time—pressing me tightly against her. For the first time I really comprehend just how serious Spencer's sickness is. Michelle tells me not to worry, but spinal meningitis can be fatal. Spencer is pretty out of it from the pain and morphine and all—plus he has this rash all over his body. Michelle asks me if I can wait with Spencer until around five—then she'll meet me with Lucy and some dinner. She wants me to spend the night at her house again if I don't mind. I tell her it's just fine.

Spencer has a private room on the third floor. It's nice enough, except for the sterile, sickening hospital smell that permeates everything. Walking in, my hands are shaking some. I really don't know what I'd do if I lost Spencer. Nobody has ever accepted me as purely and selflessly as he has. I'm terrified really, but I try hard not to show it. Seeing him lying there, stuck full of tubes and surrounded by monitors, I can't help but lower my eyes so I don't have to meet his. Spencer is a big man, but he seems to have crumpled completely, as though he's folded up on himself—shrunken, pale. The rash is a raised vibrant purple mixed with red splatters across his nearly transparent skin. He manages a smile as I walk in.

"Hey, brother," he says softly. "There must be some sort of irony in all this. I'm sorry you had to come all the way out here."

"Spencer, please, don't worry. You've seen me in much worse shape than this. Besides, I'm sure you'll be better in a couple days."

He closes his eyes. "I hope so. Right now it feels like a fucking ice pick is being driven into the center of my forehead."

"Shit, man, and you don't even get to make it with Sharon Stone first, huh?"

"What?"

"Nothing." I guess it was a dumb joke anyway. I go over to the cot at the base of the bed where Michelle must have slept last night. I sit down and pull my backpack up. "You want me to read to you or anything?" I ask.

"I'm not sure how much I'll be able to focus. They're giving me morphine injections every four hours or so. In fact, they better come give me one pretty soon, 'cause this pain is unbearable."

The curtains are open and the sun is lighting the room, though somewhat dimly. I think about morphine—or heroin, really. I see the needle going in, the excitement of pulling back the plunger and watching the blood dart up into the syringe—pushing it slowly so it disappears into your arm as if by magic. I think about the tingling numbness creeping up the back of your neck and the euphoric calm that pulses through everything. In a way, I guess, I'm looking at Spencer with a certain amount of envy. Being sick is like a Get Out of Jail Free card. I remember when I was working at that rehab in Malibu there was a middle-aged client, extremely wealthy, with a wife and kids. He would intentionally get into accidents, break limbs, or just claim crippling migraines so he could get hospital drugs—while never feeling like he was doing anything wrong.

I wonder how easy it would be to get my hands on a bottle of Dilaudid or something. I could go shoot up in the bathroom. With Spencer being in the state he's in, he probably wouldn't even notice. But then I think about Lucy and how I would be high, possibly nodding out, while she would just want to play with me, be comforted, be made to feel safe while her daddy is in the hospital. And Michelle, who gave me a job, trusted me with her child, with her home, with the dog. I just can't let them down—not now, not ever. My life has become so full, and for the first time ever, I want to take responsibility for myself and the effect I have on others.

So just then this male nurse comes in wearing green scrubs, a mask, and one of those protective hat things. He has a metal tray that he wheels in behind him. I still can't help watching with a touch of longing in my eyes.

"Nic," says Spencer.

I stand up. "Yeah?"

"They're giving me my shot now. If you feel uncomfortable, you can step outside, okay?"

"Uh . . ." I have to think for a minute. Part of me wants to see the needle go in so I can just, you know, remember. But I also just feel sort of sick about it all. When it comes down to it, I just don't even want to get high anymore. Shooting drugs was all about not having to face my life—not having to live in reality. But I don't want to escape anymore. I don't want to experience life through a veil of false emotions. I guess I just want to be authentic for a change. So I go out and pace the halls for a minute.

What can you say about hospitals? No matter how upscale they are, the air is always saturated with disinfectant and an underlying stench of chemicals. Most of the patients' doors are closed, but a few of them are open. The beds are mostly occupied by elderly men and women with brown splotchy age marks all over. They're hooked up to tubes and wires and things, like Spencer. They appear to be sleeping—or lost. It's hard for me to look at them. It's as though all the emptiness inside of all of us—regret about our past and fear about our future—has been physically manifested in these withering bodies. I shudder when I imagine getting old. Up until a few months ago, I didn't even have hope of surviving past my twenties. Now that I want to live again, all this sickness and decay makes me feel humble and even slightly humiliated. How could I have so willingly thrown my life away when all these people are fighting desperately, every day, to save theirs?

I feel a twisting inside my belly that must be guilt, or regret, or I don't know what. An elderly woman with almost no hair left on her head is sitting up on her bed. She's looking off into the distance—staring at something only she can see. A steady moan escapes her lips. She is all alone. For some reason I think of my grandfather, who died destitute and shivering under a Salvation Army blanket in a VA hospital. My mom hasn't told me much about him except that he was a miserable drunk and would pass out on the couch, screaming profanities in his sleep while my mother tried to block out his yelling with a pillow. I think about Spencer and the chance he's given me at a new life—allowing me to have a shred of hope again.

When I return to Spencer's room, he is smiling and a little overly glad to see me. Some soap opera is on TV and he talks about how amazing the colors are. I laugh and try not to let on how high he's acting. Still, he tells me that he's sorry I have to see him like this.

"It feels good," he says. "But would I give it all up for this **173** high? Would I give up Lucy? Michelle? My career? Our bike rides together? The friends I have?"

I take his hand in mine, as awkward as that feels at first.

"No," he continues. "The life I've built for myself sober is better than any high a drug could ever give me. I'm going to tell you something right now, okay?"

I nod.

"Being sober isn't just about not using. Being sober is about the joy a life of clarity and living by spiritual principles can bring. There is nothing greater than that. Forget drugs. Forget needles. Forget everything. We are living to experience the undiluted amazement of life on life's terms. And Nic, if I don't make it through this, I want you to know that I have tasted it. I have seen what *real* life has to offer and it is not cruel and oppressive—it is ecstatic. It is ecstatic far beyond a drug like Ecstasy, or this fucking morphine. It is possible to know peace. It is possible to watch all your dreams come to fruition. Nic, I promise you that."

"Spencer, please," I say. "I know you're gonna make it through this. But you don't need to tell me all this. I watch you. I watch you every day and I see the life that you've created for yourself. Don't think for a moment that I question your sincerity. I mean, I practically live with you. I've seen what this twelve-step program has done for you. My greatest hope and desire is to build a life for myself the way you have. You see what is important. You've helped me see what is important. You are a good man. I only wish I could become as good a man as you."

There are tears in both of our eyes and I fidget with my backpack nervously.

"Do you want me to read to you?" I ask.

"Yes, please. What do you want to read?"

"I have Emmet Fox's book with me—can you focus enough to listen?"

"I'll try."

I pull out Emmet Fox's *Sermon on the Mount*. I've read it so many times the pages are worn and yellow, curling around the edges. Spencer has taught me to live by it—I mean, as best I can. Actually, as embarrassing as this is, I know very little about Emmet Fox, the man. Basically all I know about him is that he was some sort of Bible scholar from England.

I sit back on the synthetic hospital pillow against the white sterile wall and begin to read.

Fox's interpretation of Jesus's Sermon on the Mount is fairly liberal. He believes, as far as I can tell, that the kingdom of heaven is inside each one of us. He also believes that our thoughts create our realities. If one is thinking only about God and constantly praising him/her/it, then they shall know nothing but peace, love, and freedom. Sickness, depression, whatever—those are all manifestations of our own negative thinking.

Apparently there are all these different laws that govern our world—physical laws, mathematical laws, chemical laws. Well, Fox says there are also spiritual laws that are just as real and unchanging as anything some scientist can prove in a test tube. On a spiritual plane, if you are open, giving, and kind, you will be rewarded these things tenfold. They may not come back to you in the same manner they were given. Often it is an internal gift that you receive. For instance, if you find a wallet on the street with five hundred dollars in it, you can keep the money and spend it on a couple pairs of shoes or something. So then you'll have those shoes. However, if you return the wallet with all the money inside, you'll be filled to overflowing with feelings of goodness and love. Basically you just replace one thought with another and, you know, it seems to work. It really does kind of change things.

So I read from *The Sermon on the Mount* to Spencer. The chapter is about Jesus's whole "blessed are the meek" thing. Meek, in this sense, being described as constantly giving God the credit for all the good things in your life. I don't know. In J. D. Salinger's *Franny and Zooey*, the Franny section is all about her trying to learn what it means in the Bible when they say that one should be in a state of constant prayer. What she does is end up repeating this specific prayer over and over in order to transcend human suffering and selfishness and nonconnection with God—assuming all the time that there is some sort of God there, or at least, a higher self.

That remains the toughest aspect of accepting this teaching for me. I just have a hard time—when I allow myself to really think about it—comprehending that there could even possibly be a God. But Spencer has given me food and helped get me a job and managed to get me somewhat stable. All I've done is follow his directions like my whole life fucking depended on it, and it seems to help.

I look at that man, lying in the hospital bed in front of me, nodding out from the morphine in him. I read to him like I'm reading to a child—like I used to read to Jasper and Daisy. And suddenly I do feel like I belong somewhere.

I keep reading. Spencer will snore for a moment, his face becoming slack and still—then he'll jerk awake and will say something. He'll look at me and I don't know what he sees—thinks—feels. I look at him and want so badly to be authentically a part of it—really a part of his family.

Michelle comes back around four thirty. I'm supposed to pick up Lucy at day care. It's all been cleared with the people at Lucy's school. Michelle has put on some makeup and her short hair has been washed and blown dry. She has an overnight bag with her.

Michelle gives me specific instructions about what to give Lucy for dinner and whatever. I listen and feel nothing but proud that she trusts me enough to leave her daughter with me again.

Driving back to their neighborhood, I stop at a local video store to get some videos for me and Lucy to watch. I look over the family selection at Cinefile and finally choose a couple of Jim Henson's Muppet movies. I always liked those as a child. I drive to their house and start the water boiling for some pasta with butter and cheese for Lucy. I cook us some food before walking down the block to her preschool.

I find her playing outside with two girls and a little boy. I just watch her at first, talking with her friends. I remember Daisy at that age. I remember volunteering with the first-grade teacher at her school in Marin. I spent my entire winter break from my school in Massachusetts working there. I got to know all the kids so well—which ones needed special attention, whatever. It was hard to leave them, you know? I mean, going back to college and all. Maybe it's an example of what the twelve-step program is all about—helping others to help yourself. It seems like when I focus on helping others, it helps me not want to get high. I just wonder how I can incorporate that more fully in my life.

So I call to Lucy and she runs over to me, giving me a big hug. I hug her back and follow her to pick up her blanket and her lunch bag and all that stuff.

We walk back along the sidewalk, stopping to pick up little Tom to take him around the block together. Lucy is full of questions. Of course she wants to know all about her daddy and why he's away. Michelle actually asked me to tell Lucy that she and Spencer were off making a movie tonight and that's why I'm staying over. I don't feel comfortable about lying, really, but I do it.

You'd think it wouldn't bother me after all the lies I've told.

I heat up our dinners in the microwave and we play with these plastic horses for a while. I pretend to be a race announcer and the horses are running in the Kentucky Derby.

Michelle calls several times to make sure everything is all right. Nothing's really changed with Spencer—he's still on morphine every four to six hours. There may be nothing more they can do than that and just let the virus run its course. Now that they've got him stabilized, they don't think he's in much danger. I guess I feel relieved, though I never really questioned whether he was gonna make it or not. I can't even begin to comprehend what my life would be like without Spencer. I can't let my mind go there.

So I go sit down next to Lucy and we watch *The Muppet Movie* and then *The Great Muppet Caper* until it's time for her to go to sleep. She nestles up against me all the while. Before bed I read her one of my stepmom's books. I found it at a used place on Sawtelle the other day and bought it for Lucy. I've read the book so many times, about a little girl who moves into this neighborhood and struggles to make friends. It's named after her mother, Henrietta—my step-grandmother. I haven't seen her since I broke into her house maybe three years ago, when I was living on the street. I fell asleep in her basement. She found me under a pile of laundry and all I wanted to do was keep sleeping, but I was so embarrassed and scared and everything, that I just ran out of there.

Nothing has really been the same between us since. She and her husband, Jeremiah, had been more like real grandparents to me than my dad's or mom's parents ever had.

Henrietta took me on hikes along the cliffs of the Marin Headlands. We'd play dominoes together and she'd teach me about sewing and cooking and things. She was so smart about politics. We would watch the presidential debates together and PBS news. When I was maybe ten or eleven I remember taking the ferry across the San Francisco Bay with her and her husband. We docked at the Port of San Francisco and walked up to eat Chinese food in North Beach. She knitted me wool socks for Christmas and embroidered a heart on the ankle.

I read the book, *Henrietta*, to Lucy.

Looking at the drawings and everything, I think about my grandparents. I think back on the times we spent together. I've alienated so many people—destroyed so many relationships—and yet here I am, lying next to Lucy, reading her this book. And, if nothing else, what Spencer stresses to me over and over is that we only have this one moment: NOW.

I am putting Lucy to bed. I am turning off the light and kissing her forehead.

That is all there is. And I have this, for now. I just wish I could figure out how to keep my fucking mind from going all over the place—dwelling on all the loss and pain and everything

I'VE DONE—then jumping off into the future to how impossible it all seems.

It's thoughts like these that used to make me stick a needle in my arm. I think about Spencer and what he would say.

"Talk to God about it, don't talk to yourself."

So I try again. I say a sort of mantra, over and over, "God, thank you for my life today. Thank you for guiding me. Thank you for protecting me."

I leave Lucy's door cracked open slightly, just like she wants it, and say good night.

Praying helps some, though I can't get my thoughts to slow down and stop torturing me with my past. I've come to rely on prayer, but it is only a minor anesthetic. Still, it is better than nothing. I hold on to it—not knowing anything better.

Thinking about all this stuff, I can't help noticing how sort of cultlike the whole thing is. Not in the financial sense—it's not like I'm giving Spencer or any of the people money. And honestly, they're not really demanding anything of me. But everyone does follow these very specific teachings and doctrines. And, like any other cult, they have offered me a place to feel safe and a part of something whereas before I was anchorless and had no direction.

But then I feel guilty questioning any of this—like I'm betraying them all. I guess I just struggle with belonging to any organization. I always feel like I should be able to do it on my own. My ego tells me I'm better than this twelve-step crap. I want to rebel against it, though of course, I don't really have any options. If this doesn't work for me, then nothing will and I'll die strung out on drugs. This program has to work. It has to.

Instead of turning on the TV, I pick up one of the twelve-step books I've got in my bag. I try to find some solace in the pages. I read over the chapter outlining the second step, all about coming to believe in a Higher Power. It's like I'm trying to pull so much meaning out of each word—maybe more meaning than is actually there. I absolutely want recovery. I need recovery. I am trying as hard as I know how to make this work. If I can turn the key somehow—unlock whatever—then I will finally find the peace offered in this program. I dig into every syllable—falling asleep like that, searching.

DAY 234

Spencer's still in the hospital, but the worst is over. He's so weak and pale. He can barely walk to the end of the hall and back. The only good thing, he says, is all the weight he's lost.

"Death-bed diet," he calls it.

I've been working at the hair salon the last few days, even though Michelle has been gone. I've stayed with Lucy every night since Spencer got sick. I've visited the hospital as much as possible. It felt good to be so busy, though I haven't been able to ride my bike or anything like that. Honestly, it's so hard for me not to exercise. I just have this feeling of total failure when I don't do it. Last night, however, I was able to go to a twelve-step meeting with some of my friends. None of them seem as crazy obsessive about everything as I am. It's strange 'cause I had the same feeling in high school that I have here in the fucking twelve-step program. It's like, well, it just seems so easy for everyone else and so difficult for me. I turn from these extremes of feeling on top of the fucking world—to feeling so despondent. They don't have to struggle like I do—or maybe that's just me comparing my goddamn insides to everyone else's outsides. But I swear to God, I just seem to wrestle with everything more than anyone else.

I talked to my father today on the phone. I called him this morning before work. We talked for almost an hour. I told him everything that was going on with me—how Spencer is in the hospital and all. He let me know a little about how Jasper and Daisy are doing. He still seems very protective of them, like he is trying to keep me from getting involved in their lives. When I asked to talk to them, he refused. I understood, but it made me cry some after I got off the phone.

My dad is not willing to help me with rent or give me any money at all, but he did offer to help pay for me to get into therapy. He believes very strongly in psychiatry and was worried when I told him I'm not on medication. I've been on different antidepressants since I was eighteen. None of them were ever like a miracle drug or anything, but they did seem to help me from falling down as deeply into my depression. I admitted to my dad that I was concerned about being off all my meds.

Spencer, of course, is intensely against taking any kind of medication for psychiatric reasons. You really can't even talk to him about it. You see, according to him, God should be able to cure everything that's wrong with me. Mental illness isn't really given any consideration. And of course I'm not denying that his teachings have been very powerful and have really helped, 'cause obviously they've changed my whole life. That is the truth. Not only am I not using anymore, but I'm not fighting cravings all day. In some ways, I can't even relate to the person I was, living out of my car—fucked up and crazy. What else can I attribute that to than following Spencer and the rest of the people in this twelve-step thing?

But at this point, I just feel like things shouldn't be so fucking hard. The depth of my isolation goes past anything I've heard my friends talk about. I'm interested in another opinion. So I accept my dad's offer and he helps set me up with a psychiatrist here in West L.A. Her office is not far from work and I made an appointment for this afternoon. I haven't told Spencer, but I figure he just doesn't understand this sort of thing. About two weeks ago I broached the subject with him on a bike ride. We were just going easy, spinning along the bike path that goes from Marina del Rey to Hermosa. Spencer didn't even let me finish my thought before going into a long monologue about the myth of antidepressants and the corrupt, manipulative drug companies.

The truth is, I agree with him in a lot of ways. The solicitation of different medications through marketing is just disgusting. I can't tell you how many doctors I've known who write prescriptions with a pen given to them by Zoloft—or drink from cups advertising Wellbutrin. But I don't think that takes away from how much certain medications can help people. Even though I never found that antidepressants solved all my problems, they did help some. And even if it is a placebo, the fact that these drugs can make things easier, well, I have to at least give them credit for that. So I don't feel like it is harmful or wrong or anything to experiment with psychiatric drugs—under a doctor's supervision, of course.

Anyway, I have to leave work a little early to go to the appointment on Wilshire. The low-hanging clouds and fog of summer mornings have burned away and it is clear and hot and penetrating as I pull away from the salon. I'm picking up Lucy again from school. Spencer and Michelle finally decided to tell Lucy the truth about Spencer's illness and I'm gonna drive Lucy to the hospital to see them. Spencer is still bedridden, but without all the tubes and everything that made him look so scary. Lucy seemed to know something was going on anyway, so I'm glad they finally told her.

I pull into a small parking space outside the high-rise office building. I finally had enough money to buy the new Secret Chiefs 3 album that came out while I was in San Francisco, so I've been listening to it over and over. As I turn off the car, the music stops abruptly and the afternoon heat makes it hard to breathe. There's an elevator that takes me to the third floor—all mirrors. I look at the fake marble flooring—anything so I don't have to stare at myself. The doctor, a woman named Rachel Levy, has her office set up just like any other psychiatrist's office I've ever been to—with the little light you switch on to call them and let them know you've arrived.

I take a seat in one of the cushioned wicker chairs, flipping through a *New Yorker* magazine. I always go right to the movie critics' page. Reading the reviews is like a religion for me. It's always been like that. In fact, I'm so engrossed in this review by Anthony Lane, I don't even notice the mousy woman with too much makeup and a short, conservative haircut who opens the door. She has to call out to me at least twice.

I stand up quickly, introducing myself, looking at the purple business suit she's wearing. We shake hands awkwardly. She has long, polished fingernails, and as she leads me into her office, I notice some very plain watercolor paintings of L.A. beaches that look like they were purchased from one of those touristy Venice galleries. There are also tons of medical books on the walls and a few framed diplomas.

I sit in the corner of the long couch while she sits in her upholstered, all-business power chair directly across from me. We both cross our legs.

Her earrings are ornate and dangling. I wonder if maybe this visit is a mistake.

"So what brings you here today?" she asks.

I'm not at all sure where to start, but I try to find a jumping-off point and just go through my story as quick as I can.

At first, you know, I'm a little embarrassed. I feel like maybe I'm just too shocking for this kind of frumpy woman. But, in the end, I figure I'm here for me and so I just lay it all out there as best I can. I talk for maybe half an hour without her doing much more than just nodding her head. When I finish, she just sits a minute, nodding like she's been doing. She makes some contemplative noises, then stands and goes to retrieve a large reference book from off the shelves. Still saying nothing, she flips through it until she finds the page she's looking for. She hands the heavy volume over to me. The heading is "Bipolar disorder (manic depression)."

"You see those bullet points there?" she asks.

I scroll my eyes down the page. "Yeah."

"Tell me if you can relate to any of those."

I read over what she's given me—a list of symptoms for what they characterize as mania. It talks about feelings of grandeur, decreased need for sleep, excessive involvement in pleasurable activities that have a high risk of painful consequences—like doing drugs, sexually acting out, or whatever.

I can relate to every last one—every last fucking one.

On the next page is a list of symptoms of what they call major depressive disorder. Mostly it's just feelings of extreme hopelessness or lack of interest in normal activities. They describe feelings of worthlessness and wanting to die.

"Do any of those seem relevant to you?"

"Yeah," I say. "They all do."

"They all do?"

"Yes."

She sits quietly a minute. "Now, here's what I'd like to try. I mean, if you're up to it."

"I am," I say. "I've got nothing to lose."

She smiles but doesn't laugh. "From what you've described," she says, in her most professional-sounding voice, "you have a form of mania, or bipolar disorder, that is classified as 'rapid cycling.' In other words, you cycle from elation to desperation throughout the day so fast that you yourself don't know which feeling to follow. In these cases, I have known drugs like lithium and Depakote to be extremely effective. I'd also like to start you on a simple antidepressant. Maybe something like Prozac would be beneficial. I'm not sure. I would even like to start you on a mild antipsychotic, like Zyprexa, just to make sure your moods don't overtake your strong desire to be sober—if that is genuine."

"It is," I say.

That is the truth.

"But to start," she continues, "I'm going to write you a prescription for Depakote and Prozac. Hopefully with these two drugs we'll be able to calm down your mood swings enough to let you focus on your day and not be so overwhelmed all the time."

I thank her. It all seems to fit. "Overwhelmed" is the perfect way to describe my general state of being. I take the flimsy piece of prescription paper she gives me with a true sense of hope and excitement, and tuck it in my wallet. On that simple piece of paper is a promise of some normalcy.

I get up and shake her hand again. We make an appointment for the following week. She wishes me luck and I just walk outta there with my head down. I take the elevator back to my car. The sun's still up and the heat stifles me to my very core. I wish it would rain.

Lucy is playing with a couple of her friends when I get to the preschool. They have some game going on in the sandbox and I feel bad breaking it up. I've dropped the prescriptions off at a local pharmacy, but I'm not gonna pick it all up till tomorrow. There's no rush.

I watch Lucy and the other kids playing at their game. When I was their age, my parents were still together. I don't really remember anything from that time. The one thing that comes to mind is walking home from school with my babysitter and finding a fuzzy caterpillar. I knew we had a garden behind our house in the Berkeley Hills. All I wanted to do was bring that caterpillar to our garden so it would have the opportunity to eat all our great plants and things. I remember carrying it the whole way home. But other than that, I have no memories of that period in my life. So maybe everything happening in Lucy's life right now is going to be a blur in her memories. Still, children seem like empty vessels who pick up on everything and are so affected by their surroundings. I mean, that's what they tell me in therapy and it seems to be true. Stuff I don't consciously remember affects my behavior every day. I see that now. So even if Lucy has no conscious memories of today, she still is taking everything in like a little sponge. And, moment by moment, she is developing her skills to cope with the situations life throws at her. If she is full of terror, she will grow up terrified. If she is made to feel safe and accepted, she will grow up trusting herself—confident and self-assured.

I want so badly to be a part of her growing up strong and comfortable with who she is—something I never experienced really.

Because Michelle has decided that she wants Lucy to finally go and visit Spencer in the hospital, I drive her out to Beverly Hills. In the car I do this imitation of Pete Seeger singing "Abiyoyo" and telling the story and everything. It's actually from a tape I used to listen to all the time with Jasper. Abiyoyo is a giant who attacks this village, and a musician boy and his father, a magician, are the only ones who can stop him. My mind can just retain information like that—reciting the story almost word for word, with all of Seeger's intonations and everything. Lucy seems entranced, and as we pull into the hospital in Beverly Hills, it's as though no time has passed. She's laughing and I'm laughing and we both sing the song: "Abiyoyo, Abiyoyo. Abiyoyo, yoyo yo, yoyo yo."

It's a little after seven when I pay the ten dollars to park at Cedars-Sinai.

The sun is still out and Lucy is wearing a colored skirt with a black tank top, ruffled socks, and white sneakers that light up red as she walks. We hold hands, walking across the asphalt to the main entrance. She skips and laughs and dances. I ask if she's scared and she says, "No."

Having visited here so many times, I don't check in at the front. We go into the elevator and climb the three floors to where Spencer is. The fluorescent lights crackle like insects. The smells of chemicals and disinfectant permeate everything. Lucy and I walk out into the sterile air, past the nurses' station, where everyone is rushing around looking busy and overworked. We follow the patterned carpet along the halls. Spencer's door is closed and I knock softly. We wait.

When Michelle opens the door she is looking better—more rested and uplifted than I have seen her since this whole thing started. I guess Spencer's situation really has improved. Spencer has gotten so much color and everything back in his face—he even seems to have gained a little weight back. He's unshaven and scraggly, but the dead, glossy clouded film over his eyes has cleared. Lucy runs to give him a hug.

"Daddy!"

She scrambles up into the bed and just nuzzles in as close as possible.

"Oh, my big girl," says Spencer. "I missed you, Squirt."

"Were you sick, Dad?"

"Yeah, pretty sick."

They hold each other and Michelle and I exchange glances. Both our eyes are red as the tears start to well up. Beyond everything, I think, we're relieved not to have to lie to Lucy anymore. Watching her with her dad—how much they love each other—how much they need each other—well, it just takes my breath from me. When Michelle puts her hand on my shoulder I can't stop from crying. Spencer is well. He'll be out of the hospital maybe tomorrow or the next day. I guess I didn't even realize what a big deal this has all been. It's like the world's gravitational pull has just lessened tenfold. Everything trapped in me, rushing in and out like the ocean against a jetty—pounding over and over, trying to crush the breaker wall with each rhythmic explosion—has finally been taken away. I cry for that and I'm not sure what else. Michelle cries too and then Spencer cries and we're standing around the hospital bed like that, until Lucy says, "Why's everyone so sad?"

And I say, "We're not sad, sweetheart, we're happy."

"Then why are you crying?"

"Because happiness goes like that too."

A little later I go pick up pizza for everyone at a place on Third. We all eat in the room, watching the opening ceremony to the Summer Olympics on the TV they have strapped to the ceiling. We're all joking about the costumes and all. Lucy seems enthralled. Björk does this whole vocal art piece and Lucy asks me all kinds of questions about her and Iceland and everything. We're like a family sitting in here, having come through this whole ordeal together. We're like veterans after a war. Laughter has never felt so effortless.

Michelle decides to go home with Lucy at her bedtime and spend the night with her. So, at least for tonight, I won't be babysitting Lucy. Spencer wants me to wait with him a while longer. The pain comes back at night and he's still on the **187** morphine—though a much smaller dose. A fat white nurse woman comes in to administer the shot and Lucy and Michelle leave for the night. The hair stands up all over my body as I watch the needle puncture the skin—as she registers and then pushes the blood/drug mixture up into his arm. I almost feel like throwing up. Sometimes, still, I long just to stick a needle in—just to feel it hit a vein. Sometimes I crave that almost as much as the drugs. I watch Spencer's eyes roll back in his head for a second as he thanks the nurse.

It takes maybe a minute or two for him to come clear again.

"I'm sorry, Nic," he says. "I know that's hard for you to watch."

"Yeah," I say, lowering my eyes. "It is. But to tell you the truth—all I feel is grateful that I don't have to be so fake and clouded by that shit."

"I'd give anything not to need it. And I'd give anything not to go through the process of stopping again."

"Is it going to be hard to stop?"

"Let's just say"—he smiles—"I'm very aware of the time and when the next shot is due. Now some of that is the pain—but some of it is just my addict getting a taste of being high again and I've missed that. You may not think you miss it—but guaranteed, somewhere in you, your addict is there—still alive—biding his time until he can get you where he wants you again. He will never be gone completely and he'll use any opportunity to bring you back."

"Yes," I say, looking away. "I know."

"I'm gonna need your help, Nic. I need you to walk with me through this. I don't know where else to turn."

"Spencer, please, don't worry. I'm here for you. I'll spend every moment with you if you need it. Spencer, beyond anything that's come before, I am your friend. I mean, you are my best friend. I could never repay you for all you've done. I love you. I mean, I do." I put my hand on his much bigger hand, standing over him as he lays there. "Whatever you need," I continue. "You can be sure of me."

Spencer smiles and rolls over slightly onto his side.

"You tired?"

"Yeah, I'll sleep in a minute. Just remember, Nic, the only thing that ever really gives us any genuine satisfaction is caring for other people. It doesn't matter how popular we are or anything. The only thing that actually makes life more fulfilling is our love for others. When I help you, I'm really helping myself—saying yes to humanity and to the connection that exists among all people. And the results speak for themselves. Like, how have you felt this last week?"

I go back over to the cot and sit down, crossing my legs. "Well, I've been scared, of course. But yeah, I haven't even really thought about myself at all. I mean, if I have time to take a shower that's a luxury. Mostly I'm just trying to make sure you're all right—or Lucy or Michelle. And I guess there is something very liberating about all that. Things have been hectic, but I feel very calm and, well, just purposeful inside."

"And that's what I wanted to point out," says Spencer, falling further away into sleep. "That is the crux of the whole twelve-step program. This is—what you're experiencing now. We are two people helping each other through life. The satisfaction of being there for someone else is unparalleled. This has been a fucked-up way to learn that lesson, but in my mind, it's been worth it. And you also get to see now, without a doubt, that the more you give to others the more gifts you receive. That is a universal truth. It will never fail you. Now I'm going to pass out, if you don't mind."

"I'll see you tomorrow." I stand up and go over to switch off the bedside lamp. The room is swallowed in darkness and I stumble toward the door.

The walk to the car and most of the drive home I'm just thinking about what Spencer said. I've always been amazed at how selflessly he took me in and helped me want to live again. Never once did I think that he might be doing it in order to help himself at the same time. As a using drug addict, all I ever really cared about was getting high myself. There were a few people around—Gack, Bullet, Lauren—but at the end of the day, all that really mattered to me was that I had whatever drugs I needed not to get sick, or come down, or whatever.

Now that Spencer has pointed it out, I realize that the times I have known some sort of inner peace in my life, those have always been times when I focused on helping others more than myself. Volunteering at Jasper and Daisy's school, babysitting, cooking dinner for my family, cleaning up the house, talking to a friend on the phone and just listening to them vent about something or other without offering an opinion or judging. Those have been the moments when I get to stop obsessing about myself and really feel a sense of liberation. "Freedom from the bondage of self," that's what they call it in twelve-step language. I never really understood that before, but now I do.

I drive back to my apartment along I-10. Los Angeles is glowing toxic and orange in the nighttime blackness. My phone rings a few times—friends from the program. Josh is calling after going on a date with some girl. He talks to me and I just try to listen. Kevin calls 'cause he's got a problem with his girlfriend, Emily. Then Emily calls to talk about Kevin. I have the stereo turned down in the car and I end up staying on the phone for about fifteen minutes after I've parked in my underground garage. Thinking about all these people in my life—all people I've met in the program—well, I'm just so grateful. I breathe out, not wanting to be anywhere but exactly where I am. As I hang up and take the elevator up to my floor, I feel like the impossible has become possible, I feel a sense of completeness and satisfaction just being in my own skin. I am comfortable being me—at least, for the moment.

I go inside and eat some Coffee Heath Bar Crunch ice cream. I put a DVD in the player. I fall asleep.

DAY 238

Yesterday I finally drove Spencer home from the hospital. He's still in a lot of pain and plagued by horrible headaches and body aches. Still, it was a huge relief to make it home. Michelle's been back at work at the salon and I've been relieved of some of my Lucy-watching duties—not that I minded them. I'm still staying pretty close, going to their house after work, making dinner and cleaning as best I can. There hasn't been more than a moment of calm, but I seem to thrive on that, reveling in the chaos.

On my lunch break today I grabbed a copy of the *LA Weekly* and saw that the L.A. film festival is coming to town. Pedro Almodóvar's new movie, *Bad Education*, is screening over the next few nights and I call my mom at her magazine to see if she can get our names on some sort of screening list. My mom is very nice on the phone and calls Sony, the film's distributor, right after we hang up. Turns out there's a screening of the film tonight at the Sony lot and my mom has gotten me and her and one guest on the list. My stepdad doesn't want to go, so I invite Josh. He seems excited and agrees to meet us at the studio a little before it starts. Michelle doesn't seem to mind, but I call Spencer, just to make sure he's not gonna need anything. Spencer happily tells me to go to the screening, so I guess it's all set. I look forward to it all day.

When I was little, especially when I visited my mom in L.A., the only escape I had was watching movies. It was the one thing that could take me out of myself—let me forget the world I lived in. I remember this one time when my mom and stepdad were fighting. My mom was screaming as she was trying to get away from Todd—trying to pack me up and take me to a hotel with her somewhere. They screamed and screamed. My mom tried to drive off and Todd blocked the car with his body, losing his glasses. I ran inside to the couch and put on this

Sergio Leone Western with the volume up real loud. I could still **191** hear them screaming, but the movie offered me some relief. For ninety minutes, I was transported into another life, another reality, another character. Basically, it let me be someone that I wasn't. It allowed me to travel, to be a part of different cultures, different world views, different societies. Plus there are all the elements of movies: music, visuals, writing, and acting. In some ways it is the perfect art form. It is the culmination of all mediums.

Throughout my whole life I have obsessively watched and studied movies, learning all about different directors and their work. It was like having my own personal film school, and for whatever reason, my mind has almost perfect recall when it comes to information about film. I remember being young, sitting by the heavy dining room table in Karen's mom's house. Her mom and I would watch *Jeopardy!* all the time on this tiny little TV that barely even got reception. One night one of the categories was movies, and she bet me a penny that I couldn't answer them all. Well, I sat there and got every single one of the questions right. More recently, Josh started working for this company that makes a DVD game called A Night at the Movies. When we played the demo version at Josh's apartment, people got sick of playing with me 'cause I knew all the answers. I'm definitely not bragging, either, it's more of a freakish phenomenon. I'm like Dustin Hoffman in *Rain Man* when it comes to this shit.

Anyway, because my mom works for a magazine, I'm able to go to these screenings and I try to take advantage of them as much as possible.

I meet my mom outside her office building on La Cienega. She takes forever coming down the stairs and I listen to Terry Gross on NPR—half getting angry that my mom is always (always) LATE. I mean, ever since I can remember my mom has always been late. I'm not sure what that means.

The sun's still keeping the sky somewhat colored, even though it's already gone down beyond the horizon. There are strips of patterned pinks and oranges layered up like sideways color bars. A Los Angeles sunset, made beautiful by a screen of haze, pollution, and trash. It says a lot about this city. It says a lot about the people who live here. But I figure my mom's all right as she comes running up to the side door, carrying all her bags and things.

I've always thought my mom was beautiful. I don't know, maybe every kid does. But my mom really is very stylish and she steps into the car wearing Jack Purcells, flared corduroy pants, and big sunglasses. She's like this mass of energy coming into the car, though. She starts talking immediately about her work, throwing stuff everywhere. I mean, she says hello to me for a second, but then she's just ranting about these "stupid celebrities." She has to go to this nightclub tomorrow night in Koreatown where Nicolas Cage met his new wife, a waitress there. Apparently, they set you up with dates when you go in and then you sing karaoke or something together. My mom is so pissed about having to go on her Friday night.

I drive across town to Sony. I listen to my mom. She had to get quotes today about Ben Affleck and Jennifer Garner's possible marriage.

We get to the Sony lot late, going in past a guard station and parking out front. Josh is sitting in his car next to us, smoking a cigarette and listening to music. He gets out when he sees us and I introduce him to my mom. He has long, tightly curled hair and a hawk nose. He shakes her hand with his skinny, pale fingers—his wrist collapsing some. Josh gives me a hug and I ask him about work and whatever. Honestly, after my relapse, he's never really been the same to me. There is a way he keeps himself guarded around me now. I guess it's the same with most of the people in my life—they're too afraid of getting hurt to let me in all the way. After relapsing I just find it impossible to be as close to my old friends as I used to be. Mostly I just pretend I don't notice it—but I always do.

We go and all sit down together in the small underground screening room. There are big plush chairs upholstered with red fabric. I've been to a couple of different screenings here. I actually came here a couple of times with my dad when he was interviewing some celebrity and we had to see a screening of their film.

The movie is sort of Hitchcockian, but tells the story of a gay transvestite heroin addict writer who is molested by a priest at a Catholic school in Spain. Josh and my mom and I just can't stop talking about it. We decide to all go out to dinner at Kate Mantalini's in Beverly Hills. For some reason they have all these pictures of Andie MacDowell on the walls. Anyway, it's open late and they have killer chicken pot pie and osso bucco. It's funny to see my mom interacting with one of my friends. Growing up, my mom was never around me and my friends. She and Josh seem to be getting on really well. She is trying to get him to help give her story ideas. Josh's twelve-step sponsor, this guy Voltaire, is a doorman at all these clubs and is friends with Paris Hilton and whoever. You can tell that Josh loves talking about it.

You know, that really is one of the oddest things about L.A. You go to twelve-step meetings and it's like a who's-who list of the Hollywood entertainment elite. And, as much as I hate to admit it, I do get sucked into that whole thing. I mean, it's intriguing and I find myself becoming more and more wrapped up in the gossiping. Plus so many of the people I've started hanging out with are in the entertainment industry. Even Spencer is involved with that stuff, producing movies and all.

And then, of course, there're my parents. As journalists, both my mom's and dad's lives have been consumed with celebrity. As much as we all want to play it off as being no big deal, at times we have all been very obsessed with fame.

Josh's lived in L.A. his whole life. His parents live in West Hollywood. He went to the USC film school and just knows a ton about movies and stars and directors. Both he and my mom are having fun talking about all these different rumors and things. My mom asks if he would want to go out to lunch with her—maybe to Mr. Chow's. He's excited and I smile, proud of my mom—though feeling awkward and left out at the same time. I tune out their conversation and stare around the dining room. I think maybe Parker Posey is in one of the booths across from us. My mom doesn't think it's her, but Josh agrees with me that it is. We watch her eating a large salad. She has horn-rimmed glasses and her hair is pulled back.

After dinner I drop my mom off at her office and Josh goes back to his place on Fairfax. I thank my mom for the whole evening—buying us dinner and all. She gives me a big hug.

"I'm proud of you," she tells me.

We hug each other again.

Back at my apartment, I can't really sleep so I go online and look at some different websites and things that I like. There's this one called Nerve.com—an online magazine where, about a year ago, they published a short story of mine. They have short movie reviews each week, and reading over them, I'm struck by how clever and creative they are.

Almodóvar's movie was so inspiring to me, I decide to write my own review and I send it off to the editor. I'm not sure what I expect, but it is fun to write and I guess that's the most important thing, right? Writing is compulsive for me. I have to write—no matter what it is. Even now, every day, I work on different short stories. I've still been trying to put together that children's book and I've been trying to write about my whole experience with Zelda and what that meant to me. Josh and I have also been working on putting together a screenplay for our zombie rehab movie. Every free moment I have at the hair salon, I'm scribbling in a notebook. Even more than exercise, writing is my outlet. It helps keep me sane.

So I work late into the night, falling asleep only after I am so tired that I'm literally nodding out at the keyboard.

It's too goddamn early and my stomach is all cramped up as I board the 747 for Honolulu. This trip was so sudden, but I feel grateful that my dad asked me to come along—though at the same time, I'm pretty nervous. I haven't seen him or Karen or the kids since before my last relapse. Actually, I did see Karen once, but that was during the whole car chase thing.

Honestly, I don't know why they decided to extend this invitation to me. I guess I've just been doing better and they're willing to give me a chance again. My dad called me to see if I wanted to come with them to Molokai, the least developed of the Hawaiian Islands. He's doing a story for the travel section of some magazine on this inexpensive beach camping resort that recently opened there. Michelle agreed to give me time off so I could visit with all of them.

Spencer was very supportive. He's home from the hospital, although he can still barely get out of bed. They have him taking Vicodin, so he has Michelle dispensing the pills to him. That way, he says, he won't be tempted to abuse them. I admire his commitment, though it's kind of scary that after fifteen years sober, Spencer still has to be so cautious. They tell you in the twelve-step program that once you are an addict, you will remain one the rest of your life. I guess there's still a part of me that wishes that wasn't true. But I look to Spencer as an example of the kind of man I want to be. As far as I can see, he is right now demonstrating his commitment and showing me what it will take for me to remain clean. It is a daunting task, but I suppose that's one of the reasons for the whole "one day at a time" philosophy.

Anyway, when I told Spencer that my dad had invited me to Hawaii, he seemed really excited for me. Of course, he cautioned me against having unrealistic expectations for what this trip might bring.

"As long as you look for someone else to validate who you are by seeking their approval, you are setting yourself up for disaster.

You have to be whole and complete in yourself. No one can give you that. You have to know who you are—what others say is irrelevant."

I know he's right, but all that is easier said than done. I respect my father and Karen. I respect Jasper and Daisy. I want them to respect me. I don't think that has ever gone away. Sure, when I'm loaded I'm able to disconnect from caring about them all, but sober, well, I want so badly to be accepted by them. I guess things might be easier if I really didn't give a fuck, but that's not the way it is.

So I walk down the dim, carpeted corridor connecting the plane to the terminal. I go past the two smiling flight attendants and walk back toward my seat, trying not to bash anyone in the head with my bags. Seems like half the goddamn plane is wearing Hawaiian shirts. They're like Mickey Mouse ear hats at Disneyland. I don't really understand why people wanna dress up like that. Somehow it must make the whole experience more satisfying, but I just don't get it.

My seat is toward the back of the plane against the window. There's no one next to me yet, so I spread out some. Sitting back, I realize just how scared I am. Mostly it's thinking about seeing Karen that freaks me out. My dad is my dad. Jasper and Daisy are my brother and sister. But Karen doesn't owe me anything, you know? I mean, she doesn't have the same connection to me that the rest of them do, and I feel like she's much less forgiving. And, honestly, I've always been sort of terrified by my stepmom. I still haven't spoken with her since before the car chase. Not that it's her fault—not at all. When she met me she'd never been around kids ever in her life and I'd never been around a stepmom. Neither of us knew what to do. I was seven and it was always me and my dad—hanging out in the city, going out to dinner or to the movies. Karen changed all that. I mean, my dad changed around her. He began pulling away from the life he'd had with me. We no longer went to all these parties. He disconnected from a lot of his old friends, so I stopped seeing them too. Suddenly we were

all sitting down for dinner together and Karen was reminding me
to chew with my mouth shut, or keep my elbows off the table. I
guess I resented her for how she changed things. My dad was
trying so hard to leave his old life behind, and I can see now that I
felt like it was a rejection of me. I felt like I was a mistake and that
my dad wanted to correct me along with everything else.

But I also really loved Karen. I mean that profoundly. In
many ways I idolized her. She used to take me to art galleries, to
museums—quiz me on the different artists. We went to movies
together. She studied French with me for hours. So much of what
I learned about in terms of art and film and literature was directly
given to me by Karen. I loved the way she dressed. I loved listening to her stories about being young in New York, or living in San
Francisco and going to the Art Institute. I also wanted so badly to
be loved by her.

But she has become very concerned about protecting her
children from me now. Sometimes I think she would just prefer it
if I was gone completely, so she wouldn't have to deal with me
and so her children would be safe. It hurts my feelings, but I don't
blame her. I know what I've done.

The plane ride takes about six hours to Oahu, then another
forty-five minutes to Molokai. The landscape is thick and green
along the coast of the small island—whereas inland it is all red dirt,
almost desert. I read almost all of Donald Goines's *Whoreson* on
the way over. His story of a ghetto pimp keeps me from thinking
about anything else. My legs are cramped and I squint against the
sun as I step out onto the stairway leading down from the plane.
I see my dad and Karen and the kids right away. They all look so
dark—tanned from a summer spent going to the beach and doing
swim team and whatever.

When I go up to Karen, I can't even meet her eyes. I just hug
her and I have tears coming down now and she does too.

Jasper and Daisy are all over me a moment later.

"Nicky, Nicky, Nicky."

They repeat my name and hug me and we all say how much

we missed one another. My dad stands at the back of the waiting area. He looks the same, with maybe a little more gray in his hair. He's wearing shorts and a ripped, dirty T-shirt. He wraps me up in a big hug and I feel like crying again.

After we get my bags we walk out to their rental car. We talk about my flight and all sorts of trivial whatevers. It's hot and the air is dense with humidity. There are scraggly trees with vines hanging down rising from the rich red soil. I get in the back between Jasper and Daisy. They are arguing and talking all at once.

"Nic," says Jasper in his high, chirpy voice. "You wanna go surfing?"

"We rented bikes," says Daisy.

"We wanna go fishing," says Jasper.

I look out on the dusty two blocks of town they have on Molokai. My dad points out a fruit stand with a bucket set up to collect the money for the otherwise unattended fruit. Jasper runs out to buy two papayas, dropping the money into the tin container. I'm playing with the kids and making jokes. It feels just like everything is back to normal. It's like we're a family again. Though, of course, things have changed. I notice myself trying harder than ever to make sure everyone knows I'm doing all right. I'm aware of a certain amount of scrutiny from everyone that I never felt before all this happened. They seem cautious—feeling me out. And then behind everything is my knowledge of the truth: I can't have their lives. I have to build my own—something I have no idea how to do.

The cabins we're staying in are right off this private beach that's down about three miles of rocky dirt road. They have outdoor showers and electricity which all run on solar power. There's an outhouse toilet and mosquito netting over each bunk. Jasper is superexcited about going surfing with me, so we drive to this nearby beach where there are supposed to be good waves. Jasper has gotten a ton bigger. So has Daisy. They look like little teenagers now—though they still maintain a child's roundness. Plus, you know, the way they act makes them seem much younger. Jasper is ten. When I was twelve I had my first sexual

relationship. Jasper seems so far away from any of that. I'm not
sure how much of it has to do with me, but my dad and Karen
have done everything they can to keep their children protected
from all the sexuality and drugs I was exposed to. Jasper and
Daisy have grown up in this little sanctuary. They're both still playing with trolls and action figures. They are really their age. I was
never my age. I always wanted to be older. I felt so inadequate
being trapped in my small, prepubescent body. Jasper and Daisy
seem very naive, but also comfortable with themselves. I'm still
not comfortable with my goddamn self. I don't know if I'll ever be.

Anyway, we pull up to the beach—jagged coral rising high
out of the water in places. The waves are big, crashing in hard
against the reef. The shape of them is just beautiful as they break
slowly down the line. It's exciting to look out there. The beach is
empty, just a few locals out bobbing in the surf on their boards.
There's one guy, a large Polynesian, who seems to be getting all
the waves. He's on a nine- or ten-foot longboard. Everyone else
is trying to get out of his way.

Me, I haven't surfed in maybe six or seven years. It used to
be my obsession, but drugs took me away from it. I wonder to
myself whether I even remember how to stand up.

Right away Karen and Jasper are fighting about whether he
can go out or not.

"Come on, Mom, please," he begs.

"Jasper, you're not going out there and that's final. Nic can
go if he wants, but we're gonna wait here on the beach. It's too
big. It's too dangerous."

"It's all right," I say. "We can go back to the cabins. I'm not
gonna make you all sit on the beach."

"No, Nic," says Karen. "You should try it out. I mean, if you
want to."

"Yeah," says my dad. "We rented these boards, you might as
well use 'em. Just go out for a minute. We'd love to watch."

"Are you all sure?"

"Yeah," they all say at once.

I put on a pair of board shorts. They're much more comfort-able than the wet suit I always had to wear in California. I grab the shorter of the two longboards, rub some wax on it, then walk cautiously out into the shore break. I get hit a couple times as I'm trying to get out and I cut my foot on a piece of coral. My heart is pounding hard as I struggle against the walls of churning white water I have to dive under. The ocean is cool, but not cold even though it's the middle of November. It's so clear you can see the patterned bottom, some ten or twenty feet below. I paddle hard, looking back to see them all playing and watching. I'm scared.

The first set that comes seems so much bigger than it looked from the beach. I watch the wave crest and set up a tube as it smashes down. All the other surfers out with me pull back, intimi-dated by the wall of water coming toward us. The sky is full of thick, billowy clouds that are being carried fast by the offshore wind. The next swell comes and I start paddling along with it. I feel the momentum of the wave carrying me, and before I can think, I'm on my feet. The sound of the wave breaking is deafening and I fall down, down, down the steep mountain of water. At the bottom, the edge of my board catches and I'm sent upward, carving into the face of the wave. All my movements are so auto-matic. I crouch down, letting my body get covered by the frothing curl. Then I emerge from the tube, breathing hard. I'm in the hot, tropical air once more. The wave is dying and I'm so close to the black rock formations on the shore. I hit the top lip and dive off into the thick salt and clear blue water. As I raise my head, my first thought is to look toward the shore. My family's all on their feet, cheering.

I wave.

I feel the adrenaline rushing in my bloodstream. My veins pulse with it. But at the same time, there is a feeling of sadness in my stomach. I paddle out, my arms strong and my lungs powerful. I duck-dive under another breaking wave. My mind is going nonstop. Why did I look at them? Why was my first response to seek their approval?

I paddle over the top of a swell and crash down on the other side, getting knocked off my board a little. Scrambling back on, I wonder to myself, what has changed? I've worked so hard on this twelve-step thing I'm in, but still, I am the same. I am still just trying to fit in. I feel like a visitor—a guest. It hurts me. I want to be a part of their lives. I want to be accepted as one of them.

Karen and my dad are almost always absorbed with the kids' needs—with their protection and care, but also with opportunities for learning and knowledge. They are both constantly teaching the kids things connected with whatever it is we're doing, whether it is educating them about sea turtles, or the leper colony on the far side of the island.

Plus, both Karen and my dad are so consistent with them. Sure they argue—all of them—but the life they've provided the kids has always been so stable. Jasper and Daisy have lived in the same house their whole lives. I envy them. I mean, of course I do. I never want to have to return to my own life, which will always be separate from theirs. I never want to go back to living by myself, struggling to make a living and forever fighting the endless brigades of depression and melancholy that attack me from my own insides. I don't want to have to face reality. I don't want to have to be a grown-up.

I take a few more waves, then paddle in—worried that they might be bored and impatient waiting for me on the beach.

We drive back to the cabins and have dinner on the sand, eating food from the resort's nightly buffet.

Before we go to sleep, I read to Jasper and Daisy from *Treasure Island*. I do all the voices of the pirates and everything. Daisy falls asleep before I finish. I stay up talking with Jasper.

"Is it weird to see me after such a long time?" I ask.

He looks down at me from his bunk. "I guess it was at first," he says. "I thought maybe, you know, you might be different or something. But you're the same old Nic."

I let that sink in.

Maybe, I think to myself, underneath it all, I am not this awful person, but a caring, loving little boy. Maybe that has never left me, even after everything. So why do I want to blot that out? Why do I want to kill off the person that I am? Why do I always want to become this unfeeling monster, fueled by whatever chemicals I can find to put in my body?

I guess I'm just selfish. My needs always come first—that need I have to escape or something.

But lying here with Jasper, all I feel is regret for having taken myself away from these people who love me. Because I do care. I do love them.

"I love you, Jasper," I say.

"I love you, too, Nicky."

I turn over on my cot and pull the covers up. I close my eyes. I go to sleep.

DAY 257

Tomorrow I have to leave to go back to L.A. I can already feel the reality of my departure setting in. There's an overwhelming sense of sadness and depression taking hold of me. I guess mostly it has to do with that same old desire I have to be a part of this wonderful family my dad has created with Karen.

Since being here we've explored the whole island, going on walks through the jungle, swimming off different isolated beaches. We've ridden bikes on backcountry trails. We've played soccer and hide-and-seek. Daisy has taken me on tours of the little forts she's made for her trolls. She is always gathering shells and pieces of wood, creating these elaborate fantasy worlds. Jasper is all about games. He's content as long as we're constantly playing *something*. Jasper and Daisy have such a loving relationship together. It's like they're always looking out for each other. If we're reading something and Jasper can sense that it might be making Daisy scared, he'll tell her to cover her ears. If Jasper gets hurt, Daisy is the first to run up and make sure he's all right.

There are all these feelings surging like breaking waves inside me. I can't help but to distance myself. I'm so easily annoyed by everything. I want to scream at my dad when he drops his coffee in the breakfast café and it spills all over the ground. Jasper keeps missing the football as we throw it back and forth on the beach and I want to just hurl it off into the bushes so he can never find it. Karen keeps trying to get us to go walk through these abandoned sugar plantations, something I would normally love to do, but the fact that she's suggested it makes me dread going.

I know this isn't fair. I try so hard to fight it. I try to just be nice. But then, gradually, I realize that all those feelings of dreading leaving are being replaced with just wanting to get the hell out of there. Suddenly I can't wait to leave—get back on my own—not have to deal with this cutesy, overprotected, sugarcoated world of my dad's family. They're keeping their children so naive, so unable to cope with the hardships of the REAL world.

But then, more logically, I wonder to myself, how well have I been able to cope with those things? Obviously, not very successfully. So maybe my dad is doing the right thing. And with that thought, I'm enveloped in sadness again.

We've driven to a western-facing beach. There's a still river that separates us from the ocean and we all have to walk across a wobbly wooden plank to reach the other side. The beach is in a protected cove. The border is all lush trees and crawling vines. We walk out onto the white sand and the sun is hot and inescapable. I'm sweating and it's almost hard to breathe in the wet, tropical air.

Quick as I can, I run into the ocean. I put my head down and swim, leaving everyone behind. It's as though I forget everything for a second. My body is working against the warm salt water and I'm just going. When I stop, breathing hard, I am far from shore, surrounded by calm ocean. I kick my legs in wide circles to tread water. My head bobs rhythmically and, slowly, I start moving back toward the beach.

Watching Karen, Daisy, and Jasper making patterns out of shells in the shore break, my dad reading farther back underneath a tree, I feel a certain calmness. Strange, I think, in the past there's no way I would have been able to pull myself out of that spiral of negativity, anger, and hopelessness. I mean, at least not that fast. Something has changed. And then it hits me—maybe it's the medication. It's been two weeks since I started that new anti-depressant and the bipolar medication. I'd forgotten about that. Sure, the change isn't very dramatic. It's not like shooting meth or something. But there is a slight difference. Keeping my head above water suddenly doesn't seem so tiring. The blackness doesn't swallow me up to such a horribly suffocating depth.

I swim back to where the kids are playing. I walk out of the surf and shake myself dry. Jasper is leaning over a sand castle that has been decorated with tiny shells. I run over and touch his shoulder.

"Tag," I say. "You're it."

I take off down the beach, Jasper chasing behind me. Daisy joins the game and soon we're all running after one another, laughing and diving into the soft grains of sand. I feel weightless. There's a burning in my eyes and a choking in my throat. I don't stop the game, but I can't stop the tears from running down. I'm so grateful to have escaped that horrible depression I was falling into. I'm so grateful to be able to be here—present—not needing anything but this moment. I'm crying from relief and thankfulness.

"What's wrong?" asks Daisy, looking scared.

"Nothing," I say. "I'm just happy to be here with you." I go kiss her wet forehead. "Ha-ha—that means you're it," I say.

"No fair."

She comes tearing after me.

As I dart away, however, I think about how what I just told her was only a half truth. There is also a feeling I have of intense, well, regret. It's like: How could I have spent my whole life battling so hard, not knowing what was wrong? Now I see a doctor and we talk for fifty minutes and this huge piece of the puzzle that was missing for me is suddenly revealed. How could I have lived so long never being treated for such an obvious mental illness? It's frustrating and sad. But Spencer's voice sounds in my head: Now is now. That's what he always tells me. There is nothing but now and I try to hold on to that. The past is gone, the future hasn't happened yet. This, right here, is all there is.

So I play with Jasper and Daisy on the beach. We go into the jungle a little ways and climb a bending-down tree that has thorns all over it. We sit talking high in the branches—not saying anything really.

As the sun sets, we have dinner on the deck of the island's only hotel. Karen and my dad both drink wine, the kids and I drink water. My dad tells me to order whatever I want, seeing as how it's my last night and all, but I just get a salad with chicken and papaya in it. We're all worn out from the sun and the heat and the ocean.

"You know," I say, "I just wanna tell you guys how much it means to me to have been invited here."

"Of course, Nic," says my dad.

"Yeah," agrees Karen. "It's great to see you. It's been so fun. I'm so happy you came. You seem to be doing so well."

"I'm trying," I say. "But thank you. Thank you for saying that."

"It's the truth. I love you, Nic."

"I love you, too."

"I love you, too," says Daisy.

"Me too," says Jasper.

"Oh, you guys—I, well, I—I'm so sorry."

"We're sorry too," says my dad. "We know how hard it's been."

We eat in silence for a while. It's dark now and the sound of crickets takes over everything.

After dinner, we watch TV in the hotel's lodge. *Pirates of the Caribbean* is on and Jasper is so excited. I sit between him and Daisy—my arms wrapped around each one on the stripe-patterned hotel couch. Daisy falls asleep with her head on my shoulder.

DAY 278

I've been back in L.A. for a couple weeks now. I was sad leaving everyone in Hawaii, but I'm also pretty grateful to be home. I've been able to ride my bike again and it's actually been great coming back to work. I've missed the girls back at the salon. They are so sweet to me, asking me questions about my trip and making me feel really appreciated.

"Nic, thank God you're back," says Ayuha. "We missed you so much. The place was going to hell without you, you know that, right?"

I just smile and maybe blush some.

"It's true," says Simone. "You better not leave us again. You're our mascot. All my clients were asking about you. They were worried you quit or something."

It feels good, the way they value me. How could I ask for a better job? Plus, because I want to pursue my writing, they let me bring my laptop to work. I set it up at the reception desk and can pick up wireless from the coffee shop across the street.

Checking my e-mail today, I have two messages that stand out. The first is from the entertainment editor at Nerve. She says they want to run my *Bad Education* review. It has to be edited some, but she says she loves where it's coming from. She also asks if I would be able to review a movie called *I Am David* for this Friday's edition. I'm so excited and I immediately tell everyone in the salon. They offer their congratulations and I go and look up *I Am David* on Yahoo. The production company is Lions Gate, so I call their publicity department.

"Hey, um, I review movies for an online magazine called Nerve.com. My editor has asked me to do a capsule review on *I Am David* and I was wondering if there were any screenings or anything coming up that I might attend." I feel so grown-up and professional making this call. It's very exciting.

The publicist tells me there're no screenings left, but she'd be happy to have a messenger drop off a VHS copy of the film at my apartment. I give her my address and then hang up. I feel so important.

The other e-mail that catches my attention is one from Zelda.

It's short and simple. "I broke up with Mike last night. I couldn't take it anymore. I've been thinking about you. My number is . . ."

I swallow hard reading this. Zelda has written to me. Zelda. I wonder whether she's still sober. She has a bad history with relapsing. Maybe she's getting high. I'm not sure what to do.

In my stomach, in the knots tying there, I know I should call Spencer—ask him his opinion. But at the same time, I know what he's going to say. I know he'll tell me to stay as far away from her as possible—not to get involved. I know he's right. Zelda is maybe the most damaged person I've ever met. She had track marks scarred all over her arms and legs. Just the fact that she cheated on Mike with me—what, almost a year ago?—makes me have a hard time trusting her. But I want her. It is a desire stronger than anything else and I'm not sure what to attribute that to. I know I'm sick. Maybe that knowledge is meaningless, though. Because I call. I just say, you know, fuck the consequences. And I call.

Zelda actually answers on the second ring. "Hello?" Her voice is soft and seductive.

"Hey Zel, it's Nic."

"Nic, oh my God, I'm so glad you called. I thought maybe you hated me or something."

"No," I say. "I've been waiting to get an e-mail like that from you since we first met."

"Oh, Nic, you know I've wanted you since then too—I was just so scared."

"Yeah, me too."

"Can you come over tonight?"

"Of course."

I take down her address and agree to come after work. Pushing all the doubt and inner warnings to the side, I convince myself that, in his perfection, this is God's will for me. I mean, isn't that what Spencer would say? I tell myself that is the truth. I don't want to hear anything different and I don't ask for any validation.

At work I'm kind of secretive. I don't tell anyone. And, you know, under any other circumstances I would be talking to everyone about it. I'm used to being very open, and hiding stuff feels uncomfortable. When Ayuha asks me what I'm doing tonight, I almost blush, stammering over my answer.

"You know, uh, nothing—just going to a meeting."

The hours at the shop advance so slowly. I call my mom and tell her about the review in Nerve. She seems excited. I refill the shampoo bottles at the washbasins. I organize the display cases and clean all the bowls filled with bleach and different dyes. I wash and fold every last towel and apron. I confirm all tomorrow's appointments. I sweep up the hair and clean off all the stylists' cutting stations.

Finally it's five o'clock. Only Fawn's still here, finishing up her last client. She assures me that she doesn't mind closing up and that I can go home. I'm actually shaking from nervousness as I drive back to my apartment. It's like I'm physically sick with it.

All the little tricks and whatever that Spencer has taught me are suddenly all blanks in my mind. I can't think of one prayer— one anything.

Not knowing what to do, I take a long shower just to relax and maybe keep busy. The heat of the water against my body calms me some. I turn the temperature up until it makes my skin red. The whole bathroom is thick with steam as I step out. I have to wipe off the mirror several times before I can see my reflection clearly. I think about how ugly I am. Maybe if I turn sideways or blink a whole lot I might look a little better, but it doesn't work. Nothing makes me feel any more beautiful.

After drying off, I get dressed quickly. I don't look in the mirror again—it's too depressing. For the first time since I stopped using I'm craving a cigarette. I resist buying a pack, though.

Eating isn't gonna be possible, so I kill time looking around the Virgin Megastore on Sunset. Zelda lives right at the base of Laurel Canyon in Hollywood. According to what she told me on the phone today, Joni Mitchell once owned the apartments where she's living. That doesn't really mean that much to me, but I guess she thinks that's pretty great.

I find the little pink stucco bungalows after missing the turn twice. Parking takes forever. I'm listening to music as loud as it'll go. It's like if the music is loud enough, I won't be able to listen to my own thoughts.

The last time I talked to Zelda, she told me she was pregnant with Mike's child and that she was going to use it as a sign that she needed to recommit to him. It was devastating. I never really thought I'd hear from her again. Now I'm walking down the slanted old Hollywood street to her apartment. She's free and, you know, that's what I've wanted all this time.

I dial her apartment number on the buzzer and a few minutes later she's downstairs, unfastening the gate.

I'm almost struck speechless seeing her again. I reach out and hug her to me tightly, inhaling the smell of her. She looks maybe a little older than I remembered—but that just makes her all the more attractive. Her red hair is cut in a sort of shag, hanging down to her shoulders. Her pale, pale skin is broken out some on her forehead. Her eyes are clear green, emerald—or so it seems. She's wearing black boots over tight jeans and two ripped T-shirts layered over each other.

"This is weird," I say.

"Yeah," she almost whispers. "Come on in."

We walk through a little garden of dense leaves and reaching-up trees. She lives at the top of a flight of stairs at the back of the apartment complex. Inside there's mostly just a bed, a large TV, a few photographs on the walls, and clothes everywhere.

"Sorry it's such a mess."

"Please. So, uh, what happened?"

We sit on the carpeted floor in front of the heater, she smoking cigarettes and me just listening. She tells me about how she broke up with Mike after she lost the baby, but that he begged for a second chance. She took him back, only to discover, last week, that he had been having two different affairs for more than a year. She was finished, and she finally moved out. I listen to her tell me about his betrayal and how hurt she is. She cries in my arms. I hold her and kiss away her tears.

"Girl," I say. "You know you're too good for him? You know he just couldn't stand himself, so he was doing whatever he could to try and feel better. I mean, it's pathetic."

"I know," she says. "But I just feel so stupid. I always thought he was safe, you know. That's why I stayed with him. What an idiot I am."

"You're not an idiot," I tell her. "You're a really good person. I wish you could see yourself like I see you. I wish you could see what an amazing, sweet, beautiful person you are."

"I'm not sweet. I'm not any of those things."

We move to her large bed. I'm kissing her on the mouth now and she's kissing back. I kiss her all down her body. I make love to her. It feels very powerful. I am so connected with her.

After some time we rest. She lies naked on the bed, letting me look at her. She smokes a cigarette and goes to eat some ice cream out of the carton. We eat it together, back on the bed—strawberry ice cream.

"Zelda, you know, I love you," I say. "I've loved you for a long time. I will devote everything to you if you'll let me."

"Oh, sweetheart," she says. "You're so young. You don't know what you're saying."

That hurts. I feel a cold shiver all through me.

"Baby," I say, "I'm so much older than my age. I've seen so much—so much."

"I know you have, my darling."

We talk for a while—just saying nothing really—and then she falls asleep. She wraps herself tight around me and I can hear her snoring loud in my ear.

Me, I can't sleep.

I can't sleep.

I'm lying here with my fantasy—my dream. She's holding me against her nakedness. I think about her—about her life—about this obsession I've had with this girl for more than a year. The thoughts just keep spinning like a record player in my mind, but eventually I fall asleep. I fall asleep next to this girl.

It's maybe six when I wake up and I feel Zelda on top of me, slipping me inside her. She moves while I just start to shake off the sleep. The gray morning is barely filtering through the blinds. She finishes on top of me and rolls off. I crouch around her body and kiss her.

"Sorry I woke you up," she says.

I tell her I don't mind. We start to drift off again, but I feel anxious and restless. My mind is going all over, and suddenly I feel guilty as hell. It's as though I can barely stand lying in this bed. I'm not sure what to do, but I decide I have to leave. Kissing Zelda good-bye, I get dressed quickly and drive all the way across town to a seven a.m. spin class. It's the only thing that makes any sense right now. I drive fast, cutting in and out of traffic—scared I'm not gonna make it on time. I listen to the Talking Heads and try not to think about anything else. Driving, I can still smell Zelda on my face and hands.

I want to call someone.

I want to call my dad or Spencer. Really.

It's too early, though, and I'm stuck with myself.

The spin class is brutal. I've never gone on so little sleep before and I feel like throwing up. But, still, I make it through. The leader of the class rides with my cycling group and has taken me under her wing. Her name is Kendra and she's actually a celebrity trainer. I think we both had a crush on each other for a time, so she agreed to train me for free. Part of that training includes being able to go to her spin class periodically, without having to pay the twenty-something-dollar fee. Hilary Swank is riding the bike three rows behind me. Welcome to L.A.

I'm sweating like I dove into the ocean—but I keep up. I have to take a shower in their bathroom, but whatever, I'm on time to work and I feel like all the money in the world. I'm strutting around like a goddamn male peacock. I may not have really slept, but I feel so damn cool.

Welcome to fucking L.A.

I call Spencer at about ten and tell him everything that happened. I guess I'm trying to impress him—is that so fucking strange?

And Spencer does seem impressed. "Just try not to get hurt," is all he can say to me.

I laugh. It seems so stupid. I mean, of course I don't wanna get hurt.

"I'll try," I say.

He's got nothing more than that to offer me and I feel pretty much fine about everything. I do my days' work at the salon and all the guilt and everything is expunged from my mind. After all, I wonder, what have I done wrong?

Nothing.

Nothing.

Nothing.

Nothing.

DAY 280

Zelda wants me to go to this twelve-step meeting with her on Bundy, so I'm gonna head over there and then I guess we'll go back to her place afterward. As I'm getting ready after work, I call Spencer and talk to him about my day.

Last night I watched that *I Am David* movie. My review started with the line: "Kicking heroin is nothing compared to the agony of sitting through ninety-something minutes of Jim Caviezel's new movie, *I Am David*." They're printing the review Friday. I get a hundred dollars for each capsule I write. Next week I'm doing *Blade: Trinity*. It feels like I found the perfect career for me.

Spencer is excited and encouraging, but then he starts grilling me on my relationship.

"Now, about this Zelda thing," he says.

I swallow hard, lying on my bed and staring at the stucco ceiling. I've been waiting for this talk.

"Nic," he continues. "First off I just want to say that I'm not going to tell you what to do or not to do. That's not my job and you're gonna do what you want anyway. But try to hear this, okay?"

"I'm listening," I say.

"This is fun," he says. "This is fun for you. You get to sleep with an older woman—a celebrity, of sorts. That's fun. That's gotta feel good. But, Nic, seriously, listen to me. That is all this will ever be—fun. If you can keep that in mind, then you're fine. If you can separate yourself from this whole thing and know that it is just a fling, well, then you'll be all right. Does that make sense?"

"Yeah, but, I mean, Spencer," I say, still just staring at nothing but the calm of my ceiling, "you know I love this person. I want to be there for her. I want to help her."

"That's very poetic, Nic, I'll say that much, but I also have to tell you that your grasp on reality right now is, uh, tenuous, at best."

"What?"

"Listen," he says. "I'll tell you right now, I mean, just to be on the record—this is going to end badly. Zelda is not, not, NOT stable. I can't say that I really even know her, but all I see is devastation in your future. If you're willing to pay that price, than you can do whatever you want. All I can ask of you is that you don't get high. Be willing to go through this and not use. That's all I've got for you."

"Spencer," I say, "I appreciate all you're trying to do. But I'm telling you, nothing bad is gonna happen."

I think I really believe that. I mean, sure the doubt comes in that maybe I should be listening to this man who helped save my life. But, really, he just doesn't get it. Besides, I want this so badly. I'd pay any price. Zelda is more important to me than anything else.

"All right," he tells me. "I'm not gonna argue with you. Just don't get high, okay?"

"No, no, of course I won't."

I hang up and get ready to drive up Sunset.

Walking down to the meeting, I see at least five hundred people in front of the church, milling about, chatting. I see Zelda, standing at the top of the steps with a black skirt, blouse, and long black leather jacket. She has on stockings and knee-high black boots. I push through the people to reach her.

"Hey, beauty," she says.

I kiss her and hold her and she kisses back.

"Thanks for coming, baby, I know how crazy this is."

"Nah, I mean, it's interesting," I say.

She guides me in through the doors. There are people everywhere and Zelda seems to know almost all of them. She introduces me, but I forget all the names. There's a sense of being her arm candy or something.

"This is Nic, my boyfriend."

Everyone seems to look me over twice and I feel very self-conscious about my age. I know how young I am and, even more, how young I appear. I mean, I even got carded the other day when I was going to see an R-rated movie. You only have to be seventeen for that. Zelda is thirty-seven. I'm twenty-two. There shouldn't be anything to your age when you consider love, but I can't help but be so incredibly aware of it.

Then, you know, as I'm being paraded around, people inevitably ask me, as they always do in L.A., "What do you do?"

I think about Spencer's words—about the importance of being humble.

I say, "I'm a receptionist at a hair salon."

Zelda always laughs. "Yeah, but he's also a writer for a bunch of different magazines, right?"

"Yeah," I say, averting my eyes. "Yeah, I am."

And, inevitably, they smile, or say something like, "Oh, how exciting."

There's something very degrading about the whole thing, but I play along. I don't know how not to.

We take our seats, near the front.

After the meeting I follow Zelda back to her apartment and we make love. In some ways, it feels like I'm making love to a cripple. She is so hurt and confused and there is something very erotic about that. Does that make sense? Probably not. I do realize I'm sick.

We flip through the movie stations on TV. She stops on late-night Cinemax.

"Oh my God," she says, laughing. "I think I'm in this movie."

It's a soft-core porn movie about a stripper who seduces men and then kills them. The stripper is Zelda. I watch her have pretend sex with this guy, then shoot him in the head while she's climaxing.

In our bed, she laughs like crazy. "That was my idea," she says. "To keep going after I killed him so I could orgasm."

"Wow," I say.

We watch most of the very bad movie, but eventually we both fall asleep. The whole time I feel uncomfortable, to say the least. I feel so much younger and less experienced than Zelda. I want to be good enough for her. I want that so badly.

DAY 309

I'm still riding bikes with the group who meet on 26th and San Vicente at six thirty in the morning, but I'm driving there from

Zelda's in Hollywood. I've stayed with her every night for the last month and we spent New Year's together. I find myself quickly moving in. We don't talk about it, but it happens instantly and it just seems natural, you know?

The only people it seems to bother is everyone else in my life. All my friends have made it very clear how stupid they think I'm being. They say Zelda is unstable and dangerous to my sobriety. Plus they've all noticed how obsessed I've become with her. I never want to leave her side. I want to sew her to me.

My dad and mom have both expressed their concern. Spencer just keeps shaking his head whenever I talk to him about it.

"I love her," I say.

"You love the idea of her, Nic," he says. "You don't love her."

"God, Spencer, you don't understand. I mean, there's no way I can explain it to you."

"No," he says. "I guess there isn't. Just try and have fun."

I hang up the phone. I'm driving home—I mean, to Zelda's—after work. The I-10 freeway is bumper to bumper, a slow-moving dinosaur of cars stretching all the way out to Pasadena—if you could see Pasadena, through all the goddamn smog. I'm listening to the Talking Heads' live album. I think about calling my dad, but know he'll just treat me like Spencer—skeptical and condescending. My mom won't be much better. But I'm nervous.

Zelda is taking me out to dinner with her dad and stepmom. Zelda's birth mom died about ten years ago; she was a recovering heroin addict who hung herself dead from a dog leash and choke chain. Now all Zelda has is her dad. He wasn't around much when she was little, but he's settled down now and they've become very close.

I'm being presented as her new boyfriend. She says her dad hated Mike, but she's sure he'll like me.

When I get back to the apartment, Zelda is lying in bed, watching *Being There* on TV. I curl up next to her. Peter Sellers is being wheeled into an elevator by some servant in this giant house. "This is a very small room, isn't it?" he asks.

Zelda and I both laugh. We talk about our days. We make love. She smokes a cigarette and we go take a shower. In the shower, she completely grooms me. She scrubs me down. She washes my hair and detangles it. After showering, she gives me stuff to put on my face and she combs my hair. She asks if I'd like to borrow some clothes. When I say that I will, she starts pulling out tons of different pants and shirts for me to wear.

"Is this real Prada?" I ask, pulling on a pair of black bell-bottom dress pants.

"Yeah," she says, laughing. "So be careful with that."

I put all the stuff on and I feel pretty cool and pretty stylish.

"Where'd you get all these clothes?" I ask.

"Oh, you know, when I was with my ex-husband, I could just go to Barney's or something and they'd close down the whole store for me. They'd pour me a glass of wine and I could buy whatever I wanted. I have so many clothes. Besides these I have a whole storage unit full of clothes. We'll go over there and you can pick out whatever you want. A lot of *his* clothes from being on tour are still in there."

"That'd be great," I say.

Looking in the mirror, I swallow. I can barely recognize myself.

"Now," she says, coming over and kissing me. "I'm a little worried about what a baby you are. I don't know what everyone's going to think. But, look, you don't have to tell them you're a receptionist. You can say you're a writer. It's not a lie."

"No, I know. I will—of course." I look in the mirror again.

"All right, let's go," she says.

We drive in the new Jetta her dad bought her, over the back hills of Hollywood to get to Studio City. I've never really spent much time in the Valley, so I don't know where we are. She listens to Cat Stevens really loud. The only songs I recognize are from *Harold and Maude*.

Zelda smokes one cigarette after another. She drives fast, barreling around the corners without any caution at all. Underneath all that makeup she's wearing I can see a face ravaged by the life she's lived. Heroin has a way of preserving people so they look sort of frozen in formaldehyde. It's not that noticeable with Zelda, but sometimes, in the right light, I can see it clearly. She still has scars on her arms from all the needles. But I don't care. I think she is the most beautiful person I've ever seen. I lean over and kiss her cheek.

"Baby," she says.

The restaurant where we're meeting her dad and stepmom is some chic Italian place on Ventura Boulevard. We don't valet park the car 'cause we don't have any money, really. Inside, the lights are very dim. Zelda waves to her dad, a really large man with gray hair and a Marine Corps tattoo on his forearm. He shakes my hand with a tight, strangling grip. Zelda's stepmom is pretty, a little overweight, with blond-dyed, very "done" hair. There's another couple at the table who are well dressed and prosperous-looking. Zelda seems to know them and everyone's talking and I just sit quietly.

Finally, her dad starts grilling me about everything—what I do, where I live, all that. He's not mean about it, but he barks questions at me like a drill sergeant. Eventually I seem to win him over. Maybe it's talking about my family, about my dad having done the *Playboy* interview with John and Yoko. Whatever it is, he turns to Zelda at a certain point and says, "I like this one."

He lets up after that and then we're all just talking. Zelda and her dad are joking about a time when she called him in the middle of the night to come get her in L.A. He was living north of L.A. and eight-year-old Zelda had gone to spend the week with her strung-out mom and one of her boyfriends. Zelda's mom had gotten really drunk and wanted to do Zelda's makeup like she'd been beaten up—a black eye and everything.

Zelda got scared and secretly called her dad as her mom got more and more belligerent.

"And you came and rescued me, Papa," she says.

"Yeah, but I wish I could've done more."

"I know."

They exchange a look and I think this man really might be **219** very sweet.

Zelda is always particular about the way she orders, asking for everything to be made a specific way. Tonight she gets fettuccine Alfredo, but she wants peas in it. Everyone laughs, but we all end up eating off her plate.

For dessert, she orders all these different things and is really cute and enthusiastic. She seems so cool and everyone there seems to respect her so much.

As I get up to leave we all shake hands. Zelda's dad gives her a couple hundred bucks and tells her how proud he is of her. He tells me good-bye and I feel like I've passed some sort of initiation.

"They liked you," she says, lighting a cigarette as we pull off onto the Hollywood Freeway. The cars and houses string along like colorful, blinking Christmas lights—draped in patterns across the Valley.

"Yeah, they seem really great."

She laughs. "Well, they can be—at times. There's also a horrible, brutal side to my father, so don't be taken in by him."

"No, of course I won't. I'm sorry." I feel so protective of Zelda. I want to take her away from all the horror she's known in her life.

"Fuck, Zel."

"Well, hell," she says, accelerating some. "We've both had a fucked-up time of things, haven't we?"

I laugh.

"'Equally Damaged,'" I say.

"What?"

"It's a song."

She tells me she loves me.

I tell her I've looked into the core of her and held it in my hand, and I will never let that go. I tell her I will be here for her as long as she allows. I tell her I love her.

"I'm not gonna leave you," I say.

She smiles. "We'll see."

We make love when we get home. I feel so connected with her. I feel like I understand her and can help her. I feel like I can be her savior. Maybe that's grandiose, but really, that's how I feel.

Zelda has known so much sadness, so much pain. I want to save her. I think I want to marry her. I want to commit myself to her like that and it just seems perfect.

If everything in life happens for a reason, as Spencer would assert, then surely this relationship is no accident. I use all his teachings to reaffirm these feelings—to validate them. I mean, if there is a God that's all-knowing and all-powerful, then surely he has orchestrated this whole thing. Why else would I have been delivered to Zelda, as I have been?

That is my logic.

DAY 351

It's February 16th, the anniversary of Zelda's mother's death. Zelda was in her mid-twenties when her mom committed suicide. It may have been almost ten years ago, but Zelda still breaks down crying and angry when she mentions her mother's death.

We're going to Forest Lawn Cemetery, where her mother is buried. It's so blue and crisp outside I have to wear sunglasses. The Valley hills are all pristine, groomed and vibrant. We drive in Zelda's Jetta, listening to the first David Crosby solo album. I think about how beautiful the day is—how beautiful she is—how incredible it is that she's taking me with her on this trip to the gravestone. She's already told me that I'm the first person since her ex-husband to visit her mom. I tell her again that I love her and that I'll never leave her. She leans over and kisses me, driving fast along the highway.

I haven't spent a night away from Zelda since we've reunited. Every day I ride my bike with Spencer, or swim, or run up the walls of Runyon Canyon—just blocks away from Zelda's. I'm exercising at least an hour every day, whether I work or not. I still haven't started smoking again, even though she smokes over a pack a day.

Spencer and I have stopped really talking about Zelda. It's like an untouchable subject. We go on our rides together and talk about movies and God and the twelve steps. My relationship with Zelda is just a given, not anything different from Spencer being married to Michelle. But I've stopped babysitting for them. And I haven't been spending as much time with Spencer and I've been going to fewer meetings. I can't stand being away from Zelda. I mean, she is definitely my priority. Spencer reminds me over and over how dangerous that is. He keeps telling me that I should "have fun" and not take everything so seriously.

"You're only twenty-two," he says. "You have your whole life ahead of you."

Obviously he doesn't understand. No one does. No one can.

But at least at work I've become the idol of some of the stylists. Ayuha can't believe I'm dating the actor's ex-wife and cousin of a famous friend of hers. In fact, everyone seems impressed and I talk about Zelda all the time. She even stopped in the other day to visit me at the shop.

"Nic," said Ayuha, after Zelda had gone. "You're dating a supermodel."

I just averted my eyes and smiled, saying nothing.

Zelda's mom is buried in a simple grave near the main church of the cemetery. Zelda remembers nodding out in that church—shooting heroin in the bathroom during her mom's funeral. We park, having to walk only a few yards to find Zelda's mother's grave.

I read the inscription. They are Zelda's words.

Zelda lies down on the grass and puts a bouquet of flowers on the headstone. She talks to her mom quietly, so I can't hear.

And me?

I try to imagine her mother. I lie there. I try to think of something to say.

Suddenly I see a picture of Zelda as a little girl, so vivid in front of me. I feel a sense of utter appreciation for Zelda's mother—the woman who gave my love her life. I begin to thank her. I tell her thank you, over and over. I thank her and I start to cry.

Zelda and I press close together on the grass—kissing like that.

I hold Zelda with such aching—never wanting to let her go. I'm going to protect her forever. The feelings are so deep in me. We both cry and I feel her tears on me.

I belong to her.

She belongs to me.

We have shared our very cores and I love her so much.

Really.

I'm crazy with it.

All I can think about is her. It fuels everything in me. It is a feeling of absolute bliss—maybe even better than crystal meth.

Zelda has become my whole world.

After Forest Lawn, Zelda and I go out to lunch at a place on Robertson. She orders for us, knowing exactly what she wants. We split a meatball sandwich, a salad, and cappuccino gelato. It's all perfect. I'm in awe of her.

Tonight, however, we're going to a screening—compliments of me. I've been reviewing movies for Nerve steadily since I first submitted that capsule for *Bad Education.* Not only that, but I've been granted an interview with Mr. Bungle's front man, Mike Patton, and Yuka Honda, the songwriter for Cibo Matto. They're paying me three hundred dollars per interview. That feels like a lot of money to me and tonight I'm taking Zelda to a screening of the new movie by the director of *City of God*. It's based on some spy novel and it stars Ralph Fiennes and Rachel Weisz. It's called the *The Constant Gardener* and I'm very excited.

Zelda seems used to the whole screening thing, and as we sit down, she falls asleep on my shoulder. I watch the whole movie like that, with her literally snoring against me. I'm embarrassed as I leave—apologizing to a few of the actors who attended the screening. Zelda is hard to wake up and I just manage to guide her home. I assume she's tired and I write the review on my laptop while she's passed out on the bed.

When she wakes up, it's around one o'clock. She jumps up just as I'm falling asleep.

"What? What's going on?" she asks, almost yelling it.

I look up. Her eyes are wide.

"Where am I?" she says.

I grab her shoulders tight. "You're here. You're here, in your apartment. You're here with me, Nic."

"Oh, Nic," she says. "I love you."

My whole body seems to shudder at that. "Zelda," I say, kissing her sweating forehead, "I love you so much. You fell asleep, you know?"

"Oh, yeah," she says slowly. "Nic, um, I have to tell you something. I'm, well, narcoleptic. You need to know that. And my sponsor doesn't allow me to take any medication. After coming off all the antidepressants and everything, my doctor has told me I'm narcoleptic. He's a great doctor. Maybe you'll meet him sometime. His name is Dr. E. I've been with him since I can remember."

Narcoleptic? I just laugh. Of course Zelda is narcoleptic. That goes along with everything else crazy and devastating in her life.

"Baby, I'm so sorry," I say.

"No, no," she says. "That's all right."

We talk for a while. Well, mostly she does all the talking and I just listen. Out of nowhere she brings up this relationship she had with the lead singer for a famous punk band.

"Have you heard this story?" she asks.

I shake my head.

"Well, I was newly sober again and I was out with some friends. As I was leaving this club, this guy comes up and hands me his number, telling me I should call him if I was brave enough. I liked that come-on and it was only later that I found out who he was."

She tells me about moving in with this guy, T, and how the first night she came home to their place, he was lying on the bed wearing a white slip and high heels. She had to stop herself from laughing.

"I mean," she says, "I'm *so* not into that."

I listen to her stories about their crazy sex—T was doing speedballs and stuff, while she couldn't, so he rubbed it in her face. He left his diary next to their bed, open to a page that was titled "Zelda: Pros and Cons." At the top of the Pros list was her connection with her ex-husband. I guess he was sort of brutal and mean to her—always putting her down. He was obsessed with the female guitar player of his band. Zelda says he could never stop talking about her.

Zelda felt more and more jealous and beaten up. Finally, one night, she relapsed on heroin. The next day she told T she was through with him. He told her that was all right, but he wanted a favor first. He wanted her to fuck him in the ass with a strap-on.

"So I did." She laughs. "I figured, why not? I gave it to him as hard as I could and, you know, I have to give him credit—he took it really well."

"Jesus," I say.

There's a coldness inside me—like a numbing chill under my skin. I know her story was supposed to be funny, but I just feel lost—intimidated—unworthy of her. It's just more proof that she's so much more sophisticated and cool than I could ever be. Most of her stories make me feel that way. The other day she was looking through a photo album and almost all her ex-boyfriends are, well, somebody. Her friends are all famous and she's met almost everybody. All my experiences, however crazy, are nothing compared with Zelda's.

But all that does is make me want her more. There's this feeling like if I can have her, then that must mean I'm worth something. If she chooses me, then I will finally be able to feel good about myself. Zelda gets up to go to the bathroom. She closes the door and I hear the lock click. I manage to turn over and fall into a deep sleep.

I hear the pounding on the door a few hours later. Looking around, I see Zelda must still be in the bathroom, 'cause the door is shut with a light just creeping out from beneath the crack. My stomach goes tight as I realize who it must be outside.

"Zelda." I hear Mike's voice coming through.

Not knowing what else to do, I call out, "Mike, man, hey, this probably isn't the best time."

The silence that follows is so long it's almost audible. I feel like I'm just writhing in the heat of the tension that is burning me alive. What is Mike doing here? I thought they were done.

I'm almost trembling. I hate confrontation.

Suddenly he calls out again, "Zelda, open the fucking door."

Zelda opens the bathroom door and leans her head out. "Who is it?"

I tell her.

"Oh, shit." She puts clothes on real quick and walks over to me.

The knocking on the door won't stop.

"Listen," she says to me, looking straight in my eyes. "Please don't worry and don't get involved."

"Okay," I say, not knowing how to get involved anyway.

Zelda opens the door and walks out and I hear Mike say, "What, did I interrupt you? Did I interrupt you fucking? Did I?" I hear her asking him to be quiet and then some muffled arguing.

I lie on the bed, holding my body in the fetal position—hyperventilating a little. I feel like a small child again, covering my ears while my parents argued. I feel this cold heat inside and I'm suddenly terrified that Zelda is going to leave me. I want to call Spencer but I know he's asleep. I lie on the bed, just trying to shut my eyes—to make it all go away.

And now I think about using. I find myself wishing so bad that I knew where to score some crystal. A shot would take all the pain away and I wouldn't care at all. But as it is, I do care. I wrap myself up tight in the blanket, pressing the pillow to my ear so I can't hear them screaming at each other.

It's fifteen minutes later when Zelda bursts back into the room.

"I called the police. He won't be back tonight." She explodes into tears, collapsing on the floor and sobbing so damn hard. I weave myself around her and she cries and cries. I tell her how much I love her and how amazing she is, but that doesn't seem to make any difference. She just keeps saying how mean he was— how hurtful.

"They're lies," I say. "None of what he said was true."

"No," she says. "He's right. You don't know me, baby. There are parts of me that, if I showed them to you, well, you'd be out the door so fast."

"That's bullshit," I say.

But she just cries on and nothing I say seems to make any difference at all. I don't know what he said exactly, but whatever it was cut right through her.

"No one who really loves you could ever treat you that way. True love is wanting what's best for that person, no matter what. Mike coming here for you is something else. It's something sick and selfish—but it's definitely not love."

"I know," she keeps saying, but it feels like she still believes whatever he said was right, and for the first time ever, I really feel like physically hurting someone. I want to tear that motherfucker apart. It's like this instinctive impulse coursing through me.

"Zelda, what did he say?"

She just cries.

"Zelda, please, tell me."

She talks into my shoulder—pressing her face against me. "He said he knew I was gonna use again and that he was going to piss on my grave after I die. He said I was worthless and was going to kill myself in the next year."

"Oh my God," I say. "He's so fucking disgusting."

"No," she says. "He knows me better than anyone. I mean,

Nic, you have to understand that there's a part of me that still
loves him. I spent the last three years with him. I can't just forget
that after one month of being with you."

That hurts so bad. I mean, it just destroys me.

"You deserve better than him," I finally say.

"I know," she says. "I know. I love you, sweetheart."

"I love you, too."

Zelda takes some pills from her purse and we lie down on
the bed. She is distant and I hold her till she falls asleep. I am
scared. I am so fucking scared.

DAY 352

I sleep some, but wake up real early and drive to that spin class
in West L.A. before work. I pedal fast, drenched in sweat and
working my legs hard. It doesn't take the pain of the night away,
but it helps some. I wonder what Spencer would tell me to do?
He'd probably say something about how I should pray for Zelda
and Mike—just pray for them. After all, seeking to help others
always takes one out of oneself. That's the way it's supposed to
work, anyway.

So I actually try it. While doing the sprints and climbs on
the stationary bike, I just hold that prayer in my thoughts. As I'm
pushing my body to its utter limit, I distract myself with a sort of
mantra—chanting a prayer for Mike and Zelda. And the thing is,
it does seem to help. I get this spiritual and physical high, feeling
so connected to whatever God is—or might be. I am suddenly
no longer an individual entity, but I am one with some sort of
greater entity—like the blanket idea in David O. Russell's *I Heart
Huckabees*. In the movie, Dustin Hoffman talks about the universe
as being a great white blanket, covering everything. Within the
blanket there are individual manifestations of existence: e.g., you,

me, the Eiffel Tower, an orgasm. They are all separate entities, created by the same coherent fabric of "the blanket." Anyway, the combination of praying and exercising to that extreme brings me to an ecstatic place—a height where I feel like I've become a part of that EVERYTHING once again.

It's like drugs.

I mean, it is.

Shooting crystal was the only way I ever got to connect with that "oneness" in the past. On the verge of death—chemicals turning my blood to poison—barely able to speak or move—in that helpless state of drug addiction, I have experienced a sense of connection with the very essence of death and life that has been unparalleled. And, similar to that, working out to the absolute furthest extremes of my body's capacity—my lungs and legs torn apart—while using Spencer's methods of prayer and talking to God, well, it is euphoric. It has replaced drugs for me, absolutely.

It is such a great high.

On my way to work from the spinning studio, I call Spencer, wanting to talk to him about everything that's happened.

He answers the phone while he's walking Lucy to school.

"Hey, Spencer," I say.

"Nic—what's up, brother?"

"Nothing," I reply. "Did you work out this morning?"

He pauses for a moment. "Uh, no. Did you?"

I tell him I have. It's weird, but I feel really kind of competitive with Spencer about our exercising. I always need to ride harder than he does. When we go out on our bikes together, I have to lead—or beat him up the hills—or something. I'm not sure what that's all about.

There's this strange rivalry that has developed between us. Honestly, it feels like the relationship I have with my dad. It's like—I admire them both, but I also want so badly to be better than them. The feeling is all-consuming. Every time I talk to my dad, all I want to do is show him how well I'm doing—maybe trying to make him jealous, because, hell, I'm jealous of him. I'm jealous of his career as a writer. I'm jealous that he has built up this wholesome family for himself that doesn't include me. I mean, I just want to be better than him.

Talking with Spencer has become something like that for me. I think about Spencer like he's my goddamn father. The parallels are undeniable.

There are certain ways in which I want so desperately to be a part of Spencer's family—really a part of the world he and Michelle have created for Lucy. I want to be her brother; I want Michelle to care about me like she cares for her daughter. I just wanna start over—with Jasper and Daisy—with Lucy.

But, sadly, I know that is all a fantasy. I have to live as myself and that I can never escape—no matter how hard I try. So, talking with Spencer as he walks Lucy to school, all I feel is this need to be better than him. Maybe there's some anger—some resentment? I don't know how to block it out from my mind, but everything is coming out so aggressively toward him. I tell him about what happened last night. He tells me that I might want to take it as a sign to not get involved in this whole mess.

I dismiss what he says. I'm not gonna argue with him, but he just obviously doesn't understand. What Zelda and I have together is something more powerful than anyone can comprehend. I almost feel sorry for Spencer as we're talking. He just doesn't get it. A love like mine and Zelda's is more incredible than anything Spencer has ever known. He seems pathetic to me.

Spencer and I get off the phone quickly. I can barely listen to him these days. It is strange because there was a time when I held on to every word Spencer said as though it were the utter gospel truth. He always says, "What you've been doing hasn't been working, so why not follow someone else's direction for once?" Only a month ago that was exactly what I was doing—following everything Spencer told me. Now I suddenly feel like things have changed—like maybe Spencer should be taking advice from me.

Going to work, I feel such spite for my job. I'm bored and irritable and I find myself really fighting to be nice to everyone. Also I'm just very freaked out about what's going to happen after last night. It's hard to focus and I make all these stupid mistakes around the salon—double-booking clients and taking appointments without getting phone numbers, or names, or something. I'm not sure if anyone notices it, but I feel slow and I just can't pay attention.

The day is long. It stretches on painfully.

When I get home to Zelda's apartment, I find that she hasn't left the bed all day. She called in sick from work. She says she's starting to feel dizzy and she wants me to go to tonight's twelve-step meeting without her. I'm concerned that she's not coming with me, but I figure she doesn't feel good, so whatever. It's hot, hot, hot and I fill our swamp cooler with ice and water to help make the room more bearable. The utilities are included with her rent, so she's not allowed to have a regular air conditioner. I kiss Zelda three times on the forehead, short, longer, longest.

"Please," she says, turning away. "I don't feel good."

That hurts. I almost panic when she says it. There's a cold terror inside and I feel needles all under my skin. I could never imagine shunning Zelda like that no matter how sick I felt. I'm worried that I'm really losing her. My mind races to try to say the right thing—do the right thing—pull her back to me.

"Do you want me to stay with you?" I ask.

"No, no, you go to the meeting."

"Can I bring you anything?"

"No, I'll be fine. I think I just have vertigo or something. I might be able to get some medicine from my doctor. Don't look so scared. Everything is all right."

That calms me some. Maybe I was overreacting.

"I love you," I say.

"Nic, I love you."

"It's just . . ."

"I know, I know," she says. "That was a really hard night."

"I'm so worried you're gonna go back to him."

"Nic, I promise, I will never go back to Mike. I swear on my mother's soul."

That's all the comfort I need. The worry and fear and everything lifts and I manage to just feel like we are back to normal again, or as normal as we can ever be.

"You sure I can't bring you anything?" I ask again, as I get ready to leave.

She tells me that she might want a milkshake from Café 101 if I have time on my way back. She also offers to let me drive her Jetta to the meeting so I don't have to worry about moving my car.

Driving to the meeting in Zelda's Jetta, I feel so cool. Secretly, I want everyone at the meeting to notice me driving her car. I wish I could broadcast it. As it is, I find some way of mentioning it to all my friends.

The meeting on Prospect and Rodney in Los Feliz is more a social thing than anything else. I've managed to work myself into the sort of elite group that sits along the back wall. There's Josh, Karen, this guy Eric, who writes Hollywood screenplays. There's Voltaire, Josh's sponsor, who is a drug counselor and a doorman at local nightclubs. Ria, the manager of the Sober Living I went to, is there, plus Vakeeza, a spray-on-tan model. I notice one really well-known actor sitting by us, along with the drummer for a punk band from the seventies. I feel confident talking with everyone—joking and whatever. Voltaire makes fun of me a little about Zelda, but I'm proud of it. He knew her from way back when she was first trying to get sober.

"That girl's a pimp, yo, I'll tell you what."

I just laugh, not even really knowing what he's talking about.

There's a speaker at the meeting, but I don't hear one word he says. Josh and Voltaire are vicious—judging everyone—relentless in their criticism. Still, they are hysterical and I have this intense desire to be accepted by them. Voltaire knows absolutely everybody in L.A. and whenever he goes to a meeting, he enters the speaker's name into the IMDb, the Internet Movie Database, on his BlackBerry so we can all know just exactly how important the person is in the Hollywood entertainment industry. There does seem to be something sort of repulsive about how superficial this all is, but I try to ignore it.

After the meeting, we all go to Café 101. There's actually a picture of Zelda when she was a little girl on the wall above one of the booths here. It's a huge crowd and we have to push about five tables together. I feel, for the first time, really a part of the whole scene there. After all, I'm a film critic and I'm dating the ex-wife of a famous actor. Suddenly I seem to have gained a level of respectability in this group that almost borders on having my own celebrity status. I can compete with anybody here and the feeling makes me high and excited. I am as much a part of the elite as the rest of them. I'm sitting next to the male star of a famous sex tape and I'm not intimidated at all. In fact, I'm almost talking down to him. The experience of being me right now is exhilarating.

I order the milkshake to go and tell everybody, sighing, "Zelda wants me to bring it to her. I swear—all she eats is ice cream." Everyone laughs as though they're all too familiar with her eating habits.

People who never would have given a shit about me are now treating me like an equal. I mean, my old friends are still concerned with my behavior, but all these new people seem nothing but impressed with me. This movie star is talking to me about his struggles getting sober—asking me questions, which I'm answering like an expert. Everything I say seems so clever and I hold the entire audience at complete attention.

Honestly, I never want this feeling to go away.

I am, finally, somebody.

That may be shallow, but it is the truth.

After the dinner, I drive Zelda's car back to the apartment. When I get inside, she is asleep—covered by a thick down comforter. The TV is on. I curl up next to her, watching some Marilyn Monroe movie with Cary Grant. She doesn't wake up. Thinking about Spencer and everything he's taught me, I thank God for Zelda, for my life—for everything that has happened. I'm

twenty-two years old and the world lies at my fingertips for the
taking. All I want is to grab hold of it—to become part of this incredible, exciting, glamorous thing called "Hollywood." Nothing could be more satisfying.

I kiss Zelda's hot forehead. She struggles awake.

"Hey, baby," she says.

"Hey. You feeling better?"

"A little. Dr. E came over here and brought some medicine. He was so great to me. I wish you could've met him."

"Me too," I say. "What'd he bring you?"

She kisses my cheek and rolls over, facing the opposite wall. Before she can answer, she's fallen back into unconsciousness. I watch the TV, feeling just so completely elated.

DAY 368

Zelda has been out of work for the past two weeks. Whatever medicine that doctor prescribed doesn't seem to have helped her nausea. I go to the salon, but when I come home, Zelda is still in bed. She seems distant recently, but I don't want to face that. I mean, we still make love every day. That hasn't changed.

It's a little after six when I wake up. I run for an hour, up and down Runyon Canyon. It is so stunning at the top. I climb this ridge that looks out over all of Hollywood, dodging the different dog walkers and hikers who crowd the path.

At work I can barely concentrate. I am now so uninterested in being there and I'm pretty sure my actions reflect that. After all, I'm practically a celebrity now because I'm dating Zelda. Why should I be a fucking receptionist at a hair salon?

I exchange text messages with Zelda all day long—just flirting. I want to be with her every second of every day.

Nothing seems more important than that.

I would die for her.

I would rather die than be away from her.

She is everything to me. She has given me a feeling of purpose, of completeness. It's what I've always wanted. She is what I've always wanted—she is better than crystal meth. I mean, she is. I'll do whatever it takes to never lose her.

No one can tell me anything different—especially not Spencer. Really, you know, I'm just tired of listening to him. What is he, after all? A wannabe movie producer who lives in West L.A. in a nothing house, with a nothing wife. I don't admire him anymore. How could I possibly take direction from him? He has nothing I want. I've just outgrown him.

Plus, he reminds me of where I was—pathetic, without a career, without a life, without a cent. Who wants to think about all that? Not me. And Spencer doesn't let me forget. But I'm somebody now. Spencer is still a nobody. Besides, he is so discouraging about my relationship with Zelda. Not that Spencer hasn't been good to me, but he just doesn't understand the direction my life has taken. He can't keep up.

I need a different sponsor. I'm sure of that. I mean, just two days ago I celebrated my one-year anniversary. I need to move on in my sobriety.

What I really want to do is ask Voltaire to sponsor me, so I call his cell phone when I go on my lunch break.

Voltaire has been a great sponsor to Josh. He's a part of that whole Hollywood scene. Paris Hilton is on his speed dial. Need I say more? Voltaire is someone who can understand me. He knows about all this celebrity shit. Anyway, I'm sure he'll introduce me to so many people. And Zelda knows him. Zelda has no idea who Spencer is.

Listening to Voltaire's phone ring, I'm nervous about what the hell I'm gonna say to him. I'm scared he'll say no, or he'll laugh at me or something. I'm scared he won't accept me.

He picks up on the fifth ring. "Haaalllloooo?"

"Voltaire, it's, uh, Nic." I stutter over my words.

"Nic Sheff—what can I do for you?"

We talk for a minute about everything that's going on with me. He seems instantly empathetic. It's like he anticipates every word I'm about to say.

"Nic, dog," he says. "I've known Zelda for fucking ever, yo. If anyone can help you navigate through this bullshit, it's me."

I tell him how grateful I am for taking me in. He tells me to meet him after work at this place on Beverly called Café Sushi. He says we'll talk about working the twelve steps together and that he'll relate our work to my relationship with Zelda. I don't tell Spencer. I'm scared of what he'll say. Even at work, I feel guilty around Michelle—like I'm betraying her and Spencer. Still, it seems like this is the right thing to do.

I call Zelda around five, right when I'm about to get off work. I tell her that I just asked Voltaire to be my sponsor.

"Oh, baby," she says. "That's so great."

"Yeah, I think it might really make a difference."

"Good, lover."

"So I'll be home as soon as I can."

"Of course."

She asks me to bring her a vegetable tempura roll and seaweed salad. I say I will.

Spencer calls me on the way to meet Voltaire. I'm driving along Crescent Heights. My phone rings over and over. I don't answer. I'm not sure what to do about our relationship. Surely we can still be friends.

Voltaire is already sitting down when I get to the restaurant. He is very thin and balding, with a thick mustache—but somehow he commands the attention of everyone there. All the waitresses know him. He even takes the liberty of ordering for me.

Talking with Voltaire is so different from my meetings with Spencer. Voltaire talks to me about how, basically, it doesn't matter what I do, so long as I stay sober and continue trying to pass the message on to newcomers in the twelve-step program. He even gives me a list of phone numbers—new people he's met who he thinks I might be able to help. He has conditions in order for him to sponsor me. I have to call every day—without fail. I have to call one new person from the list every day and talk to them about how I've managed to stay sober this long. I have to work each of the twelve steps over with Voltaire, but, other than that, I'm on my own to do whatever I want. I don't feel any of Spencer's skepticism or his misgivings about this new life of mine. Doing the twelve-step program with Voltaire doesn't seem anywhere near as strict and judgmental as it did with Spencer. I feel genuinely grateful to have changed sponsors.

When I get home, Zelda is lying down, watching some Brian De Palma movie on TV. She is still sick and is smoking cigarettes. We talk about our days, my meeting with Voltaire. She wonders aloud whether I should move in completely with her so we can save money on rent. I ask her if she's serious.

"Yes, sweetheart. You know, I love you more than anything. I'm so thankful you came into my life."

"Me too," I say, almost choking up. I am so in love.

It's around eleven thirty when she gets a call from her friend Yakuza. I've never met Yakuza before, but I've heard all about her. She is thirty-seven and the heiress to a ten-billion-dollar fortune. She just got married for the fifth time, to a twenty-five-year-old guy named Justin. Apparently, based on her phone call, he has started shooting coke again after over a year of sobriety in a twelve-step program. Yakuza says she needs help. Without hesitating, Zelda gets up and we dress quickly. Driving west on Sunset, I look back to see the lights from downtown and Hollywood reflecting off the low-hanging darkness.

Yakuza lives in Brentwood, in a house that was passed down to her as part of her trust. Zelda only became friends with her maybe two months ago, but she's already helped Zelda out financially a lot—letting her borrow various sums of money. They met at a benefit for the Musicians' Assistance Program, where Yakuza used to be on the board. Zelda tells me as we speed through the Sunset Strip that she and Yakuza have been talking about starting a clothing design business. Zelda does a lot of styling for commercials.

Yakuza's house is right off Manderville Canyon. The place is closed in with a whitewashed picket fence. The house itself is like a fairy-tale cottage. It's two stories with a shingled roof and a big yard out back.

Inside, it smells like dog shit. There's paintings and books and strange odds and ends all over the place. It's actually Justin who opens the door. He's definitely a very handsome kid. He's got dyed black hair that's long on top and shaved around the sides. He's got a square chiseled face with some scruff around the edges. The way he talks, at least when he's strung-out, is really pained—like it's all he can do to spit the words out through his clenched jaw.

"Are you the police?"

"Uh, no," I say. "I'm Nic."

"And I'm Zelda. Where's Kuza?"

"Uh, upstairs."

Zelda goes up and I stay with Justin, trying to talk to him. He keeps getting up all abruptly and shit—looking out the blinds.

"Justin," I say. "Relax. No one's coming to get you."

A little while later Yakuza comes down. She's got chopped dyed blond hair and is wearing overalls beneath a heavy wool sweater. I get up and shake her hand. From that moment on, well, she just doesn't stop talking. And, the thing of it is, I can't understand one word she's saying. I mean, she's speaking English, but her thoughts jump around so much, I can't even begin to follow her. Zelda sits next to me and I hold her close. We exchange glances. Yakuza keeps talking and Justin is catatonic. Eventually he excuses himself and goes upstairs.

"Oh my God," says Yakuza once he's gone. "He's shooting up in that bathroom. He's gonna die. His sister died of a cocaine overdose. I can't handle this. I'll get a fucking annulment. You have to help him. Nic, you're his age—help him, please."

I'm not sure what that has to do with anything, but I hike the stairs to the bathroom.

The feeling comes out of nowhere as I'm walking up there—but suddenly, I want to use real bad. I mean, I'm kinda hoping he'll have some coke I can shoot. The thought doesn't even scare me. I know how much I have to lose, but I just block that out. It's like I've switched into automatic pilot. But thankfully, when I open the bathroom door, Justin is flushing a large plastic bag of coke and two rigs down the toilet.

"It's okay," he says, looking up. "I'm not doing this shit anymore. You can go tell Kuza it's all gone. I'm so fucking sorry."

"You want to come downstairs with me?" I ask.

"Sure, sure, man. What was your name again?"

I tell him.

"Right on, right on. Kuza called you?"

"She called my girlfriend."

"Wow," he says, standing. "I'm so fucked up. Are the cops here yet?"

"No. Nobody called the cops. You're gonna be all right now, okay?"

"Thank you."

We go back downstairs. I tell Yakuza that Justin just got rid of all his coke and everything. She traps me in another barrage of monologue that makes no sense. I smile and nod, taking Zelda's hand in mine.

Justin doesn't even try to talk. In fact, he passes out a few minutes later. How anyone could fall asleep after shooting that much coke is a mystery to me. Yakuza thanks us all over the place for helping. She says if we want to get married, she'll get us wedding bands and an engagement ring. Her sister's a jewelry designer, so she can get them wholesale.

"I know Zelda would like that, Nic. I know she would. You two are perfect for each other."

I blush. "Zelda," I say, "is that something you've been thinking about—I mean, marrying me?"

"If you want to."

"Baby, I want that more than anything in the whole world."

We kiss and Yakuza tells us how fucking cute we are.

"So, is it settled then?" Yakuza asks.

"Okay," I say.

"Great. You guys will have to come over tomorrow and I'll get some rings over here for you to try on."

Zelda giggles.

Driving home, I ask her again if she's serious.

"Absolutely. I can't wait to tell my dad."

"Will he be okay with it?"

"Are you kidding, he'll be so excited. What do you think your parents will say?"

"Oh," I say, turning to look out the window at the thick growth of trees. "I'm sure they'll be really happy."

Of course, I know that's not true.

I swallow hard, something catching in my throat. How can I possibly tell them about any of this? I can already hear the horrible silence that will follow the conversation I'm going to have with my father. I've always just wanted him to be proud of me, but I can't let that influence my decisions. He's just going to have to deal with it. Everyone will. I love Zelda and I want to commit myself completely to her. Nothing can come between the connection that we have together. I will marry her and I will be with her till we're both old, in sickness and in health, for richer or poorer. With time, I'm sure, both my mom and dad will come to accept her.

Still, I'm terrified of having to tell them—terrified.

Zelda puts a cigarette in her mouth and I watch her take a few drags.

"You think I could have one of those?" I ask.

"Of course, baby." She hands me a Parliament and watches me light it. She laughs.

"I know I shouldn't say this, my love, but I'm excited to see you smoking."

"Really?"

"It makes me feel more, you know, together with you."

"Yeah—me too."

It's been over a year since I smoked a cigarette, but sitting there in the car, it seems like I never missed a day. It's so natural and I'm not even sure how I ended up with this thing in my hand. I swear, I'm so goddamn impulsive. But, well, it feels good smoking again. I know I'm just so cool, sitting here with my fiancée, smoking a cigarette, and driving out to Hollywood at two o'clock in the morning.

DAY 396

I've given my landlord notice and it only took me about two days to move all my stuff over to Zelda's. She quit her job in Beverly Hills and has started working temporarily as a wardrobe assistant for a deodorant ad. The job seems like a much better fit for her. She comes home each day, late—full of all this energy. I fall asleep in our bed, but as I wake up throughout the night, I notice that Zelda has closed herself in the bathroom. If I call out her name I hear the lock on the door click. She'll emerge a few minutes later and come out to give me a kiss, but then she immediately locks herself up in the bathroom again.

It seems like she's not sleeping nights anymore and, honestly, I'm a little suspicious. I scan her bare arms for track marks but never see any, so I guess she's not using. Still, her behavior is erratic, to say the least. I'm not sure what to think.

When I question her, she says she's been having really bad asthma attacks. She has to breathe through this machine called a nebulizer. It makes a lot of noise and she says she doesn't want to keep me up. She says she used to have to go to the emergency room all the time, but now, since she got the machine, she just uses that instead. The stuff she has to breathe in has all these steroids in it, so she gets all this nervous energy and has to paint her toenails, or whatever.

At work, Fawn told me her three-year-old daughter has to go through the same asthma treatments and she has a similar reaction—being charged with this crazy energy that makes her run all over the house. All this leads me to believe Zelda and not question her too much.

Anyway, I finally talked to Spencer about changing sponsors. He said that he'd support me, no matter what decision I made regarding how I want to work the twelve-step program. He didn't seem hurt or angry or anything. I was surprised. He told me that, no matter what, he will always be my friend and, well, I feel good about everything.

Voltaire is pretty laid-back as a sponsor. I call him every day, but he doesn't really seem that interested in talking about my personal life. We focus on the twelve steps and that's basically it. He doesn't get involved in anything else, which is great by me. Plus, we're always going out to dinner with a whole bunch of people, or going to art openings or something. I feel important, what can I say?

When I get home from work, Zelda is already back from shooting the commercial. They wrapped early and she wants to take me out to this Italian place on Robertson. I change clothes, but my stomach starts to cramp up really bad and I have to sit down for a second.

"Baby, what's wrong?" she asks. I tell her.

She says that she's sorry and asks if I want to take anything. The pain is really bad.

"What've you got?" I ask her.

She comes over and sits beside me on the bed, cradling my head in her arms.

"I missed you today," I say.

"You too." She hands me a small orange pill and tells me to take it for my stomach.

At first I want to question her about it, but I don't want to appear naive or not experienced enough for her. I want to always just seem cool and nonchalant. I think if she told me to step out into the middle of traffic with her, well, I'd do it. So I swallow the pill without water. The tightness in my stomach is still there and I'm not sure what it's from.

Yesterday Zelda told her dad and stepmom about the wedding and they were just ecstatic. Already they've started planning it—where the reception will be held, who's going to marry us. Zelda wants her old sponsor, Courtney, to perform the ceremony and she wants the wedding to take place in her dad's backyard. All that's fine, but driving home from work today, I felt like I needed to call my dad and explain what was going on to him.

Somehow, I had convinced myself that he was going to congratulate me and agree to come to the wedding. I had wanted Daisy to be a flower girl. I thought maybe if I just acted confident and excited, the feelings would be infectious or something. It didn't work. My dad told me I was making a terrible mistake. He was practically begging me not to go through with it. The conversation ended when I got angry and hung up on him, telling him that obviously he didn't care about my happiness. Maybe my stomach pain has something to do with all that and maybe it doesn't. Stomach pain isn't really anything new for me. Growing up, every time I had to fly between my dad's and mom's houses I'd get these horrible stomachaches. I remember being doubled over in pain from them. Sometimes I'd start to get the stomach problems two or three days before I left, but they would always intensify the night before. I definitely carry stress in my stomach. But I don't tell Zelda about what happened. I just go along with her like everything's all right.

It's about the time that we're walking into Al Gelato that I start to feel strange. The light from the setting sun seems to dim suddenly and it's like I'm walking through thick, thick molasses. As we sit down at a table, I almost miss my chair. I have to steady myself against the white plaster wall. My head feels too big for my body and I can't keep my eyes open.

"Nic," says Zelda, shaking me. "Nic, hey, are you all right, sweetheart?"

"Of course," I say, not meaning that at all. I look over to the **243** mirror that borders the small dining room and I see that my pupils have disappeared almost completely.

"Zelda, what was that pill you gave me?"

"Oh my God, why?" she asks, standing back up all at once.

"I feel like . . . like . . . like I just shot heroin."

She looks completely panicked. "Fuck, Nic, I think we should go."

"What? What's going on?"

"Come on." She takes my hand and leads me back out to the car, making some excuse to the heavyset waitress. I actually feel really euphoric. I mean, I'm scared and I don't know what's happening, but it doesn't seem to matter. Plus, my stomachache is completely gone. The sensations in my body are familiar and I realize how much I've missed them. I ask Zelda for a cigarette. She lights it herself, passing it over to me as she drives back toward our apartment. I don't say anything for a while, just breathing and trying to take hold of my surroundings. Suddenly, I realize Zelda is crying. I think about how beautiful she is.

"Whatever's happening," I say, "I will understand. I'm never going to leave you—no matter what."

She chokes a little, sobbing. "You promise?"

"Yes," I say. "Yes, I promise."

"Look . . . I—I swear to God I had no idea the Suboxone was going to affect you this way. I guess I've just been taking it for so long, I don't feel it anymore."

I turn my head toward her, confused.

"Nic, I'm not sober. I've been taking Suboxone for more than a year. It's like methadone, you know? It makes me unable to get high off opiates, but I guess at first it kinda feels like doing heroin. That's what you're feeling."

She's really crying hard now and I tell her not to worry, that it doesn't matter.

"No," she says. "It does matter. See, Nic, I love you and I want to be honest with you."

"Of course, baby."

So she tells me. I listen and she tells me everything.

————

Apparently, Zelda has been taking benzos and smoking crack for about three months. She started using again with this guy, Alexi, who I've actually met a couple of times. He's older than both of us and was actually shot in the head about two years ago. It was his girlfriend, Bijou, who shot him. They lived in Hollywood, and Alexi climbed up to the balcony off the bedroom—in all black, with a black mask—because he thought she was having an affair. She wasn't, but she did have a gun—his gun—and she fired at what she thought was an intruder. Half of the top of Alexi's head was blown off—but amazingly, he survived. He was going to meetings for a while and that's where Zelda met him, but then he relapsed and moved with Bijou to Las Vegas. He still comes to L.A. all the time, though, and I guess he finally talked Zelda into smoking crack with him. Not only that, but her doctor—Dr. E—is basically just a drug dealer and will write prescriptions for anything she wants. She tells me I can leave her now if I want.

"No, baby," I say. "If this is what you're going through, I want to be with you. I want to be with you on every journey you take in your life."

Despite the Suboxone, as soon as I speak these words I feel the tightness swell up inside me again. Is Zelda really worth this? Will I fall back into that same horror I lived out with Lauren? No. Zelda is different. I would throw my whole life away for just one more night with her. Besides, I have learned so much about sobriety and God and everything Spencer helped teach me. Surely those lessons will carry me through this. Zelda and I will come out stronger than ever. Our love will conquer addiction. Our love will conquer everything.

It will.

It has to.

"We're in this together," I say.

"Oh, beautiful boy, I love you so much."

She's stopped crying and we kiss each other for a long time at a red light.

Zelda asks me if I want to go to a party at Yakuza and Justin's new apartment they just moved into in Beverly Hills. I'm still pretty fucked up from the Suboxone, so nothing seems like a bad idea right now. The sun has gone down, and the streetlamps streak past.

"Zelda," I ask. "Wasn't Yakuza all concerned about Justin relapsing?"

"Yeah, but I guess she's using now. She can be pretty crazy sometimes."

I nod.

Yakuza and Justin's place looks down on Sunset, off Wilshire Boulevard. It's a high-rise apartment with a doorman and a garage. We have to be buzzed up. The lobby is huge, with indoor palms and a little fountain waterfall. We go up to the eighth floor, then head down a corridor to the last suite on the left. Someone has painted a messy white X on the door. We ring the buzzer and Justin answers. He's high as can be—his jaw going back and forth. We go in.

The place is really big, with a full-size pool table in the middle of the living room and a view of the Sunset Strip. There's also a pile of crystal meth and a pile of coke on one of the dining-room tables. Seeing the meth there, I almost can't breathe with anticipation. There aren't any clean needles, but Yakuza lets us use one of hers. She also has the wedding bands and engagement rings to try on. Zelda has never tried meth and just shoots the cocaine, but I of course immediately cook up the crystal. I let her stick my arm with the needle and push off.

The feeling is just indescribable.

I don't know how I could've possibly made it over a year without doing this shit. I light a cigarette and feel so high. Then we start looking through the rings.

We decide to get the wedding bands specially engraved on the insides, but Zelda chooses an engagement ring right away. Yakuza says the one Zelda wants is seven thousand dollars wholesale. I write her a check for three hundred 'cause that's all I can afford right now, but she says I can pay the rest in installments.

We all hang out talking nonsense for a couple hours. There's some pain in my arm where I shot the meth, but I ignore it. At some point Yakuza disappears into the bathroom with all the drugs and refuses to come out. She starts yelling from behind the door about how she's going to get evicted from the apartment and how she's calling her lawyer to sue the building management. She says something about the front door and how they know it was her and I figure she must have been the one who painted that X. Zelda tries to console her, but Kuza's just completely fucking lost it. I can hear her mumbling in there. Justin is passed out on a black leather couch. It seems like it's time to leave so I ask Zelda if she wants to go check out the pool on the roof. She agrees and we go.

The pool is closed. It's like three in the morning, but I strip naked and dive in anyway. Zelda watches and laughs. I managed to steal a bunch of crystal and a rig from Kuza. And even though Zelda is hesitant about doing meth, we both shoot up right there—me dripping wet. I choke on the chemical fumes as they rush up the back of my throat. We go home—me driving and talking, talking, talking.

Around six in the morning I pass out on the bed. I'm not sure how long I sleep, but when I come to, Zelda is standing over me holding this Prada bag of hers.

"I can't believe you did this," she shrieks. Her eyes are glassed-over and crazy.

"What?"

"Don't play dumb. I'm not fucking stupid, Nic. You tore out this lining and put it back together, right? There are drugs in here, aren't there? I already found all the drugs in the bathroom tile."

"Zelda, what are you talking about?"

"Oh, sure. Yeah, right."

"No, no, I'm serious."

I follow her into the bathroom and see that she's removed all the tile paneling along the base of the white painted walls. She shows me a little pile of white flakes.

"Tell me that isn't meth," she says.

"It's not meth," I say. "Those are fucking paint chips. Zelda, you're in a psychosis or something. You're not thinking right."

"I'm not even high," she says. "You're fucking high—you're hiding drugs all over this apartment."

"Uh, no, baby, I'm not. I mean, I haven't."

"Tell the truth, Nic."

"Zelda, I am."

She starts trying to tear more of the paneling apart.

"Zelda, please, there's nothing there. You'll see. Look, I'll make a deal with you. Wait till tomorrow—the drugs won't go anywhere—then, if you still want to, we'll take it apart together. But baby, really, there's nothing going on. I've never lied to you and I never will."

She doesn't believe me. She's just gone.

I mix up another shot of whatever's left and give it to Zelda. That actually seems to calm her down some and I suggest we go take a drive somewhere. She agrees and we go down to the Rite Aid on Franklin and Sunset. It's almost midday already and the sun is so goddamn bright. I buy a carton of cigarettes and Zelda steals three pints of ice cream, a box of Lucky Charms, and some makeup. She just puts it in her purse. It's that easy.

I kiss her on the steps and everything seems okay again. We drive home and she apologizes for freaking out. She says she never wants to shoot meth again. We fall back into a half sleep, watching TV.

I've been out of work since last Friday. I showed up at the salon in a total blackout, having stayed up all night shooting coke with Zelda. Her friend gave us the number of her dealer, this guy, Adam. Most times we have to meet him down in the neighborhood surrounding Larchmont. It's actually really close to Dr. E's, who I've also started seeing with Zelda. He writes me prescriptions for Xanax and gives us free packs of Seroquel. Between him and Adam we can always get anything we want.

Despite the occasional freakouts Zelda continues to have, where she thinks I've been hiding drugs in the apartment, our relationship seems better than ever. We are so close and we do everything together. We make love and talk and watch movies and I'm still trying to write. Unfortunately, I took apart my computer with Zelda's toolbox the other day because I wanted to fix it. Now all that's left of my Mac is a pile of unusable parts. It reminds me of what Gack used to do.

As far as what happened at work to make them fire me, well, I honestly don't remember. All I know is that when I got back to our apartment, Fawn had called and left me a message saying that they were changing the locks and I wasn't allowed back for any reason. That shook me up, you know? I mean, I really had loved, and still do love, those girls. I would never intentionally hurt them. I can't believe they were so scared of me they actually changed the locks. I think back to breaking into my parents' house in Point Reyes. There's no way I can live with doing anything like that again. The guilt and shame are just too unbearable. So maybe it's a good thing that I got fired, before I did any real damage. Besides, I can't stand being away from Zelda— not ever.

Still, though, I'm not sure what the hell I'm gonna do for money now. Zelda is getting unemployment every two weeks now that the commercial finished shooting, but that's not anywhere near enough.

Not only that, but ever since that night at Yakuza's there's been a swollen, painful lump growing on my arm. Zelda tells me it must have been from a dirty needle. Over the last week it has gotten even bigger, turning purple, and sort of yellowish. The growth is about the size of a baseball. I keep thinking it'll go down, but it's just getting worse. It hurts so bad.

Because we're running out of money, Zelda calls her friend Lisa, to see if she wants to buy some of Zelda's never-worn designer clothes. Lisa, it turns out, is going out with this kid Jordan, whom I've known since before I was born. He grew up in New York in the same apartment complex as one of my best friends.

Anyway, Lisa agrees to buy some clothes, so we head over to her house up Rockingham Street. I'm starting to get really sick on account of my arm and Zelda tells me that the infection is starting to smell—so I ask to be dropped off at an emergency room in Santa Monica. I figure I'll just take a taxi to Lisa and Jordan's. Zelda drops me at the UCLA ER. I give my insurance card to the woman at the front counter. My whole arm is fucking swollen as hell and the abscess has turned orange and brown. The woman takes a look at it and I'm rushed in pretty quickly.

The first doctor who comes, this chubby-faced man with a close-cut mullet, frowns and tells me he thinks the arm is going to have to come off.

My eyes go wide.

"You're joking."

"No. Son, why did you wait so long to have this thing looked at?"

"I didn't think it was that bad."

"Not that bad? The infection's almost eaten straight through the entire arm. I guess we'll try to just cut it locally at first."

"Yeah, I'm sure that'll be fine. It's not that bad."

"Kid, listen to me—it is bad. I'll try to save the arm, but I can't promise anything."

I just don't get it, you know? I can't see how it could possibly be as serious as he says. A nurse comes in and gives me a shot of morphine. I swear I don't feel a fucking thing from it.

"Hey," I say. "I'm on this opiate blocker called Suboxone. You're gonna have to give me more morphine than that."

The nurse is this haggard-looking white woman. She asks the doctor, but he tells her I can't have any more. Another nurse comes in, a man with a light beard and glasses. He holds my arm down and slices a big X in the top of the abscess. It hurts. It really hurts.

As he makes the incision a white, yellow, bloody pus comes oozing out. It smells awful—just like rotten flesh or shit or something. The two nurses squeeze and squeeze and I feel like maybe I'll pass out.

After they drain the whole thing there's this giant, gaping hole in my arm. Then the nurse tells me I need to pay attention to how he packs the wound, because I'm going to have to do it myself. They take a long wooden Q-tip and this bottle of sterilized bandage and they begin stuffing the hole with it. They have to push it hard down around the bone and I grit my teeth and maybe there are even tears in my eyes. They're just shoving the stuff in there—forcing it in every possible little space that's been eaten out of my arm. It takes around fifteen minutes. Then they bandage it up and tell me to stand up and pull down my pants. I do and they give me a shot of antibiotics right in the ass. That hurts almost more than everything else.

The doctor comes in a few minutes later, telling me how lucky I was the bone wasn't infected. He gives me a prescription for Vicodin and antibiotics. They give me a bunch of extra bandage tape and some of those long wooden Q-tip things. I have blood all over me, but I finally get to leave. I go to the end of the block and call a cab. The driver comes quick but almost doesn't let me in the cab 'cause of all the blood.

"Jesus Christ, what happened to you?"

"Oh, uh, I just came from the emergency room."

As if that explains everything.

Jordan and Lisa live up Rockingham in this beautiful gated-in house with a swimming pool. I haven't seen Jordan since I was a little kid, but he's so sweet to me. He pays for my cab and gives me a big hug.

He's a little heavy—short with long black hair and a scraggly beard. He makes me feel welcome and is full of questions about my parents, who he says he thinks about all the time.

We talk on a plush white couch, while Lisa tries on the different clothes. She is thin and barely says anything to me. Lisa is the daughter of this very famous couple. She has a bunch of brothers—one of whom is a kind of successful actor—but as far as I know, Lisa has never done anything with her life. Still, she buys almost five thousand dollars' worth of clothes from Zelda.

Jordan gives me his phone number, hugging me and telling me to call anytime. Zelda and I head home, stopping at Rite Aid to get my prescription filled and to steal more ice cream. It seems like our money problems are over for a while. Zelda and I make love—even with the hole in my arm.

DAY 427

That guy Alexi, who got shot in the head, has offered to fly Zelda up to Las Vegas to help organize his office. He says he'll pay her five hundred dollars for three days' work. She won't go without me, though, so he agrees to pay for my ticket as well. We're all set to leave, but Alexi wants us to pick up two hundred dollars' worth of crack from his connection, who'll meet us at the airport. I drop Zelda off at the terminal and then go park the car. By the time I get the bus back to Southwest, the transaction has already taken place. Zelda has the crack hidden in her underwear and we check in at the ticket counter. It's hot in Burbank and I'm sweating and nervous going through the security checkpoint. For some reason both Zelda and I have to go through the whole "take off your shoes and empty your bag" procedure. They search through everything. They wave that metal wand all over us. But they don't find the crack on Zelda and we make it to the gate.

I steal a prepackaged salad and two ice-cream sandwiches from a coffee shop. We go eat at the gate. It's the first food we've had in a long time. The ice-cream sandwiches are the kind with chocolate chip cookies on the outside and they're pretty great. We wait till the last moment to get on the flight. We sit next to each other in the very back and Zelda sleeps on my shoulder. I still have the hole in my arm, but it is closing up some.

Arriving at the airport in Las Vegas is really bizarre. Alexi meets us out front and we immediately start smoking crack. He has this very broken crack pipe, which we pass between us. I've never smoked crack before, but I don't tell anyone that. Honestly, I don't see what the big deal is. You always hear about crack being the most addictive, insidious drug of them all. I even had a counselor at a rehab tell me that, if I relapsed, the one drug I should never do was crack. She said that it was the hardest drug of all to kick and at the time that really scared me.

But here I am smoking crack in the backseat of Alexi's old Land Cruiser, driving through the hood in downtown Las Vegas. And the thing is, I don't even like the feeling it gives me. You get high for about ten seconds and then you instantly want more. It's so unsatisfying, but at the same time, I feel like I can't stop doing it. It's actually kind of scary. Before I even know what I'm doing I find myself looking for bits of crack that might have fallen on the car's floor, picking up pieces of lint and things, sure that they're crack.

Alexi drives with one hand and hits the pipe with the other. He has light blond hair and green eyes. He looks Northern European, with hard, masculine features. He is tall and thick, but speaks and moves with incredible sensuality—especially toward Zelda. It makes me uncomfortable, but of course, I keep that to myself.

Zelda actually starts having a really terrible asthma attack right when we get to Alexi's house, and she realizes she forgot her inhaler. We go in and the house is very nice, really. It's just one story, painted white, but there's a big backyard. We put our bags down in the room Alexi uses as his office studio. Then we all get into the car and drive to a pharmacy. Zelda goes in and I wait with Alexi in the car. He turns back toward me, staring me straight in the eye—challenging me maybe.

"So you're getting married?"

"I guess, yeah."

He smiles, showing his yellow teeth.

"You really think you can commit to being with Zelda for the rest of your life?"

"Absolutely."

"But you're only twenty-two. You're gonna have many lovers in your life. I can't see someone like you settling down so early."

I have no idea what that means. "I love Zelda," I say. "I'm totally committed to her. I mean, what can I say? Time will prove me right."

"Yeah, maybe. What if she were to cheat on you?"

I swallow hard, feeling angry and helpless all at once. "I don't know. I'd be crushed."

He hits the crack pipe and passes it over, saying, "I think Bijou may be cheating on me. I'm not sure if that's the truth or not—but I definitely, you know, think she might be."

"Really?" I ask stupidly. I've never met Bijou and I really don't even know Alexi that well.

While Zelda's in the drugstore, Alexi begins asking me all these questions about my past and everything. I feel really almost scared of him. He is so aggressive. I'm just hoping Zelda will come back soon.

Also, he keeps yelling at me about people seeing me as I'm smoking the crack. He's very paranoid and I'm not sure whether it's the drugs or his brain injury that makes him act this way, but suddenly I wish we'd never come down here.

Zelda finally comes back with an inhaler and her asthma seems a little better—though she still has trouble breathing. We go back to Alexi's and he immediately starts freaking out 'cause Bijou's gonna be home and he doesn't want her to know he's high. He starts yelling at me because my eyes are bloodshot and I tell him I'll do my best to look as normal as possible.

We order hamburgers to pick up and I'm absolutely not hungry, but Alexi makes me go with him. He keeps asking me if I know whether I'm clean or not—like whether I have HIV or hep C or something. He tells me if I get Zelda sick that he'll kill me and by the time we get back to the house, I feel like I've really got to get away from here somehow.

We walk up and Bijou opens the door to help us with the dinner bags. She's very conservative-looking. I can't believe she's Alexi's girlfriend. They're both in their late forties and the dynamic is suddenly very clear. She tells us about the two jobs she holds to basically support Alexi. Maybe she's stuck with him out of guilt for shooting him in the head. Either way, I can't understand how she doesn't see how crazy he is.

Eventually, Zelda and I disappear into the studio where there's a foldout couch, while Bijou and Alexi go to bed. We smoke a little bit of the crack Alexi gave us in the closet and burn incense to hide the smell and cough whenever we click the lighter on.

"Zelda," I say. "Alexi was being really weird—like asking me all this shit about what I'd do if you cheated on me and stuff. He was really kind of mean. You know?"

"I noticed that too," she says. "He's acting different. I'm not sure what's going on. I know he really didn't want you to come. Maybe that has something to do with it."

"Maybe."

Zelda tells me I should go look behind Alexi's computer to see if there's any crack spilled there. She says he always leaves crack lying around. Pretty soon we're both crawling around on hands and knees searching for microscopic crack rocks—almost frenzied. My mind can't seem to focus on anything but finding more crack. We get a little pile together and start hitting the pipe some more.

Alexi comes into the studio after he waits for Bijou to fall asleep. We smoke crack till early in the morning. He seems a little more calm and I think that maybe things are getting better. Zelda and I lie down to sleep around four or five. I manage to pass out, while Zelda stays awake.

It's around twelve the next day when we run out of crack. None of us have done any work on Alexi's office space, but now that we're out of drugs, he's really starting to scream at both of us about the project not getting done. I'm not sure what the hell I'm even supposed to do, so I just try to clean up some—mopping the kitchen floor and all. But then Alexi yells at me about how I shouldn't be doing that, I should be helping in the office. He calls me lazy and ungrateful. He says I'm spoiled and just won't stop lecturing me.

Finally, we go and drive around looking to score some crack in downtown Las Vegas. Alexi circles the blocks over and over.

"Why can't any of these kids have fucking phones?"

I guess he's looking for someone in particular, too, because he keeps saying, "Where is he? Fuck."

It takes over an hour for Alexi to find him. He's a skinny child, really—maybe sixteen years old. He's riding an old BMX bike around, and as Alexi passes, he raises his hand up to the sky. We pull over and Alexi orders me into the backseat. The boy, who says his name is T, crawls into the front.

"I only got forty," he says.

Alexi hands him the money and the kid produces a very small plastic-wrapped bundle of crack rocks. Alexi throws it back to me and yells for me to put it in my sock. I do what he says. Then the kid jumps out of the car and we pull away quickly from the curb. I climb back to the front and look at the Baggie for the first time. There's almost nothing in it. Both Alexi and I feel the panic of the drugs running out and you can see it in our faces.

"Fuck," he growls.

As soon as we get back to his house, Alexi disappears into his room. He doesn't offer either of us more than a tiny hit, then he starts screaming at us for not working hard enough. He tells Zelda she has no work ethic and is completely unreliable. Zelda tells him he's acting like an asshole. He storms off down into the basement.

"Zelda," I say. "We've got to get out of here."

She's pacing, angry and cursing.

"I can't believe him," she says. "I've never seen him act this way before. He's totally lost it."

"I know, baby, I'm so sorry. What can we do?"

"We gotta leave. Alexi's gonna give us a ride to the airport, right now. Pack our stuff."

I run to the room we've been staying in, while Zelda rushes downstairs. I get our bags packed, and suddenly Zelda bursts back into the room, sobbing.

"He says he's not gonna help us. He won't even buy us a ticket home. He was so mean."

I press her to me. "Come on," I say. "It'll be all right."

"But we don't have any money. I just deposited that check from Lisa. My bank account's still negative." She cries hard into my shoulder.

So, you know, I feel like I have no choice.

I've still been lying to my parents about my sobriety, and, because I didn't want my dad to worry about me being in Las Vegas, I told him Zelda and I were taking a trip out to the desert southeast of L.A. But now I realize I'm going to have to call everyone I know to try and get help.

I go out to the backyard and start making calls. I dial my mom's number first. I tell her some story about how we came up here to work for one of Zelda's friends and then we found out he was using. I tell her we're stuck here and don't want to relapse, so I beg her: Please, please, please can she get us a plane ticket home?

She doesn't buy it. "Nic, I know you're high. I've already talked to Spencer and Michelle."

Those are her exact words.

"I can't help you," she says. She hangs up on me.

I call this girl in the program, Julia, who I went out with a couple of times. She won't help me either. I leave messages all over the place. I call Jordan, Josh, even Lauren. No one answers and I'm really starting to freak out.

I call my godfather. I call Karen. The only person I don't call is my dad because I just can't handle that.

When Bijou gets home from work, Alexi and Zelda are fighting. Zelda tells Bijou exactly what's going on—except she leaves out the fact that we've all been smoking crack. Alexi flips out and actually hits Bijou on the side of her head.

When I come in, Bijou and Alexi are screaming at each other loudly and violently.

Zelda huddles close to me in the studio and we just listen, cowering. Alexi is accusing Bijou of intentionally shooting him. He keeps saying, "You wish I was dead, don't you?"

It reminds me of being a little kid and hiding in the other room while my mom and stepdad fought. There's a feeling in my body—an internal, shaking terror that I can't let go of. My throat is dry and I just hold Zelda as she shrinks into my arms.

Finally Bijou comes in and tells us to follow her to the car. She has gotten plane tickets for us and she apologizes over and over.

"Come on," she says. "I'll take you to a hotel by the airport— you can fly out from there in the morning."

"Bijou, are you sure?" asks Zelda.

"Yes, of course."

We get into the car without saying anything to Alexi. Bijou drives a little Audi and I sit in the back with our bags.

Almost immediately Bijou goes into excuses about why Alexi behaves the way he does. She talks and talks about his brain injury. Never once does she mention drugs. Zelda comes right out and tells her straight up that she should drug-test Alexi, the way he's acting.

Bijou says, "No, no—I'd know if he was using again."

I say nothing, but I sort of feel like screaming at her.

"Bijou, you know, you don't deserve to put up with this," says Zelda.

"I know," she replies, but with such resignation and hopelessness that I feel sick.

She drives us to a couple different hotels before we find a vacancy. She gives us some cash and we go up to the room and it's like I can finally breathe.

I take a shower and Zelda orders pizza with some of the money Bijou gave us. We watch TV and try to eat some.

"Zelda," I say finally. "We can't go on like this."

"No," she says. "No, we can't. We gotta stop using."

"I know," I say, meaning it. "I'm ready. This is so gross, you know?"

"Yeah, it is."

"I want to build a life with you," I say. "A real life, where we can have babies and a house and all."

"I want that too," she says, kissing me.

"So we'll stop?"

"Yes, baby. We have to."

I wrap my body around hers and we fall asleep. I feel some hope, maybe, for the first time since I relapsed with her.

DAY 555

We managed to stay clean three days before we started using again. Actually, we never stopped taking the Klonopin, Xanax, and Suboxone because otherwise we'd go into withdrawals. Still, we didn't shoot any drugs for three days and that was the last time I was clean in almost four months. We've been shooting cocaine, meth, and even some heroin. Zelda continues freaking out about me hiding drugs in the apartment almost every time we do meth, but that doesn't stop her. She and I have actually been fighting a lot. She watched one of her ex-husband's movies the other day and I got really upset and jealous and we both ended up screaming at each other.

Plus, my dad has been calling almost every day, begging me to get back into recovery—demanding to talk to Zelda and trying to talk her into helping me. My mom showed up here once, but I screamed at her so much, she left without getting a chance to really say anything. Even Spencer came here, asking me to go for a ride with him. I refused and told him to leave me the hell alone.

Honestly, I'm so ashamed around them that I have no choice but to yell angrily. I know how much progress I made and how well I was doing. Nothing can really excuse my relapsing. It's like being back in San Francisco all over again. The difference, of course, is Zelda. If I stopped using, or let Spencer or my mom in, I would have to lose Zelda. I cannot even bear the thought of that. So I lash out at everyone who tries to help me, just trying to scare them away so they can stop giving a damn about me and let me throw my life away in peace.

And, you know, today things have been relatively quiet. Zelda and I haven't left the bathroom for over three hours, sitting naked on the side of the bathtub—just shooting coke and more coke. When the shots are strong enough you get this feeling like your head is just pounding with energy. Your ears ring and you almost pass out and it is just amazing. So I mix up a shot and hit myself with it—but it's still not enough. I take another syringe already filled with a mixture of Zelda's blood and cocaine. I slam that right away and suddenly I fall off the side of the bathtub, convulsing on the floor. Zelda is right there standing over me and as I start to black out, she claps her hands in front of my face, yelling at me to talk to her. That's not really possible, but I manage to start singing this old video game song. It's, like, some long-buried memory that comes back from my childhood when I would play Nintendo all the time. It's the song from the game Dr. Mario. I just keep singing it over and over so I don't lose consciousness. My legs are kicking rhythmically and my eyelids are just flickering, flickering, flickering.

I'm not sure how long it lasts, but Zelda stays right with me. As I come more and more out of it she kisses me and holds me and I realize I must be pretty lucky to be alive.

We go over to the bed. I'm not sure what the eroticism around how close I came to death is all about, but we are both really turned on. Zelda is more beautiful than ever and we make love until morning—our bodies washed in sweat.

I get up from the bed around seven and do another shot of cocaine. I actually end up going into convulsions again. Zelda gets mad and yells at me while I'm twitching there on the floor. I think she's scared—but that translates into anger.

Anyway, Zelda's phone rings right as I'm coming out of the convulsions. It turns out to be this girl, Sam, who's an old friend of Zelda's. She's been up all night shooting cocaine as well. She lives in Culver City and invites us to come over and, well, shoot cocaine with her.

Zelda and I get into the car after a little bit and we drive past Sony Studios to the second-floor apartment Sam shares with her three roommates. When we walk in the front door, we're immediately met by a potbellied, balding little man who introduces himself as Sam's boyfriend. His name is Freddy.

"Sam's in there," he says, pointing to a closed door down the dark wooden hallway. "She doesn't let me around when she's using needles."

So we go in and Sam is digging around her arm, looking for a vein, seated cross-legged on her bed. She's very light-skinned and short with small rolls around her belly. She's very welcoming to both of us. She lets me use her computer to check my e-mail and there's a note from the father of a friend of mine in New York.

I'd asked to borrow money and he has told me that he can't help me as long as I'm using.

I'm crushed and kind of scared because we have no money left. Zelda and I have been selling clothes—books—CDs—anything—but that's not gonna last and I know that. Still, I don't mention the e-mail to Zelda. I choose to treat it like I treat everything these days—that if I just ignore stuff it'll go away, or get better, or whatever. I'm already about to lose my cell phone through an inability to pay the bill and my car has been towed and I have no means of getting it because the storage fee is so high. Add that to the twenty-something parking tickets I have that are racking up penalty charges and the unpaid hospital and therapy bills and, well, you get an idea of how much I've already fucked everything up—and we're only a couple months into our run.

These thoughts are quickly pushed aside, however, as Sam hands this huge bag of cocaine over to Zelda so we can make up some shots. We go into the bathroom.

"Is she just giving us all that coke?" I ask.

"I guess so. Sam's a trust-fund kid."

"Of course. How come everyone we know, besides us, has a fucking trust fund?"

"'Cause we live in L.A."

"Right."

Zelda insists on hitting me and making up my shot cause of all my convulsions. What she gives me is just perfect—head-banging without leaving me flopping like a fish on the floor. We go back out and sit around talking with Sam and Freddy, who's been let back in the room. Sam's dad is a sculptor who lives near Buenos Aires. Freddy is friends with all these people I knew in New York, so we talk about that stuff and music and books. We actually get on real well together and the girls go on the back porch together—I guess to shoot more coke.

We've been there about two hours when Zelda's dad calls. I'm not sure why she answers, but she does. Immediately I hear her start screaming and I run out onto the porch. She's yelling at her father in these shrill bursts and I'm actually kind of scared to go up to her.

"No! No, that's fucking bullshit."

"What?" I ask. "What?"

She hangs up the phone and then turns all her anger toward me.

"You! Your fucking mom called my dad to tell her we relapsed."

"That bitch."

"Jesus Christ," she rants. "What are you, twelve? Your fucking mommy has to try and rescue you? Why doesn't she just leave us the hell alone? Do you know what's going to happen? Do you know how crazy my father is?"

I put my hand on her shoulder. "It's gonna be all right."

"Don't touch me." She howls that, pulling away, swinging back her arm as though she were going to hit me. I cringe back and she just starts going on and on about how she'll never be able to forgive me for this. I try to remind her that we've been up for three days and that everything might seem better after we sleep. She doesn't really hear anything I say. She screams until she can't scream anymore and then she breaks down crying—collapsed on the splintering wooden deck.

Finally, she reaches her arms out to me and I bend down and hold her. She tells me she's sorry. She tells me that over and over.

I apologize to Sam and Freddy when we get back in. They seem understanding, but Zelda and I decide to leave anyway, and we walk out into the afternoon sun. I'm starving and need some food so we get In-N-Out burgers and a couple of milkshakes. At this point we have no money left. Both our bank accounts are overdrawn. We asked our landlord if we could hold a garage sale out front of our apartment complex and he agreed to let us do it sometime early next month. Zelda rents a storage unit in the Valley where she has a lot of really valuable furniture and clothes and expensive prints of people like Neil Young, Jerry Garcia, and

Duane Allman. We're planning on going there this weekend. We've also contacted some guy Yakuza knows who'll buy Zelda's wedding band from her first husband and a Tiffany diamond ring she has. I feel really bad about Zelda having to sell all her stuff, but there's just no other way.

On the way home Zelda reminds me that the needle exchange is open off Santa Monica Boulevard, so we turn left and head over to get some new needles and tourniquets. They have big cotton balls there too, but the last time I used their cotton a piece of it got drawn up in the needle and I ended up shooting it. When the bit of cotton fiber reached my brain it felt like someone smashed my head as hard as they could into the pavement. Then I started throwing up until Zelda could get a clean shot in me. I passed out for several hours after that.

The woman at the needle exchange remembers me and she fills in my drug of choice on her sheet without me having to say anything. She marks the crystal meth box and tells me I can have ten needles and two tourniquets. I get back in the car and Zelda is asleep, so I just drive around awhile listening to music. I wonder how my life has fallen apart again and how—AGAIN—I've lost everything. It was all going so well. I don't know why the ground falls away underneath me so fast. I never even see it happening.

Or do I?

Either way, all I am aware of right now is a longing to just get home and stick a fresh needle in my vein with whatever drugs are left in our apartment. I pull our car into the parking space.

"Baby, we're home," I say, kissing Zelda's forehead.

Her eyelids flicker open.

"Where?" she asks.

"Home."

We get out and go up to the apartment.

Tomorrow's the garage sale, so we drive early to Zelda's storage unit. We managed to stay clean for two days after the fight we had at Sam's. But then we sold some clothes at Wasteland on Melrose and we've been shooting cocaine and meth since last night. There was this halogen bulb in one of Zelda's cosmetic mirrors that exploded in the middle of the night, right as she was getting into the shower. She couldn't find the pieces anywhere, so she went ahead into the shower. She washed her hair and scrubbed over her body, while I was writing in a notebook on the bed. Pretty soon I heard her cursing and calling out for help. By the time I ran into the bathroom, Zelda was crying from the pain.

I guess what happened was the halogen bulb must have exploded into her hair. When she was washing her body she embedded the tiny pieces of glass all over her skin. Now you can see her legs and arms and face and chest covered in the splintered lightbulb.

We've just been digging the pieces out for the last seven hours. Zelda's pretty good about it and we have the drugs to kill her pain—or at least, some of the pain. Still, now she's bleeding all over and scabbed and everything. We actually decided to videotape some of our picking session in hopes of maybe suing the company that made the lightbulb and failed to put any warning label on the package. I mean, maybe it was a stupid idea, but there was no way of getting all the glass out. When you tried to pull out the shards they would break off into a thousand new pieces beneath the skin.

Zelda called her dad's lawyers this morning about what happened, but I wouldn't be surprised if they don't respond. I mean, they are her dad's lawyers and her dad isn't exactly happy with us right now.

Finally we get dressed, and even though Zelda still has tons of glass in her, we drive over the Hollywood Freeway to her storage unit. The sky is all brown haze and black smog in the Valley. The light is dull and the heat is oppressive, but I still have to wear long-sleeved shirts 'cause my arms are so marked from needle tracks and the scar from my abscess.

The storage unit is deep in the Valley and it just keeps getting hotter the farther inland we drive. We pull in and Zelda enters her code to the gate. She has one of the bigger units on the lot. It's ground-level, with a large corrugated metal door that she unlocks and we both struggle to push open. Inside, there are boxes upon boxes of clothes, lots of Moroccan furniture, some books, knick-knacks, whatever.

I bring out a large couch and various benches and things. Zelda keeps telling me to slow down, but I just want to get through this as quickly as possible because so much of the stuff belonged to her ex-husband. There are old reels and posters and tons of photos. I feel really uncomfortable going through every-thing and I just have to keep moving so I don't have to deal with it. I'm sweating and hot—moving almost spastically fast. I can't stop. It's gotten totally compulsive. It's like I'm in psychosis or something—like I don't really know what I'm doing. I empty the entire unit, pretty much, and then suddenly I pass out completely onto the asphalt. I start throwing up and Zelda tries to force-feed water down my throat. I take it in, but then keep choking up this bubbling foam.

I'm not sure what's happening or why she's pouring the water in my mouth. I crawl over to the couch I brought out and fall asleep—or pass out on it. Time passes.

I wake up to Zelda sticking me with a syringe and shooting me up with some coke. Zelda's loaded up whatever she thinks we can sell at the garage sale but she needs me to help put the rest of the shit back in the storage unit. The sun is setting. I help her with the couch and this big mirror thing. That's when I come out with it.

"Zelda, it would really mean a lot to me if you would throw that shit of your ex-husband's away."

She pauses. "I can't. A lot of it belongs to his production company, and besides, that stuff was my life. I'm not gonna throw it away so you don't have to be fucking jealous."

That makes me angry, so I yell at her, saying, "You're so stuck in your past! This place is like a fucking tomb."

She bursts into tears at that. "Some of this was my mom's stuff—stuff I've never even looked at. I can't believe you don't understand that."

Of course I feel bad and I try to comfort her. "I'm sorry," I say, softly now. "I just think it's time to start moving on."

"I know," she says, after a while. "I will. Give it time, Nic. It'll come. I know that with you, I'll be able to start over. Be patient with me, please."

"I will. I love you. It's hard for me, you know? I get very jealous."

"I get really jealous too," she says.

I get into the front seat and kiss Zelda's tears away, apologizing. We drive home and I'm still sick and exhausted. I'm concentration-camp skinny—everything all sunken in. We fall asleep early in bed, both loaded up on Seroquel. We're supposed to get up, you know, really fucking early to set up for the garage sale.

I guess it's around twelve when I hear Zelda screaming incoherently. I jerk awake, just as she starts digging her fingernails into the sides of my face. I try to push her off and she bites the bridge of my nose hard. She starts screaming about how she's gonna call the fucking cops. I have to push her off again because she's just flipping out and really hurting me. I'm scared and I don't know what to do.

I run to the bathroom and slam the door, but she's right behind me. I lock myself in and she pounds against it, saying she'll call the cops if I don't come out. I tell her she has to calm down before I do. She's bashing against the bathroom door with something, trying to break it, and I keep pleading with her to stop. I'm not sure how long that goes on, but I'm cowering in the bathroom for a long time before I finally hear her slide to the ground, sobbing.

I open the door slowly and she's collapsed there, crying and

crying. I hold her and she starts apologizing, saying she didn't
know what she was doing. She's really crying so hard. I kiss her
forehead and hold her. She keeps asking if I'll forgive her and, of
course, I say yes. I love her, I tell her. We get back into bed and fall
back asleep. I'm bleeding some from her fingernails.

DAY 578

We sleep all the next day—missing the garage sale entirely.

It's around six when Zelda wakes me up and I'm pretty well
fucked up from everything that happened yesterday. We have a
small bit of cocaine left, so we shoot that and start trying to figure
out what the hell we're gonna do about money. It's a pale gray
outside—the hot sun almost set behind the polluted Los Angeles
ocean. We eat some ice cream and Zelda calls Lisa. Lisa agrees to
buy Zelda's Duane Allman print for six hundred dollars—she says
she'll leave the check with Jordan if we go and drop the photo off.
We get into the car after taking a shower together. I'm wearing
these bell-bottom cords and one of Zelda's ex-husband's jackets
that she designed. I feel weird about wearing his clothes—but
whatever. Zelda drives down Sunset to Lisa and Jordan's house
up Mandeville Canyon. The road is crowded with traffic. We're
going around the turns at a stop-and-go pace.

Neither one of us mentions the way she flipped out last night,
though my face still bears the scars.

It's dark, dark by the time we pull into Jordan and Lisa's
driveway. Zelda brings in a full-length leather coat she hopes Lisa
might buy. Jordan welcomes us. He looks the same as ever—long
hair tied back, a little heavy, wearing a faded T-shirt. He's super-
sweet to us, offering us food. He's impressed by the print and
accepts the coat, saying he'll try to talk Lisa into buying it. He
asks me about what I've been doing. We just talk for a while.

Eventually, I ask if he has any heroin we could smoke with him. He claims to be out.

"I'm sorry," I say. "I didn't mean to assume."

"No, no," he says, in that sleepy voice of his. "You assumed correctly. I'm just out."

He then takes us outside to see the new motorcycle he just bought. It's a Ducati and he tells us how it's the only thing that really makes him happy anymore. We look it over and act impressed. I actually really love riding motorcycles and have always wanted a racing bike like this.

"It just gives me so much pleasure," he says. "Like nothing else."

Zelda and I drive home. She's managed to get me an interview tomorrow with the head of *Flaunt* magazine, so I know I really shouldn't use speed tonight. Besides, we're both out of money. But Zelda has a connection downtown that'll front us some crack—if we want it. His name is Carlos and he deals off the street.

We head downtown and call him. He agrees to let us have eighty dollars' worth of crack cocaine. We stop at a gas station and buy one of those flowers in the glass tubes that are basically only purchased for crack smoking. I know we shouldn't be using anymore and that shit's really falling apart, but the thought of not using now is basically unbearable.

We drive along a street downtown. Carlos reaches his arm through the window and hands over a very full Baggie of crack rocks. Zelda tells me he's always had a crush on her, so that's why he gives her such good deals. The guy is a scrawny little Hispanic kid, handsome, but strung-out-looking—maybe more than me.

We start smoking the crack on the way home and already I'm feeling better. I have to hold the wheel while she hits the pipe. The high is short-lived, but I guess that's what we need, what with the interview and all. We go back to our apartment.

Our downstairs neighbor—this gay makeup artist from the South somewhere—gives us a very penetrating look like we're just too disgusting for words as we walk into the courtyard. We go up past him, saying hello casually, and then we lock ourselves in our room. We smoke crack for a while and then make love.

We don't sleep at all and as morning comes we're still smoking crack and shooting the last of the cocaine. I do this complicated drawing and I tape it all up with string and pieces of that computer I took apart. Zelda stands in the bathroom and picks at her skin for hours. I listen to music on my headphones. Eventually I pull Zelda out of her face-picking trance and we take a shower. I eat some Lucky Charms and we make coffee.

Before my interview with the *Flaunt* guy, I figure I should print out all my clips and writing samples at Kinko's. Zelda and I drive down to the one on Sunset and we're both about to go in, when Zelda decides to call Lisa and see if she's interested in buying her leather trench coat. It's actually raining a little—a muggy, dirty rain. The haze from the sky is just bleeding down on the stucco buildings along Sunset. I smoke a cigarette with the windows up and Zelda holds the phone, listening to it ring. I'm not sure who it is that answers, but Zelda keeps saying, "What?" over and over again—then, "Oh my God." She hangs up and turns to me.

Jordan is dead. He crashed his motorcycle into a tree.

We stare at each other and then, at the same time, start crying all at once.

I'm actually bawling and I can't stop. I'm not sure what to do. I call my friends in New York who knew Jordan so well, but no one answers any of the numbers. I call my dad and leave him a message. I figure maybe he can get in touch with Jordan's mom—I know Jordan's father died last year. Then I call my mom and she answers. I try to explain what happened, but before I can she is yelling at me—saying she knows I'm high.

"Mom, Jordan's dead—what the hell are you talking about? I'm not high—I'm fucking flipping out. I thought you could get in touch with his mom, or something."

"I'm not interested in Jordan, I'm interested in you. I haven't heard from you in months and now you call me crying. What the hell is wrong with you?"

"Mom," I say, curling my legs up to my chest on the front seat, "Jordan's dead. I'm telling you, Jordan had a motorcycle accident and he's fucking dead."

"You're high, aren't you? I can tell by your voice. You need to get help. You're throwing your life away with that woman."

"Mom, this isn't about that. This is about Jordan. But anyway, I am sober. I've been sober for two weeks."

She doesn't buy it. She's almost yelling at me. Then suddenly Zelda flips out and starts screaming at my mom, through me. She starts calling her a nosy bitch—saying she's heartless. She's pissed that my mom called her family about us using again. She's telling my mom (again, through me) about how crazy her father is and how my mom had no right to involve them.

"You don't understand what he's like. You don't understand what he'll do."

I pass the message along—though I know my mom can hear Zelda just fine. Somehow the whole Jordan being dead thing has completely gotten lost in all of this. I'm screaming, Zelda's screaming, my mom's screaming. Somewhere in the chaos Zelda's phone rings. The guy from *Flaunt* is calling, rescheduling our appointment—which, under the circumstances, seems like a good thing. We stop driving, but the argument keeps moving along. I'm so fried out, I kinda wish Zelda would be quiet so I could yell at my mom by myself. Finally, I just hang up the phone and then I cry some more about Jordan being gone and how hopeless everything is.

We call our dealer and meet him in Larchmont, where we're almost at anyway. We buy lots of cocaine and crystal and some pills. We're basically out of money. I'm not sure how we're going to pay rent, or eat, or anything. I have this hope that maybe I can get a job somehow, but that is fleeting.

There are very few things I'm sure of anymore. I love Zelda—I know that. But we fight so often, and honestly I'm scared of losing her all the time. I just don't know if I'll ever be able to trust her. I've watched her lie so many times.

And then there's the drugs. We shoot up in the car and my arms are so scarred and I don't know how to stop—if I even want to stop. I feel like I'm living with death so close every day and Jordan crashing his bike only adds to this.

I'm scared.

I need to get my life together, I know that. I need to start working again. But I don't have a computer and can't possibly do movie reviews and stuff without one.

Yes, I reason. Work will fix everything. I need a computer.

We go back to the apartment and spend hours shooting drugs and talking about money and what the hell we should do. We talk about my mom and how angry we are at her for treating us like this. I talk about how angry I am with my stepdad for the way he's treated me and my mom, really.

We shoot drugs and now it's three o'clock in the morning and we're pacing the apartment like caged animals.

"Zelda," I say—the thought just coming to me like that. "Let's go to my mom's. I know how to break in and I can steal Todd's computer."

"Perfect," she says. "You need a computer."

We spend a long time getting dressed. We get in the car and I drive and we are very high and Amon Tobin is on the stereo. The early morning dark is cold and I'm holding my jaw tight, too tight. I mean, more than normal. I'm talking real angry about my mom and my stepdad and blah, blah, blah.

When we get to my mom's neighborhood, Pacific Palisades, we decide, first off, to stop and get some stuff at a supermarket down the street from my mom's. It's still only, like, four o'clock in the morning. We park in the lot and shoot up more crystal. Wandering around the too-bright aisles of the grocery store, we laugh to ourselves and make out and I wonder who the hell is looking at us and what they're thinking. I'm kind of paranoid, and I keep my eyes on the floor. After all, we are the only two people in here.

Anyway, we get some ice cream and Lucky Charms and we

want to buy a bottle of wine, but they won't sell it to us until six, so I tell Zelda I'll be right back—I'm just gonna go get the computer. She kisses me bye and I go drive up to my mom's house.

The fear takes hold about the time I make it to their driveway. I park far away and walk up slow. I suddenly remember my mom's dogs and how they're gonna bark like hell if I make any noise. I'm really very scared. I feel like all the neighbors are looking at me—watching me. The computer is in the garage, so I figure I can get in there, no problem. For some reason, though, I decide to climb on the roof of the garage and I think maybe I can break through the shingles in the roof. I start tearing 'em off.

I don't get very far.

They're hard as hell to get off. I slide down a tree, hurting my arms real bad—then I run into the garage and lock the door.

I'm not sure what happens at this point. I guess I kind of lose hold of reality for a little bit. The garage is full of boxes and hanging clothes and clothes piled up on the floor and just stuff everywhere. Quickly, I empty one box and put the computer in it. But then, well, I'm not thinking too clearly 'cause I start just going through everything. I'm emptying boxes and throwing things and climbing up into the rafters. I'm tearing at the roof again and hours pass with me just crawling around—gathering things in little piles—just totally tweaking out.

I find these two porn movies that I'm pretty sure are my stepfather's and I break them with my foot. I feel like a giant oozing insect or something, climbing over everything—maybe a worm, or a writhing slug, or who knows what. Then, in the crosshatched beams that hold the roof together, I'm like a long-legged spider scurrying in the shadows.

More time passes.

I'm hot and thirsty.

It's midday now. The sun is streaming through the cracks in the shingles. Beams of yellow light pierce through the dusty, thick air of the garage. I dodge these shafts of brightness. I feel like maybe they will turn me to ash—like a vampire.

Thoughts race through my head and I'm losing it. Suddenly I can't find the door and I realize I'm trapped and I've no way out. I go into a dream where I see myself as a child, cowering in this same garage—shaking with fear and almost throwing up as I hide from the fighting. My mom and Todd are screaming at each other and I am little and terrified. My mom keeps trying to get me to go with her to a hotel, but I am too scared. I don't want to betray Todd.

Next I remember a time, driving down the freeway to San Diego. My mom and Todd are fighting while I pretend to be asleep in the backseat. My mom grabs the steering wheel and begins trying to turn the car around while Todd is driving.

Lying in the backseat, I feel so guilty, like it's all my fault.

Then another memory begins to crawl into my mind. It's so dim and clouded that I can't see what is happening. I feel sick and throw up some foamy liquid in a corner.

It's been over five hours when the knock comes at the door. Somehow I come out of my psychosis long enough to open it. Spencer is standing there and I'm pretty sure that's real, not a hallucination—especially once he starts talking to me all about twelve-step stuff. My mom is there too—looking appropriately freaked out. I'm not too sure why she's not at work. Standing next to her is my older brother, Ron—my mom's son from her first marriage, who I've met only a couple of times.

All three of them are talking at once. They tell me that Zelda is freaked out because I left her in that grocery store for, like, half the goddamn day. She's called my mom along with a million other people and she had to borrow all this money from Yakuza to get a taxi back to Hollywood. Zelda told everyone she wants me to go into rehab—no more fucking around. Spencer wants me to go to rehab. My mom wants me to go into rehab. Even Ron says I need help.

I'm not sure how long we're talking there, but soon a cop from the Los Angeles Police Department shows up to make a report. I'm pretty sure my stepdad must have called him. I guess Todd is staying inside—away from me. The cop—square-jawed, with a crew cut and all—threatens to arrest me, but my mom agrees to hold off pressing charges so long as I agree to check into rehab.

I don't want to go to jail, so I tell them what they want to hear. They allow me to return to Hollywood and pack and whatever. I drive back home, cursing and wondering, for the thousandth time in my life, "How the hell am I gonna get out of this one?"

Zelda beats me up when I walk through the door.

Everything of mine is in a cardboard box in the middle of the room. She's crying and yelling and I try to grab her arms to keep from getting slapped. I try to get her to understand, even though there isn't really an explanation that could possibly make the situation any better. I mean, I left her in a supermarket for five hours because I had a drug-induced psychotic breakdown.

After a few minutes I manage to calm her down. I make up some lie about hearing my brother outside and having to hide and being trapped in there. She seems to accept my excuse, but still wants me to get help. We shoot more drugs while we talk about it.

Zelda's phone rings a little later and it's my dad calling. He and Zelda talk for a while about I'm not sure what. Zelda puts on this whole "responsible party" persona with my dad. She's suddenly the voice of reason and maturity and manages to remove herself from my drug use. I'm not sure how much of it my dad actually believes, but she does put on a good act.

So eventually the phone is passed over to me and my dad sounds concerned and worried. He is stern and talking fast. Apparently they've talked to lawyers. Basically I'm looking at ninety days and they might even be able to get Zelda as an accomplice. That would mean both of us having to detox on the jail cell floor—kicking the Suboxone, Xanax, and Klonopin—which could make us go into seizures and could even kill us.

I'm so fucking angry at myself. I have no choice but to agree to everything my dad's saying. He tells me there's a treatment center in Oregon that has an open bed. He's arranged for an interview with them. They're gonna call Zelda's cell phone in about an hour. I hang up.

"Baby," I say, "they want me to go to Oregon."

"What? Why can't you stay in L.A.?" She's wearing little boxer shorts and a tank top. She looks unbelievably cute and she's suddenly very clingy and scared of me leaving. I kiss her and just want to die, really. This is all so depressing. Zelda and I are so damn strung-out and emaciated. My body has actually stopped producing stool, a doctor called it "compacting." The shit in me is like this hard, petrified rock. I have to spend hours in the bathroom literally digging out these pellets with my hand. My eyes are sunken in, my skin yellow and scaly—my sweat smelling like chemicals. My body is just bones at this point.

We make love until the phone rings.

I answer and than everything kind of goes black again for a while. I know the caller from the treatment center is a woman, but I can't remember much else about the conversation. I think I talk a lot about Zelda and how I don't want to live without her. I guess that freaks the woman out or something, because I don't get into that place in Oregon. I mean, they won't take me. They just will not let me in there. I'm not sure why that is, exactly, but anyway, I gotta figure out something else to do.

My dad is very upset with me. I think he feels like I did it on purpose or something. Like I faked out the interview lady—intentionally said stuff to not get accepted. But that's just not true. I answered her honestly.

So now I'm waiting again, shooting drugs with Zelda.

Around nine o'clock at night my dad calls again. He says there's this detox in the Valley that'll take me. He says I better go, or I'm gonna be arrested right away. I'm not sure how true that is, but I'm not willing to chance it.

So I go.

Well, first I take a shower and Zelda packs for me. She also gets a photo album ready with lots of photos of her. Plus she writes me a long letter promising to never leave me. We're still gonna get married, after all. We kiss, cry, and tell each other over and over that we love each other.

I'm thinking ten days in detox, max—then I'll just be sober and living with Zelda and writing again and everything will be perfect. Still, I'm scared of losing Zelda.

She drives to the detox and I'm snorting, shooting, smoking, swallowing any goddamn thing I can get my hands on. I'm deliriously high and the fear around this detox has subsided some. I show up there looking like a rock star. It's around two in the morning, but I got these big sunglasses on, bell-bottoms, a jacket with all this fringe, and a crazy, multicolored hat thing made by some designer. Zelda kisses me good-bye and I give her some stuff, like my wallet and all, because I'm not sure how bad this place is gonna be. This is actually the first exclusive hospital detox I've ever been to. All the other places have always been connected to twenty-eight-day programs. And after Lauren's I just kinda did it on the floor. With meth and coke, all you have to do is sleep a lot. With benzos and Suboxone, well, I don't know what to expect.

Anyway, Zelda says good-bye and I want to cry as she drives away. I feel totally defeated. But I'm high as hell, so I talk myself into a place of everything being all right.

The Mission Community detox is a hospital and, well, it looks like a hospital. The whole thing is very antiseptic with flickering fluorescent lights and white tile. The beds have plastic coverings and it's freezing as hell all the time. There are two TV rooms with a VCR and a lot of videos. There's a little kitchen area with a refrigerator full of cheap junk food and stale sandwiches. A short little Hispanic guy with a goatee and a Hawaiian-print shirt checks me in. A teddy-bear-like, extremely fat woman who is also short takes my blood pressure. But goddamn is she nice. Both of them are really just so nice. They're polite and gentle and they don't seem too horrified at the amount and variety of drugs in my system. It's a relief not to have to lie for once. I just tell them everything—meth, coke, heroin, Xanax, Klonopin, Somas, and Suboxone. They smile and nod and take my picture and draw my blood.

The guy takes me down for a cigarette outside in the warm **277** Valley air. After that they give me a bunch of meds to knock me out. They search my clothes and I try to sleep. Well, first I mess around with the window and draw a little. Whatever they gave me works fast, though, because I pretty much pass right out.

I wake up only twice in the night and both times this tall, hollow, vacant-eyed kid—probably younger than me—is sneaking into my room. He's got a shaved head and a basketball player's body and a jersey thing. I think he's holding toiletries in his hand. Maybe a towel.

"Dude, what the fuck are you doing?" I manage to say.

He freezes. His wide eyes open wider.

"I'm scared," he says. "Can I sleep with you?"

"Hell, no. Go get them to give you some shit to knock you out."

At that moment a nurse, this very masculine black woman who looks like she could break me in half with her littlest toe, comes clamoring into my room. Her hair is all standing up and she yells at the kid to leave me alone. He jumps about ten feet and scurries off.

She apologizes to me and winks. I say, "Just give him some shit so he can sleep."

And then that's what I do: I sleep.

DAY 581

I basically just sleep for three days straight. They keep having to wake me up so I'll take my meds. I can't eat—don't wanna eat and don't really wanna move much either. This plump, long-nosed, gray-bearded doctor guy tries to talk me into eating and maybe getting up, but I only ask to be left alone. I have this feeling, like I just wish I didn't have to exist. I wish it would all just go away.

It's not as though I'd want to do anything proactive, like

actually dying. No, I just want to disappear—to simply become part of the ethos, or whatever. I don't know who I am and my body feels beyond repair. It is sunken down to nothing.

At one point another big lady nurse shakes me awake and takes my blood pressure. It's one of those electronic machines and I see the digital electronic numbers pop up: sixty-three over something. She doesn't like that. They ask me to stand up and, well, that's hard.

"Please," I say. "Just let me die."

"Not a chance, honey—not on my watch."

The next reading is still pretty bad.

"Okay, sweetie, you gotta work with us here. There's a fruit plate in the kitchen. I'm gonna walk you down there. I also need you to drink some juices. We gotta get that blood pressure of yours up."

So she helps me stagger down the hall. She also takes the Clonidine patch off my shoulder. I guess that shit has something to do with making one's blood pressure low.

The other stuff they got me on, Phenobarbital, is supposed to keep me from having seizures, but makes me feel like I'm walking through, like, bubble world or something. Or maybe I'm just a floating head. I can't get thoughts to come out straight—or go in straight, or something.

Anyway, I do eat some melon and whatever else is on the fruit plate. I manage to keep that down, but I'm so nauseous. Immediately I stumble back to bed and sleep.

At some point the director of the detox, this sleazy-looking car salesman type named Gill, makes me go out and talk to him about my discharge plan and where I'm gonna go. I did manage to have a few hysterical crying conversations with Zelda on the phone. I'm allowed to use the phone whenever I want and there is basically no schedule here. The hospital is designed only for short stays, just to get you through the physical detox. There are visiting hours every day from four to six and visitors are allowed all day on the weekends. Zelda actually almost came for visiting hours one

night, but she was too high from shooting coke and she turned
around halfway. She says she'll come on the weekend.

Gill gets me up and actually outside. We smoke and he tells
me I look like the guy who started Woodstock. I guess that's fine
by me. He asks me about myself and I tell him a little bit. I do
say something about not really knowing who I am or something.
I also tell him a little about Zelda and then the interview is pretty
much over.

There are some other people from the detox outside with
us. I haven't said much of anything to any of the other patients.
Basically I just want to get back home to Zelda. That's all I care
about. But this one fat, tall guy with no hair and a goatee comes
over to me. I guess he overheard me telling Gill I was a writer—or
trying to be one.

He says, "Son, I've been writing TV shows for twenty years.
Turn back, before it's too late."

I try to impress him with saying I want to write a book.

"Ah," he says. "We all start out with big dreams, but we end
up writing cartoons about talking horses."

I like this guy instantly. He's cynical and surly and he's carrying a Henry Miller book under his arm. His name is Bobby, and,
as bad as I feel, I actually manage to talk to him a little bit. Turns
out we know a lot of the same people. He knows (and despises)
Dr. E, Zelda's doctor, and he was married to that woman, Ria,
who runs the Sober Living where I went.

"Holy shit," I say. "Bobby. Did you write Ria this two-page,
unpunctuated, all-lowercase letter about how you still loved her
about a year ago?"

"Uh, sounds like me."

"Dude, I read that fucking letter."

"You read my letter?"

"Yeah, man, she gave it to me to read."

"That bitch," he says, joking—and then, in typical writer's
fashion, "What did you think?"

"It was well written."

Which is true.

"And, uh, you know," I continue, "I think she's still got a thing for you."

He nods and pulls at his chin with his cigar-butt fingers. "That Ria, she was something else. I know she's gotten sort of—well, matronly, but she was wild, boy. I'll tell you."

"I bet. Yeah, I had a crush on her for fucking ever."

We have to go up now and I've talked myself back into catatonic sleep—but I feel like I have an ally with Bobby and I fucking can't wait to tell Zelda I met him. I mean, he's world famous. At least Ria has made him so through her stories.

When I wake up it is already night and I make a few phone calls. Zelda is missing me bad and is gonna come tomorrow. Apparently she's gonna get into a detox on Monday. She's been talking to my dad a whole bunch and he says he's going to help her get into the hospital at UCLA. My mom is actually going to drive her there.

After talking to Zelda and after the nurses have finished trying to get me to eat something, I call my dad. He sounds very relieved. But I just try to convince him to let me out of here.

"Dad," I say, "I'm so grateful to be sober now. I'm definitely not gonna use anymore, so I think I can probably go home—maybe tomorrow or something."

"No, Nic, absolutely not. Your mom and I are working on getting you into a longer program. We just have to figure out what place would be the best for you."

"Dad, come on, I don't need that."

He sighs. "Yes, you do. Nic, right now you're like a little baby, just learning how to crawl. Or maybe even back further, just learning to hold your head up. You wouldn't ask a newborn to run a marathon, would you?"

"Maybe if I was a sadist—which I'm not saying I'm not."

"Well, there's no point even discussing it. You will be arrested if you leave."

"Can I stay in L.A.? Can I go to treatment around here?"

"I don't think so. No, none of the places in L.A. can deal with the issues you have."

I get mad now. "What fucking issues are those?"

"Drugs and your relationship problems."

I tell him I don't have any relationship problems and he tells me he's not going to discuss it with me. I can either do what he says, or go to jail. Goddamn, my dad can be so manipulative. I wish he'd just leave me the hell alone.

"Look, I don't want to get high," I continue. "I just want to go back home and lie in bed with Zelda and watch movies."

There's a pregnant silence.

"You know what that sounds like to me? That sounds like shooting heroin. Don't you want to be able to really live again?"

"I don't know," I answer, and that's the truth.

My dad tells me to be patient. He assures me that he and my mom are working together around the clock to try and find the right place for me. I imagine half their objective, at least, is to get me as far away from Zelda as geographically possible. Maybe I'll be going to rehab in Norway.

So my dad and I hang up. I feel very sick, but I'm not ready to sleep. I stumble into the TV room. Bobby is in there, passed out on the couch. He's been shooting heroin for so long that all his veins have collapsed. Even the doctors and nurses can't find a vein to draw blood from. All he's got is this hole in his arm—an open wound the size of a softball. The flesh and everything has been eaten away to the bone. It's really one of the most repulsive things I've ever seen and I have a hard time not staring at it. I sit as far away from him as possible.

Besides Bobby, there's this new patient who wanders by every twenty minutes or so. He weighs three hundred pounds and his face is bright red. His pants are usually around his ankles and his bulbous tongue dangles out of his bulbous mouth. His eyes hold the helpless confusion of a little puppy dog. He is most always covered in excrement. Plus, I guess he's wet-brained or something, 'cause all he ever says is:

"Is it lunchtime?"

Or: "Where's the hallway?"

He usually asks the hallway question from the hallway. He almost trampled me one time when he couldn't find a spoon and felt sure that I must have one. The guy eats a lot. He packs that hospital food away.

But anyway, Bobby is sleeping and I start looking through the video selection. Their selection is pretty bad, but I notice a Lars von Trier movie called *Breaking the Waves*. At least it's something I've been wanting to see. I put the movie in and the sound wakes Bobby up. He was actually sleeping with his head buried under a copy of that James Frey book.

"You bastard," he says, sounding like Templeton, the rat from *Charlotte's Web*. "I can't believe you read my letters. What're you watching?"

I tell him.

"Great flick, man. A little heavy maybe."

Bobby is right. It's a good movie, but goddamn—if I thought I was depressed before, after watching three hours of this sweet, innocent little Emily Watson turning herself into a whore for her quadriplegic husband—well, I was ready to pretty much end it. They say suicide is a permanent solution to a temporary problem. Well, the problem of being human isn't really so temporary and sometimes a permanent solution seems like the best possible way out.

Bobby snores through most of the movie. Every once in a while he'll roll over and say something about how great an actress Emily Watson is—or about how lucky I am to be young. I nod, watching the screen. Three hours pass and finally I take some chloral hydrate, drifting into a sleep filled with nightmares about an airplane flown by large monkeys.

Zelda visited me yesterday and brought In-N-Out burgers—the first solid food I've eaten in quite a long time. I was actually a little embarrassed by her while she was on the unit. I guess she'd been shooting coke ever since I left, and then she tried to counteract that by swallowing a bunch of pills before coming up.

The result was that she ended up nodding out over and over while she was sitting with me in the TV room. What made everything worse was that they'd already started cutting back my Phenobarbital. I can no longer sit still. I'm squirming constantly and my skin feels like bugs are crawling all over it and like there's an electrical storm surging through my body. And my stomach is fucked up as hell. It feels like there are acid fires raging in my belly—or like those oil fires you see on TV in Iraq.

All of this made it extremely difficult to just sit still with Zelda while she was falling asleep on me. Today, however, she seems more sober and has snuck me in a bunch of Somas and some more Suboxone, so I should be feeling better shortly. Plus, she talked to a friend, who's been thrown in jail a bunch of times. According to him, the crime I committed will, at the most, get me thirty days. That means I'll only have to serve five, tops. And if I say I'm gay, they'll put me in a separate cell with a bunch of queens and I'll just be able to watch TV and it'll be totally safe and actually kind of fun. Besides that, we can maybe hide out at Zelda's friend Juliet's house.

I want to leave and I figure they can't stop me, so I'll just get my stuff and walk out with Zelda. I'm detoxed enough. We can get into some sort of outpatient program. She seems pretty sober at the moment.

So I go into my room with Zelda and start packing.

She paces nervously. "You know," she says, "maybe I'll still go into detox tomorrow. Then we can be clean together, right? I mean, I should probably throw away all the coke I have in the car."

I stop and look up at her. "You have coke in the car?"

"Yeah, I stayed at Sam's last night. She gave me so much coke. But if you're coming home, I'll throw it all away."

I just stare at her silently. Suddenly I realize I can't go with Zelda. I'll just get high again and all these days of hell in detox will have been wasted. I also see an image, very clear, of Zelda and me sitting together in her car—dressed in our designer clothes—cell phones to our ears—both OD'ed—dead, cold, purple.

I didn't even really think I wanted to live, but I guess I do.

"Zelda, baby," I say. "I love you, but if you've been using all night, I can't go with you."

She freezes. "Uh, yeah, of course. I . . . uh . . . that makes sense."

"I love you and I want to be with you more than anything in the whole world. But we both need to get clean. We need to do this if we want to have a life together."

Zelda's eyes are filled with tears. "I know, baby. You're right." She hugs me and cries all over my shoulder.

I'm not sure where this clarity comes from. It hits me somewhat miraculously. Maybe I've been given the faintest glimmer of hope over these last few days. I wasn't asking for it. Spencer would probably say it was God or something, but I just can't believe that anymore.

Regardless, I don't leave with Zelda. I ask her, again, to go into detox. She promises me she will. Then a woman nurse takes us all out to smoke with our visitors. The drugs Zelda snuck in start to hit me out there in the sun and suddenly I feel a whole lot better. I mean, a whole lot. Everything's gonna be fine, just fine. Why was I worrying so much? I say good-bye to my Zelda and go upstairs to sleep.

"You think you have the world on a string, don't you, kid?" says Bobby. "Just try being forty-five with a hole the size of a grapefruit in your arm—writing talking horse cartoons for TV. I even got a fucking kid. What happened to me? The time goes so fast, so goddamn fast."

DAY 586

My dad and mom are forcing me to check into a treatment center in Arizona that deals with dual diagnosis patients—people who have addiction along with other psychological disorders. I absolutely do not want to go, but it's not like I have any real choice.

The usual stay is one month, but due to my feeling like I need to crawl out of my skin, turn inside out, and tear out my veins—well, they want me to stay an extra two weeks. Initially I go into a program they've named Serenity, but after that I go into a more in-depth group. The center apparently deals with trauma, as well as chemical dependency issues. I don't really think I'm much of a trauma survivor, but it beats jail. At least, I hope it does.

The last two nights have been hell. My body can't figure out how to fall asleep on its own anymore and the doctors here have cut back all my medication. I have these surges of electricity pulsing through me. The bugs are still crawling all over me and I have the worst diarrhea.

But despite all that, at six thirty in the morning my mom is helping me carry my bags to the elevator. All the nurses say goodbye to me, and, once again, they're so nice. They tell me to call, like, five hundred times. I know I never will, but I'm like, "Oh, of course, thank you so much."

My mom is sweet if somewhat nervous around me. She definitely acts a little strange and makes lighthearted jokes about things that aren't funny.

In the car, she says I'm like a worm in hot ashes. I can't stop moving. My body is gyrating uncontrollably and it's actually completely embarrassing.

I do tell my mom how sorry I am about everything, though I'm sure my words are meaningless. There's nothing I could possibly say at this point to make anything better. I've fucked it all up beyond repair, maybe forever. My mom definitely doesn't trust me. She even insists on getting a special medical pass from the flight attendant so she can make sure I get on the plane.

My mom tells me Zelda got into UCLA detox last night. It's sort of hard to believe. I text-message her from my mom's phone, telling her that I will, no matter what, come back for her.

The flight is terrible. I'm terrified of having to sit in such close quarters with people—my body convulsing like it is. Plus, there are tons of little kids on the plane. It takes me a while to figure it out, but I finally realize that in three days, it'll be Thanksgiving. Great—another holiday in rehab. At least I don't have to be with my goddamn family.

I keep jumping around and I have to go to the bathroom, like, five hundred times. I'm going totally out of my mind so I have to try reading as best I can. I actually forgot a pen, so I can't draw or anything. The book I have is this one Zelda gave me called *The Painted Bird*. Once again I find myself in the same position I was in with *Breaking the Waves*. The book is great, but it's dark and brutal and actually kind of hard to read. I mean, I'm into stuff like that and this is still almost too much for me.

I finally have to put it down when this peasant scoops out the eyes of his wife's admirer with a spoon. It makes me think of Mike and Zelda, and I must still be hallucinating because I kind of drift in and out of being a part of the story. By the time the plane lands in Phoenix, I'm just gripping the armrest and trying not to scream. I'm sweating but cold, and everything feels so surreal.

The airport in Phoenix leaves me in total culture shock. First of all, it is very small and there are military personnel all over the place.

I'm so jacked up because of that electrical current thing surging through me, I almost walk past the guy holding the sign with my name on it. But he recognizes me from my mom's description and calls out to me.

I stop and we talk some. He is so sweet and soft-spoken

I want to slap him. He looks a little like Jimmy Stewart, but with white hair and thick glasses. His name is Jerome. He is gentle and calm and I don't think I can take much more of him at present.

What makes it all worse is that he tells me he actually used to live in L.A. He moved to Arizona after attending the program I'm about to go into. He says the pace of Los Angeles was too much for him. All I want to do is get back to Zelda. I am completely uninterested in going into another rehab. I am just frustrated talking with Jerome, and, despite my present condition, I feel I'm much better than he is. I want to say to him, "Don't you know who I am? Who I know?" I sit quietly, though, trying to answer his questions politely.

Arizona is desolate and ugly. Everything is brown and dusty and strip-malled and windswept. Jerome and I drive along the two-lane highway and he talks to me about where I'm headed and what a wonderful place it is. I feel like I'm in a wasteland. Sitting still in the car is almost worse than the airplane. It's just me and Jerome and I'm vibrating like a maniac. I miss Zelda so bad. I feel anchorless without her.

The Safe Passage Center is high in the Arizona mountains, about an hour and a half away from Phoenix. It's basically just a trailer park on a mound of dirt. There are faux log cabins where we sleep and a couple of buildings where groups are held.

The first thing that bothers me is that when I introduce myself, people refuse to shake my hand because there's a "no touch" policy. Also, half the women can't talk to me because they're not allowed to talk to men. Then the guy who does my bag search is so weaselly, old, and mealymouthed that I can't stand to even look at him. He wears these baggy-butt jeans that are just awful. Plus, I can't stop moving 'cause of the bugs and all. If this is what sobriety is gonna be like I don't think I can cut it. My roommate asks me why I'm here and I say, "Drugs."

He smiles, a tattooed kid who's very punk-looking—maybe a year or two older than me. "Yeah," he says. "That's what I thought when I got here too. But that's just the beginning."

I'm too fried out to think of anything biting and sarcastic to say. Besides, I have to sit through a mountain of intake paperwork and sitting through anything right now is nearly impossible.

James, my roommate, shows me around and then makes me a necklace with my name on it. The food at dinner looks so good compared to the hospital stuff that I eat way too much and throw up all night. I'm freezing always. I don't sleep for four days and nights and the fucking bugs won't leave me alone. There are groups and different meetings I'm supposed to be going to all day long, but I can't imagine trying to sit still through anything. I go into the counselors' office and demand to be taken to a hospital. A silver-haired Austrian woman with shimmering blue eyes suggests, "Why don't you just lie down and invite the bugs in? Experience the bugs crawling on you. Become one with the bugs."

I tell her what I think about that idea.

I eat no Thanksgiving dinner because I'm still too sick. I can't get through to Zelda in her detox and the cold is so deep inside me. I snarl at anyone who tries to talk to me.

I think I'm definitely in the wrong place and I imagine the few counselors I've had interactions with probably think I'm in the wrong place too. I'm not sure why the hell they let me in, but I've got no choice but to ride this out.

DAY 589

I spent the weekend at the Safe Passage Center basically just watching movies and praying no one would talk to me. I finally got in to see a shrink lady, who prescribed me some medication for sleep and for the seizures I've been having. I guess that's what the electric feeling was—little seizures throughout my body. Anyway, that's what she told me. But they've gotten me on an antiseizure drug called Neurontin, which has calmed me down.

Also they've prescribed me enough Seroquel to knock out a fuck-ing hippopotamus. **289**

The best thing about the weekend was this chef they had working named Bing. I mean, his food was amazing. Oven-fried chicken; baked French toast; quesadillas; pozole; Caesar salad; made-to-order omelets; mozzarella, tomato, and basil salad; ribs. He was fantastic. But also he was just really great to talk to. He told me he was from San Francisco and he worked all over the city—even running a little bakery in Glen Ellen, where I lived when I was three. His face was all smashed in like a boxer's, so I figure he'd been through a lot. He gave me some encouragement about hanging in there. He was just gentle as hell and I felt like I could really connect with him.

The routine here is pretty simple. I wake up early and eat breakfast and then go to a morning group that lasts until lunch. In the afternoons I go to different groups about chemical dependency, codependency, sexual dependency, or men's issues. There's also a class called Living in the Body where we have to do exercises with movement, sort of like yoga. They also have eating disorder groups and body image groups, but I don't go to those.

Besides all that, I talked to Zelda. She's in detox and doing all right. This friend of mine, Eric, who was just a pinnacle of sobriety, was in detox with her, so I feel a little better about having relapsed and all.

Zelda is still pretty high and hearing the sweetness of her voice just destroys me. I can't talk very long. It's horrible. I want to leave so badly and not use, but just lie in bed and watch movies with her—make love, whatever. I feel very alone. I write her a long letter professing my commitment to her, but it's all so tiring.

I'm overwhelmed all over again by the reality that I have, in truth, destroyed everything in my life. That weighs on me so heavily. I just keep thinking about how I had everything and I threw it all away. It seems like trying to build it back is an impossible task. I'm not even sure how to begin. I guess just being here in Arizona is a start.

I'm finally meeting with my primary therapist—this woman, Annie. The way it works here is that you have a psychiatrist who does your meds, then there are the people who run your morning group, where each person spends time discussing whatever is bothering them. The name of my group is Serenity. Then there are different therapists who run the afternoon groups.

In addition to these groups, everyone has a main therapist who handles their case. They meet with you individually, though everything you tell them is shared with the entire staff, so there's no confidentiality. Plus there are these counselor aid people on the grounds twenty-four hours a day who are everywhere and are constantly calling your individual therapist, telling them all the things you've been doing that are wrong.

Anyway, it's complicated.

Annie, my therapist, resembles a large barnyard animal—most specifically a pig wearing way too much makeup. She snorts when she laughs and her butt is wider than her entire body from the waist up. She invites me into her office and I sit down in an uncomfortable office chair. There are motivational slogans on the wall and a few personal photos—mostly of a young boy who's probably ten or eleven. She introduces herself to me and then asks me to just tell her my history. I try to get through it as quickly as possible.

When I finish she sets about organizing my treatment plan, telling me which of the afternoon groups she wants me to attend.

"I want you to go to chemical dependency and sexual dependency twice a week. I want you to go to anger group and also to the group that helps you discover spirituality."

I try to tell her I've tried all that before.

"Well, obviously it didn't work, so you better try to get something different out of it this time. This treatment program is all about what you make it. If you put a lot into your recovery, you will reap the benefits. If you skate through here, well, you're not going to change."

I'm so sick of this recovery twelve-step psychobabble. There's

just no way I can make it through another round of rehab. It never
works and I feel really hopeless about this whole process.

"Look," I say. "I've done this so many times. I don't think it's going to make a difference. I can't stay sober."

"Yes," she says. "You can. Maybe you 'won't,' but you absolutely 'can.' You know, just watching you I notice how closed off your body posture is. If you're going to be open to doing this work you need to adopt an attitude of willingness. I want you to put your feet flat on the floor and sit up straight and just breathe quietly for a minute."

Everything Annie has said to me just sounds like the same old shit, but I comply just to make things easier. I put my feet down and sit with my back arched. I close my eyes and breathe. It does seem to center me slightly.

"Now," she continues, "I've talked to your father and we both agree that we want you to stay here for at least three months to fully immerse yourself in this work. How do you feel about that?"

There's actually a panic that surges through me when I think about being away from Zelda that long. In three months I imagine that she will forget all about me. I need to get back to her quickly. I remember when she was having the affair with me and she was lying in my bed. Her phone rang over and over, so she finally answered it. I listened to her telling Mike that she was at her sponsor's house. Her lies were so convincing. I mean, I was literally holding her naked next to me and she was talking on the phone to Mike—telling him "I love you, too," before hanging up.

Besides, I'm worried that when she gets sober she will finally realize what a total loser I am. I've always figured it was just a matter of time till she woke up and asked herself what the hell she was doing with me. I have to get back to Zelda as soon as possible.

However, I know about rehab and all and this whole codependency thing they always talk about. Every program I've ever been in has had groups centered around treating codependency. I know that if I talk about my feelings for Zelda, Annie will see it as a sure sign that our relationship is unhealthy. I also know that if I resist her telling me to stay for three months, she'll say that my addict self just wants to use again and there'll be no way I can get out of here any sooner. I want to play this rehab game perfectly and I think I'll be able to do it too, because I've been in so many of these goddamn places.

"I'm not sure I need to stay here that long," I say. "But I'm definitely open to talking about it."

"Good," she says. "That's all I ask. Now, I've received reports from several of the therapists and counselor assistants who've observed you that you have very leaky sexual energy."

"What?" I ask, kind of angrily.

"They've just told me that they think you come off as being very flirty. You also have sort of an androgynous look about you that is very sexual. Have you ever thought about cutting your hair?"

This all seems to come out of nowhere and really pisses me off.

"Look, just because I'm not some fucking football-loving ass-hole guy and I'm comfortable with my femininity doesn't mean there's something wrong with me."

"That's just it," she tells me. "You don't seem very comfortable with yourself. I think you use your sexuality to try to control and influence other people. That's what you did as a sex worker, isn't it?"

I almost want to cry I'm so frustrated with her.

"This is bullshit. You're just some hack therapist, not even a doctor, who thinks you know something about addiction 'cause you read some goddamn statistics in a book. Well, I'm not a statistic and I'm never gonna drink the Kool-Aid at this place, so you might as well not even try. I've been around some amazing people in my life who've inspired me to want to change, but you will never be one of them."

She just laughs, snorting. "Good, I knew there was some anger in you somewhere," she said. "Now, from what your father has told me, you don't have any options other than being here, so, unless you want to hitchhike back to Los Angeles, I suggest you comply with the rules here. Just to test your willingness, I'm gonna put you on a no-female contract. That means if you are caught talking to any women, you will have to meet with a panel of therapists. If you do it again, you will be asked to leave. I want you to go to the art room and do some drawings around the feelings our meeting has brought up for you. I want you to draw your anger, okay?"

I don't know what to say. I feel this heat all in my body. I am so utterly defeated. Annie tells me she'll see me in two days and I go up and smoke a cigarette, wanting to scream as loud as I can and cry and just go home—home to Zelda.

DAY 590

This morning, when I go to my core group, I notice a huge pile of different stuffed animals, dolls, toys, scattered across the floor. The two facilitators of the group, Wayne and Melissa, ask me if I'd like to do something called Animal Farm. So I have to stand up and walk over into the middle of this pile of toys and things.

I really don't want to be here and I feel so resistant, but, at the same time, there is a tiny piece of me that does want to change. I'm just afraid it won't work. Also, I am worried that to really embrace the process here, I will be forced to let go of Zelda. I mean, I hated everything Annie said to me yesterday, but what she said really made me question how much my insecurities have played a role in my acting out. I even began to wonder if my time as a sex worker was more a result of my hunger for acceptance than just needing money. My mind has just been going and going all night long. I feel like at least, since I'm here, I might as well just play along for now. Besides, what Annie said was true. I have no real options.

Anyway, Melissa and Wayne sit together and ask me to go

reach down and choose different items to represent things in my life—like my families, my different addictions, traumas, myself, my relationships, all that. Melissa is fat and cherubic, with dimples, rosy cheeks, and a sweetness that is a little overdone. Wayne is so slow and deliberate and gentle that I think he must be really stupid—but the more I actually listen to what he says, I realize he is pretty insightful. He has a long pointy nose and always talks in a loud whisper. It actually snowed last night, but now sunshine reflects through the windows. There are, of course, stupid, obligatory twelve-step slogans all over the walls.

So, first off, Wayne "invites" me to go into the pile and pick out something to be my two families in San Francisco and L.A. I search around for a minute, but he interrupts me.

"Try not to think about it. Just pick things intuitively."

I nod, getting out this hard plastic alligator to be my stepmom and these two polished stone eggs to be her children. I have her turning away from me and protecting her kids. My dad is a bear of some kind—soft and furry and standing in between me and Karen and the kids. I'm a stuffed cat under a hard hat, with Zelda, a fluffy dog, hidden under there with me. Todd is a plastic tyrannosaurus with gnashing teeth. It goes on like that.

After I finish, people in the group are encouraged to point out what they notice regarding color similarities and placement— whatever. This one girl with a shaved head notices that I've used the same animal to represent Zelda and my mom. They are also lying in the same position. Someone else points out that they are even the same color. It is just a coincidence, but it does make me think.

Wayne asks me if I can notice any connections between my mom and Zelda in real life. It actually seems pretty obvious to me.

"Sure, I mean, they are both these sort of unattainable women who I've always been afraid of losing. Plus I always wanted to rescue my mom from her husband, and with Zelda, I was sort of able to do that. I mean, I rescued her from her boyfriend, Mike, who reminds me a lot of my stepdad."

"So," asks Melissa, "do you think maybe you are reenacting your relationship with your mom with Zelda? And do you think that maybe the fear of abandonment you have with your mom since she moved away when you were so little has transferred to your fear of losing Zelda?"

It makes sense and it's not really that shocking of a revelation. I've been in therapy forever. I don't think I have that difficult a time recognizing these patterns in my life.

"Yeah," I say. "I mean, that's pretty obvious, but what am I supposed to do about it?"

"Just acknowledge it," says Wayne. "Hopefully someday you will love yourself enough to choose a partner who instills peace in you, not fear. But for now just try and feel it. Try to feel that you may have unconsciously chosen your girlfriend because she is emotionally unavailable, like your mother. Try to experience that feeling in your body. Put your feet flat on the floor, breathe, and let yourself sit with that. You must not like yourself very much if that's the kind of woman you would choose to marry."

I'm all curled up on my chair so I try to straighten out. The whole time Wayne was talking I felt really angry and defensive, but as I sit up and push my feet into the ground, I feel just more sad than anything else.

"But I love Zelda more than anything," I say. "We are meant to be together."

"That's true," says Melissa. "But only so long as you are willing to keep bringing self-hatred to the relationship. If you were to get healthy, to feel good about who you are, I don't think the two of you would fit so well anymore."

"And that leaves you with an interesting choice," says Wayne. "Do you sacrifice your own happiness and feelings of peace in order to have this relationship, or do you start to get well and choose a real life that maybe doesn't include Zelda?"

This all feels like too much pressure on me and I want them to just move on to somebody else. I don't look at anyone, but I can feel all their eyes on me.

"I'm happy," I say. "As long as I can make Zelda happy."

Everyone is silent. Finally Melissa speaks.

"If that were true, then why did you end up nearly killing yourself with drugs?"

"And," says Wayne, "from what little you've said about Zelda, it sounds like making her happy is an impossible task, so you are just setting yourself up for failure and, frankly, a miserable life."

"But it's your choice," says Melissa.

I want to argue with them, but Melissa tells me just to sit with it all.

"Why don't you do some drawings around what's come up for you in group today."

That seems like their answer for everything. I try to think about what they've said, but it's just too much for me. I can't even go there right now. All I want to do is smoke a cigarette and not deal with any of this crap. I do want to love myself and not need to seek approval from other people, but that just feels impossible. I'll never get to that place. If all the other rehabs couldn't help me, then why should this place be any different?

It isn't. It won't be.

I can't change.

Trying is terrifying because I know I will just fail. But I do want things to be different. I do. If I'm going to live then I have to find something here at the Safe Passage Center to help me. It's the only chance I have. I know that. But what can that possibly be? I am so afraid. I'm afraid to hope again.

DAY 596

I've finally moved out of the Serenity group, transferring into the all-male core group called Empowerment. Annie actually thinks I'm making a lot of progress and I agree, you know? I mean, I have decided to try and that is a big step. I'm not sure what exactly made me start opening up. I guess the will to live is stronger in me than I thought.

The people who lead the Empowerment group are these two complete opposites. The man, Ray, is older—looks like a Hell's Angel or something, with a long ponytail and Marine Corps tattoos. He is big and surly, but still sweet somehow. The woman who co-leads the group, Kris, well, I like her all right.

I sit down on a worn-out blue couch in the group room. There are signs with the word EMPOWERMENT painted on them all over the walls. Besides me there are five other guys in the group. There's James and Jim, an older guy named Justice, a kid around eighteen named Henry, and a big Irish guy with a knee brace named Brian. We all take turns checking in. Because it's my first day in group, I have to tell my story for about half an hour—just explaining why I'm in treatment and what I've been through. At this point I'm really just trying to be as honest as possible. I still really have my doubts about this place, but I am here and I don't want to go back to using like I was. So I tell my story as best I can.

When I finish we all go take a cigarette break and then return to the group room so everyone can give me their feedback. I sit nervously on the couch, trying not to look at anyone. Right off Kris asks me to sit straight and make eye contact with everyone individually. I feel very exposed having just told all these strangers everything that's happened and, for some reason, having to look them in their eyes just makes it all feel more real. By the time I get to Justice I see that he has tears in his eyes and that makes me start crying. I look down at the floor again, but Kris tells me I have to keep going around the circle looking each person in the eye. It is so hard. I just want to disappear, but I follow her directions.

"Good," says Ray in this gruff voice. "Nic, what was really disturbing to me as you were telling your story was how disconnected you seemed from what had happened. You just described some pretty terrible things, but you talked about them as though they were happening to somebody else. It's nice to see you feeling it finally."

"Also," says Kris, "it was obviously really interesting how much your life has been surrounded by celebrities. The way you talk about it, well, it feels kind of like you're bragging. I wonder how much your obsession with fame and celebrities contributed to you being so obsessed with your current relationship."

I feel defensive when she says this and also just very embarrassed.

"I'm not one of those people," I say, sort of angrily.

"Okay," says Kris. "Well then, why don't we try a little experiment. For the rest of your time here, I'm putting you on a no-name-dropping contract. Now, group, I want you to help Nic with this. If you guys notice him talking about any famous people he knows, I want you to remind him to honor his contract."

Everyone nods in agreement. I feel humiliated, but I try to just keep my feet on the floor, my arms uncrossed. Ray notices my agitation and encourages me to sit with the feelings this has brought up. The truth is, I've always known, at least somewhere inside me, that Zelda was partly just a status symbol. I felt important with her. Hanging out with my celebrity friends I always felt important—cool—whatever. But underneath that, I can see now, was a deep-seated feeling of worthlessness. Surrounding myself with famous people helped me to hide that ever-expanding chasm in me. Was Zelda a part of that? I guess it makes sense. But what am I without her? I can't possibly stand on my own. There's no way.

After group we all go up and smoke cigarettes. Everyone tells me how proud they are of me for being so open. They tell me they support me.

James and Jim have emerged as real friends to me. These guys are fucking funny as hell. Plus James is really very cool. He's reading this biography of Georges Bataille and lived in Brooklyn for the last couple of years. I enjoy just talking to him and we play a lot of cards and stuff.

When the cigarette break is over I have to walk back down the dusty path leading to one of the group rooms. I'm scheduled for this thing called SE with a woman named Georgia. SE is Somatic Experiencing, but that's as much as I know about it. Georgia is tall and thin with pixieish gray hair, librarian glasses, and a color-coordinated little suit. The color she's coordinated is brown. I have to sign a release in order to do whatever it is we're about to do. We shake hands and I sign. What does Dylan say in one of his songs? "When you ain't got nothing, you got nothing to lose."

Exactly.

I sit in a chair opposite her and she smiles.

"Okay, well," she begins. "Why don't you put both feet on the floor and uncross your arms?"

I didn't realize my arms were crossed, but I do as she says. Then she asks me about my past. She asks what I've been focusing on. I talk to her about different stuff, eventually getting to the part about getting beat up when I was on the street—prostituting myself.

"Great," she says, somewhat incongruously. "Where do you feel that in your body?"

"What?"

"Go inside. What are you feeling? Is it shame? Terror? Anger?"

"Maybe all those," I say, swallowing hard.

"And where do you experience that in your body?"

I try to check in with myself.

"I guess I feel it in my chest and stomach."

"What does it feel like in your chest and stomach?"

"It's a tightness in my chest and maybe a nausea in my stomach."

She talks me back through the night. She has me describe it to her. "What happened?"

"I don't really remember," I say. "I mean, it's all just blurred out. I met him at a bar somewhere downtown. It was him and his boyfriend."

"Can you remember what they looked like?"

"No. Well, the boyfriend was maybe Eastern European, I think. He had an accent and, uh, long hair. The first guy was really muscular, like a body-builder type. He had a shaved head."

"What did they do to you?"

"My ribs were broken," I say. Then, suddenly, I have this horrible memory/sensation of the muscular guy on top of me. I feel like I'm gonna throw up. It's like I can't control my breathing and I'm hyperventilating some. I'm choking all at once—like something is being shoved against the back of my throat. I can't breathe and I start crying. Georgia helps me get back, grounded, feeling my feet pressed against the floor.

I can't stop crying. I feel very out of control. I'm really feeling this stuff in my body and memories are jarred loose that I would've been content to have kept hidden. According to Georgia, the body traps memories of trauma within it. Animals in the world will shake or something until the trauma is released, but humans aren't connected with how to do that. We need guidance. I guess the concept makes sense, as far as it goes. The session's only a half hour long, but by the end I need to just take off running up the hill. I feel genuine sadness over what I put myself through. I mean, I can actually feel it, which is different for me. It's weird actually starting to own all that's happened.

This is all made more acute by the appearance of Patrick.

Patrick had been at Safe Passage Center before, but I guess it hadn't quite done the trick. What I'm struck by immediately with Patrick is that he reminds me of someone who I had back when I was working the streets. I mean, I know I've never actually seen this guy before, but I can't even be in the same fucking room with him. He looks like Steve Buscemi in *Fargo*, with yellow, crooked teeth, and thick, wet lips. He has pasty skin and an obvious comb-over. His eyes are strangely perverse. He blubbers constantly, crying with the wild abandon of a forgotten child. He snivels and squirms and nobody is really sure why he's even here. But I can't stand to look at him. I run from every interaction I might have to have with him.

I explain the situation to James and Jim. They try to buffer the impact by keeping us separate, but it's not that easy.

In codependency group, we have to do these role-plays to help us learn how to assert ourselves. This is, like, fifteen minutes after the stuff about my time as a sex worker came up with Georgia. And, of course, I randomly get paired with Patrick. So here's my chance to confront my past and walk through the fear. Wayne from my old Serenity group co-leads with this Emily woman. It's weird, but almost all the female therapists here look alike. They are all fat and strong and dress very similarly. It's like they harvested them all from the same gene pool.

Today Wayne and Emily have us focusing on boundaries. Boundaries are where you practice standing up for yourself, saying what you will or won't do, take, etc. We have to role-play it out. For instance, Patrick is getting a divorce from his wife and she's guilt-tripping him about money. I'm supposed to play Patrick's wife and he's gonna set the boundary that he's not giving her any more.

"So," he says in a voice that is overly sweet and insincere. "You be my wife and I'll tell you that I don't owe you anything else. Are you all right with that, Nic?"

Sitting this close to him I am barely able to speak. I'm very hot and sweating and I want to run screaming from the room. Worse, I'm supposed to maintain eye contact. I start to actually think I might fucking pass out. I just can't take it.

"I'm sorry," I murmur. "I have to . . . I have to go."

I mostly stumble toward the door.

"You all right?" asks Emily after me.

"I'll be back," I say.

I never come back—or, at least, not until the next class.

I go into my cabin and am suddenly very cold. I get under the covers and shake. I shake all over the place, like an animal who just escaped from a predator. It goes on for nearly an hour and a half. I try singing a little to myself. It doesn't help much.

DAY 635

It's the day after Christmas and I've started to really value the time I've spent at Safe Passage Center. Ray, the core group leader, has almost taken on a sort of surrogate father role for me and a lot of the boys. He is so strong, yet gentle, and just a sweetheart. He embodies a sensitive masculinity, ying and yang—something I never knew was possible. Somehow he manages to make everything we've been through seem less shameful. He helps us love ourselves more through his complete acceptance and openness.

The focus here is really on loving yourself. That idea is something I never really understood before Ray. He talks to us with such honesty about his own struggles hating himself—not feeling like he was good enough. As Ray shares, I can see so many similarities in our stories. Maybe it was my self-loathing and insecurities that made me act the way I did. That's sort of an amazing realization for me. I never really thought about the fact that I'd have to learn how to really care about myself in order to stay sober. I always thought it was more about learning to care about other people. Like, I should stay sober for Jasper and Daisy, my dad, Spencer, friends, girlfriends. I never understood that I have to really want to live for myself and as myself—not as anyone else. If I could be content with who I am, I wouldn't have to escape myself always. That sounds simple, I guess, but it seems impossible. I don't even really know how to begin. Maybe being here and going to groups and everything is a start. At least, I'm starting to feel a difference—a clarity or something.

Basically I've just really been trusting in the process here. I want it to work. I want to change and I actually have hope that it might be possible. A lot of this is due to some of the more intense alternative therapies they offer here, like Somatic Experiencing. Through these sessions I've been able to recall events from my

childhood that I had completely suppressed from my memory. **303**
There was one event in particular that I was able to confront through
these therapies. They say in the twelve-step program that the only
people who can't stay sober are the ones who are constitutionally
incapable of being honest with themselves. I didn't know it, but I
was constitutionally incapable of being honest with myself. Now
that I have discovered some of these truths about myself and have
been helped to move through them, my mind isn't such a scary
place anymore.

They talk a lot here about the grieving process, citing the
work of Elisabeth Kübler-Ross's *On Death and Dying*. In her book
she describes the phases of grief one must go through in order to
move on from the death of a loved one. Here they say that those
same phases of grieving have to apply to any trauma that occurs
in our lives. Suppressing the pain, ignoring it, blocking it out, or
getting high so I don't have to feel it—those coping methods just
don't work. And I believe that. My insides always felt like they were
consuming themselves. I felt fear for no reason, panic in response
to everyday situations, and, of course, that terrible, violent self-
loathing that controlled my life.

At the Safe Passage Center I am taken back through the
trauma, re-experiencing it so that I can finally grieve in a healthy
way. Maybe this all sounds crazy. But as new age and touchy-feely
as it seems, I have really seen my life change. I am embracing who
I am. I am not hiding anymore.

Today they have me doing this therapy they call Breath Work.
They have me get up real early so I can do it before morning group.
It is very cold this morning and I have to wrap myself in this army
jacket that James gave me. I drink a little coffee and walk down
to another group room. I've never worked with the woman who
leads Breath Work, but I've seen her around the treatment center.
She is very old and spindly with gray hair and no makeup. She
looks really cool, with blue jeans and big boots on.

On the floor of her office she's constructed a sort of crucifix-
looking thing made out of pillows. It actually reminds me of the

things they strap you to when they execute you with lethal injection on death row—or at least the way they made it look in *Dead Man Walking*.

Anyway, the woman, Gertrude, asks me to take off my shoes and lie down on the pillows.

"Now," she says, "just clear your mind. Don't try to control your thoughts at all. Let go completely."

I try my best to do what she says. I want to get as much as I can out of everything they are offering me here. These regression therapies are always very frightening. Usually I'll end up going back to a time when I was on the street, or some other sexual stuff that happened to me when I was young. It is always very painful and I'm nervous.

Gertrude puts her hand with wax-paper skin on my chest. She tells me to breathe fast and deep—never stopping. She doesn't want me to talk. I'm just supposed to hyperventilate and she'll guide me through it.

So I begin.

At first I notice just how dry my lips feel as the breath goes in and out. I feel light-headed and my stomach and legs start to cramp up. My mind races through many different things, but never stays with any one memory. Then, suddenly, I can't stop thinking about that time at Zelda's when I went into convulsions shooting cocaine. My body seizes up. I remember the song I sang to keep myself conscious. I remember it all, but I'm also feeling it inside me. I am scared. I am terrified I am going to die. It is just so frightening. I never really got that before, you know? I never felt how scary it was to come that close to death. I feel it now and I'm shaking, shaking, shaking and then I have to stop all at once and throw up into a trash can next to me. Nothing really comes out, but I just retch again and again.

Gertrude rubs my back and tells me everything will be all right. It's not easy feeling everything so strongly and it makes it a lot harder to dismiss what I've been through. It just all seems so real now, whereas it never really did before. And, as difficult as it is to feel all this stuff, I believe that it is my only chance to **305** really heal—to have a Safe Passage, which is the promise of this treatment center.

After doing Breath Work I have enough time to call Zelda, who just got out of detox and has moved into a Sober Living. I want to share all these new experiences with her. I want to believe that she can fit into my life as a healthier person. None of the therapists here agree with me, but I still want to try. My relationship with Zelda is the one aspect of my life that I haven't completely given over to this process. It's the one thing that I'm still protecting, though, honestly, I am beginning to have my doubts as to whether I could really ever be with Zelda.

Zelda is really having the roughest time ever getting sober. She's had two big seizures and had to have her gall bladder removed. All the drugs we were shooting dehydrated her or something. That caused stones to form inside her and I guess it hurts real bad.

But when she answers her phone I listen to her voice and it doesn't fill me with the same crazy feeling of passion it used to. She sounds distant and still just so caught up in that world I left behind. She tells me all about what's happening with Yakuza and Justin and all our friends there. I can't talk to her for very long. I have to get to group.

"I love you," I tell her.

"I know," she says. "I hear you. I just don't even know who I am. It's hard to imagine anyone loving me."

I feel this profound emptiness at the other end of the line—an emptiness that I used to feel within myself, but that is lessening as each day passes. I realize suddenly very clearly that loving Zelda is like loving a black hole. I'm not saying I'm willing to act on that yet, but it is an awareness that I want to share in core group.

When I get to the group room, they tell me Ray isn't going to be in today, which is frustrating because I really wanted to talk to him about all this. Instead I just tell Kris and the rest of the group. I stammer over my words.

"You know," I say, "I talked to Zelda this morning and I'm really scared that I'm not going to be able to work things out with her."

Everyone seems shocked, except Kris, who says, "Uh, you think? It's about time."

I laugh. "It's just that, you know, here I am having all these opportunities for healing, while she's back in Sober Living, basically doing the same stuff we all did there two or three years ago. It's not her fault, but it's so hard for me to envision her changing. Not to say that it can't happen—but I have a sense of independence now that I never had with Zelda."

"Look," says Kris. "Whether she changes or not, you need to learn to be on your own—not to depend on others to complete you. Until you have that, you have nothing. So, yeah, I suggest you separate from Zelda. And it doesn't have to be forever. But, honestly, it'll probably have to be."

I'm not sure what to say. I know I'm not ready for that yet. Or at least I don't think I am. I just try to sit with all this.

After group Kris tells us they're having an emergency community meeting today and, of course, I immediately assume I'm in trouble. It's been surprisingly warm over Christmas, even though I've had bronchitis and am on antibiotics and shit. We didn't really do anything for the holiday, which is fine by me. This is the third Christmas I've spent in rehab. It's definitely easier than being with my family.

I'm one of the first people in the community building aside from a wall of staff. My eyes make contact with Wayne's and my stomach drops out of me.

"What's wrong?"

I see the tears in Wayne's eyes. I sit next to him.

"Ray's dead," he tells me. "He died suddenly last night of a heart attack."

I find it hard to breathe and I'm crying all at once. The rest of the clients and therapists take their seats around the room and I just cry.

Jim is hit hardest by Ray's death. Ray had really become like Jim's father—and they both acknowledged this. Jim gets, like, physically sick from the shock of it. He's crying so much and I hear him run off to the bathroom and throw up. Those who knew Ray each take turns saying a word or two about his impact on us. Kris is really crying and the air just seems thick with sadness and grief.

Jim's strong, thick body is crumpled on mine. I actually kiss him on the forehead before I am able to think long enough to stop myself. He immediately runs up to his cabin and slams the door once the assembly is over. I walk up to go smoke. I really don't talk to anyone. I try to go to my next group, but this strange cold feeling keeps shivering through my body. I literally can't control it. It jerks and spasms. My body seems to be reacting completely independent of me. I'm forced to excuse myself and I go to lie down in my cabin.

The fit of shaking lasts for several hours. I'm so cold, it's like the chill has buried itself into the very depth of my being. My legs jerk involuntarily and my mind seems sick with fever. Faces come out of the wooden screens that are set up around my bed to separate me from my roommate's side of the cabin. The knots and lines in the grain of wood become shapes that I can't blink away. There's something amazing about being able to actually feel stuff now. I'm not sure what it is exactly that they've done to me here, but as hard as it is, I am so grateful to actually be connected with what's going on with me. Annie says it's the first step: dropping in—feeling my feelings—owning my past. I'm really just in it—acknowledging the pain and hurt I've caused to people who love me—to people I love.

Anyway, Annie wants me to do this family weekend thing with both my mom and my dad next month. They've agreed to come even though I haven't been with the two of them together in over five years. I'm nervous about it, obviously. There is so much I want to say to them, but words seem like they could never express my sorrow and regret enough. Even just saying I'm sorry feels so meaningless—like I'm trying to put a Band-Aid on a shotgun wound. Repairing any of the damage I've done to them seems impossible. In fact, building my life back seems impossible. I keep thinking just over and over about how I've managed to ruin everything once again. I've torn my world down, then built it back up, then torn it down again, then built it back and on and on. It feels so overwhelming.

The thing is, though, every time I think I'm just gonna give up—that I can't possibly do it, that I'm just going to curl up alone somewhere and waste away, well, I always keep trying. I mean, for some reason I manage to make it through another day and then another day after that. I'm not sure what there is, inside me, that enables me to keep pushing my boulder up the mountain. I guess I've managed to retain the tiniest bit of hope that this time, *this time*, I can climb a little higher and then higher still. This time I won't fall back, or tumble down as far. There is a will to live in me that, though weak at times, propels me forward. And the longer I've been here, the more committed I've become.

Even more than my relationships with the therapists, it's the clients who really make the most difference for me.

The people here are just incredible and, well, I don't feel like such a freak after being around them. Everyone is just as fucked up as I am—if not more so.

The bond among all of us is amazing. In a way, my days here have been some of the best in my whole life. When we're not in groups we're hanging out at the "smoke pit," talking shit and laughing like crazy. These are people who I've really started to trust and when they tell me things about myself, I listen. I respect them and I respect the work they're doing here. So I wonder: Why can't I listen to their advice about Zelda? Why am I so afraid to lose her? I suddenly feel like I'm cheating this place and all the friends I've made here and Ray and everyone if I don't start getting honest. I ask myself the question: Can I stay sober and resume my life with Zelda?

I think about what our life might be like after I get out of here. I'll be back in Sober Living, no car, no phone, no career, no promise of any future. Can I imagine Zelda sticking around through all that? Honestly, I can't. Besides, I feel so completely inadequate compared to her. The only way I can feel confident around her is to get high. Without drugs, well, it's hard enough to face my own life on a day-to-day basis. I think being around Zelda would be absolutely impossible for me. I mean, just trying to live outside this treatment center seems almost unimaginable. Mostly I'd prefer to hide in bed all day.

But I manage to get myself up. The shaking has subsided and I want to wash away the sweat from my body. As I strip off my clothes in the bathroom, I look down at my foot.

I think maybe I hit my toe against something while I was blacked out in detox. The nail has gotten all discolored—sort of yellow and dead-looking. It hasn't grown at all over the past month. I've been waiting for the nail to just drop off, but it actually keeps getting worse. It's changed colors and there's a sort of greenish-white pus underneath it. I guess the thing must be infected.

I took only one shower when I was at the detox. It was the first day Zelda was coming to visit me. I wanted to look good for her, you know, and that must have been when I got this goddamn fungus in my toe. It kinda makes me sick to look at it, but there seems to be some irony in the whole thing.

I rinse off under water that's as hot as I can possibly stand, then I get dressed and walk down the dirt path to Annie's office. I smoke a cigarette. By the time I get down there I have so much I want to say, it's like I can't possibly get my thoughts out fast enough. Annie has to remind me several times to breathe, which is pretty hard.

As I start talking about Zelda, Annie asks me a very simple question. "If you felt that inadequate with her, why did you stay?"

I look at Annie, sitting there across from me in that cramped office, with her splotchy makeup and turned-up pig nose. I know the answer, I think, but I'm embarrassed to say it out loud. I've known it all along, I guess, but to voice it will make it real. And how can I ever take it back after it has been made real?

I am with Zelda because I think that, if she accepts me, I will finally feel good about myself.

I tell that to Annie.

I voice it aloud for the first time.

"Why?" she asks. "Because of who she is?"

I am ashamed, but I nod my head. There is something so pathetic about admitting this that I want to just disappear—fold up on myself—implode somehow. Annie doesn't let me. She makes me uncross my arms and legs and sit up straight. She makes me hold our eye contact.

"I'm not good enough on my own," I say. "I mean, I am just nothing."

I'm crying a little now, the tears hot on my face.

"You're not nothing," she says. "Stay here with us, Nic. Trust in this process. We can teach you how to feel confident about who you are. You don't need to escape through drugs, or sex, or anything anymore. Don't deny yourself the gift of recovery. You deserve it. You deserve to love yourself."

"How long did you think I should stay again?" I ask.

She smiles.

"Three months, at least."

I look down at the paisley carpeting.

"Okay . . . yes . . . fine," I say.

Annie gives me a hug and I don't pull away.

DAY 642

My parents are set to arrive for family weekend in a couple of hours. I have to say, I'm pretty goddamn nervous. I haven't seen my mom since she drove me to the airport and I haven't seen my dad since before I relapsed. When my mom told my stepdad she was coming to visit me, he threw a fit, saying he was going on a hunger strike. It seems pretty ridiculous to me. My relationship with my stepfather feels just completely irreparable. It's sad because he is married to my mom and he will always be connected with my life. My mom agreed to come despite Todd's protests and I feel very grateful to her for that. I've come to believe in the Safe Passage Center more and more with each passing day and I imagine that the family weekend here will be really powerful.

Of course, I know that my recovery will be looked at skeptically by my family, especially my dad. He's already been through these kind of programs at other rehabs and they have never made a difference. Still, I feel like this place here in Arizona is special.

I am changing here—or maybe not changing, but reconnecting with who I really am. Someone who has been lost to me for a long time. I am separating from my past life. I haven't spoken to Zelda in a few weeks and already I feel like I have been able to disentangle myself emotionally from her.

I wake up early the day my parents are scheduled to visit—so early, in fact, that the sun hasn't even risen yet. I go make coffee in the community kitchen. There are actually a few other clients up, reading the paper or whatever. We say good morning to one another.

Then I basically smoke one cigarette after the other for the next three hours and drink way too much coffee. I'm not sure what I'm going to say to either of my parents. We have a session all together with Annie at nine thirty, and then we're doing the family program for the rest of the weekend. There are two therapists who facilitate the whole thing. There are usually only three families who participate, though this weekend there are going to be four. The first day we all write our goals for the weekend, then each family does an art therapy exercise. The second day each family takes turns sitting in the middle of the circle and having an hour-long therapy session in front of everyone else. No one observing the session can comment during the hour of therapy, but afterward we all get to give feedback. The third day we do a movement exercise and then do some sort of project helping us make plans for the future. I'm sure it is going to be really intense and, well, I'm scared.

It is cold this morning. The wind in the desert mountains chills me to my core. It feels like I can never get warm. I just keep smoking cigarettes.

I see my dad pull up in his rental car before my mom. He's driving a big blue minivan and he parks right next to where I'm smoking. When he gets out of the car I just stare at him. He looks older. His hair is thinning and almost all white now. He looks tired and he's dressed pretty conservatively—his button-down shirt tucked in and all.

He sees me right away and starts walking over. I have to look at the ground. I feel so sorry—so full of regret. My dad says, "Oh, Nic," and then hugs me tightly. I smell him. It is that smell of my dad I've always held with me. There's nothing I can say now. I want to cry, but I'm maybe too scared to let the tears out.

"How are you?" he asks.

I shake my head, saying, "I don't know. Good, I guess. I mean, considering everything."

"Yeah," he says. "You look good. You have life in your eyes again."

I put my arm around him. "Thanks, Dad. Come on, I'll show you around."

We walk together through the compound and I introduce him to various people. I ask him about Jasper and Daisy. He tells me they're fine but doesn't really want to talk about it. Neither one of us even mention Karen.

I take my dad down to Annie's office. My mom hasn't shown up yet, but that's not surprising. Annie greets us and tells my dad she feels like she already knows him since they've talked on the phone so much. Annie has actually spoken to me about my dad calling—maybe trying to be a little overcontrolling or something. I asked my dad not to do it, but he didn't really listen.

Anyway, we sit down and Annie smiles at me.

"So," she says, "how's it feel to see your dad again?"

I look at her and not my dad. "It feels sad. But, I mean, also it's just really great, too. I missed him. He's my friend."

"And how do you feel?" she asks my dad.

He looks at me, then at the floor, then back at me.

"I feel the same way," he says. "I missed Nic. He is my friend. But there's a large part of me that is also just completely blocked off to him. I don't trust him and I don't want to let him in because I don't want to be hurt again. I'm not sure I even have the ability to let him in. And, honestly, I'm skeptical about this whole weekend. I feel like I've been right here before and it has never made a difference."

I swallow hard. Of course, I expected this and I completely understand, but it is still very sad.

"I thought you'd feel that way," I say. "And you know, I'm not sure what to tell you. I think you will see that things are changing for me. I hope you will give me a chance."

"Nic," he says, "I've given you so many."

"But you are here," Annie says to my dad. "You are here supporting your son and that means you are open, if only the tiniest bit."

"Yes," says my dad. "Yes, I suppose that's true."

There's a knock at the door and Annie gets up to open it. One of the counselor's assistants, a girl named Laura, has led my mom down to Annie's office. My mom comes inside, telling us she's sorry that she's late. I stand up and give her a hug. She's wearing sunglasses and a knit poncho with her jeans tucked into a pair of thigh-high boots. She looks very pretty and young and hip. I wonder what my dad is thinking.

When my mom takes her seat, Annie tries to catch her up on what we've been talking about.

"Nic's father has just been expressing his concern that this weekend is going to be a waste of time, that Nic cannot change. How do you feel about that?"

My mom sighs. "I agree. I have the same concern. Nic, I love you, I really do, but we've done this so many times."

"I know," I say, not looking at anyone.

"I don't think you do," says my dad. "I don't think you do know. I have a life I have to live. I have to be a father for Jasper and Daisy. I have to be a husband to Karen. I have to work. But when you are using, my life is completely consumed by my worry for you. I can't function. So I've had to shut you out. I've had to close myself off to you so I can survive. It's just not fair."

I breathe out long and slow. There's a sick feeling in my stomach. My voice shakes as I speak.

"Dad, Mom, I do know. I understand. I talked to Annie about not even wanting you guys to come because I didn't want to give you hope again. I'm afraid of that responsibility and, well, I can't promise you anything. But we all have a lot of hurt, you know, and maybe just talking it out can help us heal or something. I mean, that's what Annie has told me. And I don't know if we will ever be able to have a relationship again. I want to. I think I do, anyway, but I know I can't control that."

"That's right," says Annie. "This weekend is about having a chance to confront the past and begin the healing process. No one can predict what will come from this."

My mom shifts around in her chair over and over. "Well," she says. "If we are going to be honestly talking about the past, then right away I want to say that I believe that if Nic comes back to L.A. he will die. I just don't think he has a chance if he stays with Zelda."

"I agree," I say quickly. "That's one of the things I've come to understand here. I know that I have an addiction to these sick relationships and I am working on that here."

"Yes," says Annie. "Nic has made a lot of progress along those lines."

"Good," says my mom. "Because I don't feel comfortable with Nic being in L.A."

"And," says my dad, "I don't feel comfortable with Nic moving back to San Francisco. He'll just be too close to Karen and me and the kids."

"All right," says Annie. "Well, those are all things you can **315** address on the third day of family weekend, when you make plans for the future."

I don't say anything. My parents don't want me in the same city as them.

We finish the therapy session with Annie around lunchtime. I take my parents up to the lunchroom and show them where to eat and all. I leave them there to smoke a cigarette. James sees me and gives me a hug, saying, "So, how was it?"

"Rough, man. This is gonna be even harder than I thought."

I put some headphones on and listen to music to just calm down. I smoke a cigarette, listening to this Daniel Johnston song. I listen to him sing, "When I'm down, nothing matters. nothing does. Please hear my cry for help, and save me from myself. . . ."

I'm crying now as I finish my cigarette. I turn off my CD player and go splash water on my face, then I walk into the lunchroom and sit down next to my parents. We haven't all been together since I graduated high school. And, even then, Karen, Jasper, and Daisy were there, so it wasn't just the three of us together. I actually can't remember a single time in my life where I've been alone with just my two parents and we were sitting down together eating lunch or whatever. I've heard both my mom and my dad say so many hurtful things about each other. I always felt so divided between the two of them. When I was with my mom in L.A. my allegiance was to her. When I was with my dad's family in San Francisco my allegiance was to them. I always just wanted to make everyone happy, but then I completely tore everyone apart. How did my good intentions turn into such an explosive nightmare? I am the only one to blame. There is this pressure building and building around me and I feel like I'm being crushed from all sides.

The three other families who are in the family group with us are already sitting down when we get to the room. The two therapists greet us. They are both short with flowing dresses and they look very new agey or whatever. The smaller one with fading blond hair is named Patricia and the other woman is Teresa. Teresa is taller but thinner and has short black hair and thick glasses.

I sit down between my mom and dad. The first thing we do is go around the circle and state our goals for the weekend. When it comes to my dad, he repeats what he said in Annie's office. He has a ton of anger toward me and is skeptical about this whole process.

"But I do love Nic," he says, choking up. "I love him so much. I'm just scared. I'm really scared."

He cries and then I cry too and I glance over and see that my mom is crying. I hate watching them cry. It is just so defeating. It feels like all the life is just drained out of me.

I sit low in my chair. My dad finishes and now it's my turn to state my goals. I have a hard time talking through my crying.

"I just, well, I don't know what I want from all this. I mean, I have been hurt by my parents, but then I have hurt them back so badly. I guess I want to use this weekend as a chance to address some of the resentments I have toward both my mom and my dad. But also, I want to show them how sorry I am. I don't think they will ever know just how much I regret what I've done to them. I am sorry, but that doesn't even begin to describe how I feel. And I want them to know how hard this is for me, too. Living with myself is hell. It's not like I'm just having a good time when I'm using and saying 'fuck you' to everyone. It is all pain. I mean, maybe four years ago when I first started this was all fun. But now it is just desperate and pathetic. I have been completely out of control and it is the worst feeling in the world. I'm not trying to say, like, 'poor me' or whatever. I want to take full responsibility for what I've done. But I just need my parents to know that this has been very hard for me, too. We have all suffered just so much."

My dad actually puts his hand on my shoulder and that makes me cry harder. He is still crying too and now my mom gets ready to speak.

"You know," my mom says, "I am really angry at Nic. He's hurt me and this whole thing has been terrible. But I know that I have made a lot of mistakes and so has Nic's father. I want for me and Nic's dad to both try and admit to some of the ways we've been unfair to Nic over the years. We have both been selfish with Nic, putting him in the middle of things that had nothing to do with him. So, as much as I don't want to, I am willing to face that. And, Nic, I want you to know that you can say anything to me. I don't want you to worry about protecting my feelings or your father's or Todd's or anybody's. When you were little you always tried to make everyone happy. Then it was like one day you just exploded. I don't want you to hold all that stuff inside of you anymore. It hasn't worked for you and it hasn't worked for me. I just want you healthy, Nic. That's all I want."

I hold her hand for a minute. I feel so grateful to her for everything she said. It's like for the first time my mom and dad and I will be able to be really honest with one another. Annie has taught me here that every resentment I hold inside me eventually will fester and come bursting to the surface. I just want to get rid of all the anger that has been building inside me for all these years. I want to get rid of it in a way where I don't end up hurting myself. It means so much to me that my mom sees this. It means so much to me that she says she wants to take some responsibility for everything. I've never heard my mom speak like this before and it gives me a lot of hope. I take her hand in mine and we both cry together.

The art therapy exercise we do is pretty simple. We have a piece of paper divided three ways and my mom and dad and I each get to draw in our own section. We are sitting on the floor and my dad is working with oil pastels and my mom has watercolors and I'm drawing with colored pencils.

As I watch my mom's drawing unfold, at first I am a little wary. She has painted a nice little blue sky with clouds and a sunset. This seems so typical of my mom, just trying to run from anything difficult—covering it up with a happy exterior. I wonder how she could have shifted so quickly from a few minutes ago when she was talking in group. But then the dark colors come in. There are swirling storm clouds covering the blue and turning the sky black and threatening. In the middle of the darkness is a solitary red balloon, drifting upward, almost too small to be seen. I guess that is her hope, so insignificant-looking in the overwhelming storm. I am very sad looking at this.

My dad draws something that looks like a giant vein, with lots of red and orange and drops of blood. It looks like pressure and pounding and worry and pain. He pushes the pastels into the paper so hard that they keep breaking in his hand. I try to focus on my own drawing.

At first I don't really know what I'm doing. I sketch a heart with veins and aortas and the different ventricles and things. Then I draw faces morphing together out of the heart, stretching up—screaming faces, terrified faces, desperate faces. And then, before I can even think about it, I write the words "I am sorry."

I write it over and over and over and over again. The words fill the whole page. When I look up I see my dad staring at my picture. He is crying again.

"I'm sorry," I say to him.

My dad gives me a hug, saying, "I'm sorry too. I'm sorry you've had to go through all this. I really am. I forget sometimes how hard this has been for you."

I let him hug me and I don't pull away.

"I love you, Dad. I love you, too, Mom. I really do."

I want to just collapse I'm feeling so much right now. I feel love, sadness, hurt, gratitude, fear, hope, hopelessness, regret— so many conflicting emotions. As we end group I know I'm allowed to go out to dinner with my mom and dad, but I decide not to. I need the support of the community and my friends here. I can process everything with them and they make me feel so supported. I talk to James and Jim. We go to a twelve-step meeting.

Later, me and a bunch of people sit around the TV room and watch *Labyrinth*, with David Bowie. Everyone's making jokes and I'm just laughing so hard—so genuinely. It's a feeling I thought maybe I'd lost.

I laugh and eat popcorn and drink hot chocolate.

This feels more like living than anything I've known in a long time. I realize how hard tomorrow is going to be, but for now, I feel so thankful to be exactly where I am. I feel independent. I feel like my own person.

James sees me and remarks, "Jesus Christ, my friend's become an adult."

It seems to fit. I feel comfortable in my own skin. I feel like I'm able to claim my own person. At least I'm making a start. I'm learning to stand on my own.

EPILOGUE

It's a few days before New Year's and it's gotten cold here. I've been living with a friend in Savannah for almost a year now. I actually drove cross-country with her twice before settling down here where she goes to school. We stayed in Yellowstone on the drive and I saw my first wild grizzly and black bears. We camped on cliffs overlooking the ocean and snuck into a hot spring in Calistoga.

Savannah is definitely not a place I ever imagined ending up, but it's not so bad. It's safe for now and I'm able to live much more simply here. And that's what I've come to value more than anything—simplicity.

So I'm sitting here writing, still smoking too many cigarettes and drinking too much coffee—though I guess there are worse things. Our apartment is small, but I've set up a little desk in the corner and I'm listening to the newest Fantômas record as loud as I can take it. There's a big tuxedo cat who probably hates the music lying on my lap. He's basically on top of me all day when I'm working. My kitten, who I rescued from the Humane Society a few months ago, is chasing a sparkly colored ball across the floor.

The family of my friend who I live with here has taken me in. They live close and I just celebrated Christmas with them. They were so open and made me feel completely welcome. I really do stick out here in the South, but her family has never been anything but accepting of me. I can't thank them enough.

It took me four months to complete treatment at the Safe Passage Center and I've been sober since then. Using just has no place in my life now and I can't see that ever changing. The feeling of vacancy I always had really isn't there anymore. I mean, I still struggle with depression and mania and whatever—but I guess I just don't hate myself like I used to. I actually really like my life now and I'm trying very hard to live with honesty and integrity.

My friend is at work right now, so I have the cats to myself. There's some leftover fried chicken in the fridge, so I cut it up and put it in the bowl for my kitten. She loves fried chicken.

I've been working on this book for more than a year now and have been trying to get some other writing projects together. I just finished the screenplay about zombies who take over a rehab and also a children's story based on the characters I made up for Jasper and Daisy. My friend here has a little cousin who's only fourteen months old. He's too young to listen to my stories yet, but I still hang out with him all the time. For Christmas I made him a mix CD with all my favorite childhood songs on it.

It's interesting because writing a memoir is really a foreign idea for most people I've met so far living in the South. It is so important here to keep family secrets private and a lot depends on never admitting to anything embarrassing or shameful. For myself, I've come to discover that holding on to secrets about who I am and where I come from is toxic. My secrets will kill me. If I don't get honest about my life, I cannot have recovery. I've learned that from the twelve steps and I've learned that from my own experience. I need to admit to what I've done, who I've been. That is how I have been able to survive.

And though I have done many shameful things, I am not ashamed of who I am. I am not ashamed of who I am because I know who I am. I have tried to rip myself open and expose everything inside—accepting my weaknesses and strengths—not trying to be anyone else. 'Cause that never works, does it?

So my challenge is to be authentic. And I believe I am today. I believe I am.

ACKNOWLEDGMENTS

Thank you, Ginee Seo. I mean, thank you so, so much.
You are really amazing and inspiring.

Thank you, Binky. Thank you for sticking by me.

Thank you, Debbie, George, Quincy, Jack, Cameron, and Liam.

Thank you to my dad, mom, Karen, Jasper, Daisy, Joe, Mark, Jenny, Becca, Bear, Nancy, Don, Susan, Lucy, Steve, Mark, Debbie, Joan, and Sumner.

Thank you, Randy, Susan, Sophia, and Carmine.

Thank you, Hillel, Shannon, Katie, and Spencer.

Thank you, Zan and Jace.

Thank you, Armistead, Terry, and Peggy.

Thank you, D. B.

Thank you, Sean.

Thank you to the Saint John Coltrane African Orthodox Church.

Thank you to Glide Memorial Church.

Thank you to my friends at LHC.

AFTERWORD

Walking my dog this morning, I had this memory come back to me that I'd blocked out completely. That happens sometimes, you know—still, after more than two years off shit.

The memory was from when I lived in the apartment off La Brea.

Me'n my girlfriend had been up all night in our one room apartment off Franklin, shooting cocaine. I had to work the next day, but I'd passed out sometime in the morning, and I guess my girlfriend couldn't wake me up.

Suddenly I jerked into consciousness and saw her staring down at me, her glossy blue eyes darting and unfocused.

"You all right?" she asked, voice stuttering.

"Huh? What? Why?"

"I couldn't wake you up, so I just gave you a shot of coke. Are you going to work?"

I looked at my arm, and there was a line of blood dripping down it.

"Yeah," I told her. "I feel pretty good. Let's go take a shower."

That's the memory I got back this morning—hiking up through Griffith Park, looking out at brown haze endlessly clinging to the downtown skyline.

This sickness tightened in my stomach, crawling up and out my throat.

Where I've been, where I come from—it's always gonna be with me. I'm a drug addict. That's who I am. I shot cocaine and heroin and crystal meth off and on for six years. I took pills, mushrooms, acid, Ketamine, GHB. I even smoked crack. Drugs were my whole life and death and whatever. They were everything, and they took everything from me. Or, actually, that's not true. It wasn't drugs. It was me. I threw everything away. I was the coward, too afraid to face life without sticking a needle in my arm.

So how do I move on from that? How do I go forward?

I guess that's the fucking question, right?

Ever since I can remember, I've had this pain inside me—this vacancy, this hole opening up wide. I always felt so alone, like I was this worthless little nothing. I guess the biggest fear I had in the whole world was that someone would see what's inside of me and discover what an ugly, disgusting, horrible person I really am. So I spent a whole lotta time trying to do everything I could to escape those feelings storming inside me. I ran from myself—using drugs, exercising compulsively, trying to find validation through sex and relationships. None of it ever worked. I remained myself.

But, when I was growing up, the one thing that did help me not to feel so isolated and crazy was reading—especially books by authors who fearlessly examined and exposed their highly imperfect inner lives. Books like *Confessions of a Mask* by Yukio Mishima; *Tropic of Cancer* by Henry Miller; *Try* by Dennis Cooper; and, of course, the works of authors like Bukowski, Salinger, Hesse, Bataille, Iceberg Slim, and Murakami. These writers revealed the things that existed beneath most humans' seemingly secure and confident exteriors. I suddenly realized, after reading their work, that I wasn't unique—that my doubts and fears and insecurities were more universal than I could've ever imagined. Their words gave me strength. They gave me permission to start trying to accept my flaws, my darkness, my insanity. They let me know that it was okay not to fit in with everyone else—to be a sensitive person—and that others struggled just like I did. It was such a relief when I finally began to understand this. It was like I could breathe—maybe for the first time.

So reading became an obsession for me, and I devoted myself to discovering new authors and trying to teach myself how to write. It was actually in one of Herman Hesse's books that I first read about the idea of art as a conversation. According to Hesse, each person's work is a response to someone else's work—a conversation that spans decades, or even centuries. When I look at an Egon Schiele painting, it affects me. And so when I write, that's like my answer back—to all the art that has meant something to me in my life. It's a cool idea and I believe in it.

Anyway, I've been inspired by reading to respond with my own work, and I'm constantly trying to participate in that conversation.

Writing *Tweak* was like that for me. I wanted to tell my story—to contribute to the conversation. And it was my life, too, so I knew there would be something cathartic in that, like that song where Yoko Ono just screams "Why?" over and over—releasing everything.

Now that the book's finished and been put out there for everyone to see, I have conflicting feelings about what I've done. On the one hand, the process of writing everything down and sharing my story was like performing an exorcism—minus the projectile vomiting and my head spinning around. Actually, it was like a purging or something. It was totally a kind of therapy for me.

Going on book tour and talking with groups of people about my experience and listening to their stories was just like a continuation of that process. The readings and talks felt like being in groups at rehab. The level of honesty and intimacy that was shared with me was overwhelming. I think exposing our pain and insecurity and fear allows others to do the same, and that is very beautiful. Connecting on that level feels so much more meaningful than most human interactions I have in my life.

So all that's been amazing.

And learning to handle criticism and negative, sometimes hostile, feedback has been super important for me in terms of developing strength and conviction in my beliefs.

But, looking back, well, I think the one thing that is hard for me to reconcile is the fact that I exposed other peoples' lives in my writing. Of course, I tried to disguise their identities, but they know who they are. I'm not sure if their stories were mine to tell.

I wrote about myself, but I exposed them. This is particularly true with the portrayal of my ex-girlfriend, whom I called Zelda in the book. She has suffered a ton, right? I regret very much adding to that and I can't help but feel some guilt for what I've done.

Of course, when I wrote *Tweak* I was more immature than I am now. I didn't understand how sharing someone else's secrets, even anonymously, is a violation of their right to their own story. I genuinely had no way of knowing that. It was only through the process of publishing this book that I began to see the error in my actions.

Other writers have done it, of course. Henry Miller and Charles Bukowski are the two authors I admire most who consistently wrote about the people in their lives, exposing their most intimate secrets. I respect them both very much, and I guess I partly used their example to go forward with telling these other peoples' stories in my book.

Like I said, I feel fairly conflicted about this now.

I'm not saying I'd take it back. What I can say is that I'm committed to not doing it again. I want to focus on writing only about myself.

Maybe that's a strange thing to include in an afterword, but I feel like it's important to acknowledge what I feel like are my mistakes. That has become an integral part of my recovery.

So, that said, since publishing *Tweak*, I have relapsed. It was brief and not on hard drugs at all. I relapsed on pills that I had justified taking, but quickly saw how the obsession had taken hold of me again. Actually it was sort of miraculous that I got myself into treatment before things could spiral out of control. I think more than anything else, I understand now that if I keep running from my feelings, I will never grow and, ultimately, I'll fucking get myself dead. If I don't figure out who I am now and learn to live with myself, I'll never have any kind of life at all. I have to face my shit one day. The longer I wait, the harder it'll be.

So I have about a hundred days clean again. I'm living with a friend in East Hollywood. I go to an outpatient program twice a week, and I have this totally amazing therapist. I'm in the process of getting on medication for depression, as well as for bipolar disorder. I have a dog that is just the best thing ever. Things are good— Well, a lot of the time.

Honestly, I struggle every day, but I *am* moving forward.

I opened the book with a John Lennon quote and, recently, there's been this one song of his that I just play over and over. Sometimes it makes me fucking cry and sometimes it fills me with hope.

John's voice is so beautiful, singing, "Hold on, John. John, Hold on. It's gonna be all right."

I have to believe that.

It's gonna be all right.

I just know it will.

—Nic Sheff, Hollywoodland, 2008

READING GROUP GUIDE FOR *TWEAK*

DISCUSSION QUESTIONS

What are some of the reasons Nic gives for turning to drugs? What are his insecurities? In what ways do the drugs help him to escape them?

Is Nic happy when he is on drugs? Does he enjoy his life at these times? What does he mean when he calls his addiction a "horrible vicious cycle"?

When Nic relapses in L.A. in the second part of the book, what is his reason for using again? Were the other people in his life surprised that he relapsed? Was he? Did you see the relapse coming? Why or why not?

What does Nic want from his father? Why does his father react to Nic the way he does? How much do you think Nic's childhood relationship with his father contributed to his addiction?

What does it mean for Nic to give himself over to a higher power? Why is it so difficult for him to do this?

A number of the people in the book come close to dying—Lauren ODs on heroin, Spencer gets meningitis, and Nic suffers through various overdoses and infections. How do these brushes with death affect Nic's outlook on life? Does he ever believe that any of these people are actually going to die? How does Nic react when Jordan really does die?

Discuss Nic's relationship with Zelda. Why is he so drawn to her? Why does everyone in Nic's life caution him against becoming involved with her? How does she contribute to his addiction? Is there anything healthy about their relationship?

What causes Nic to get help each time he relapsed? What does hitting bottom look like for him? Why is his stay at Safe Passage more effective than his other attempts at rehab? Do you think it's because of what they do there, or what led up to his going there . . . or both?

Nic's addiction—and attempts at rehab—make him part of a specific subculture, one with its own language, values, and network of people. Why does this aspect of the drug culture appeal to him? Would you consider the friends that he makes while using to be good friends?

Nic mentions many times that he feels worthless, and that his addiction has caused him to irreparably damage his relationships with others. Do the actions of his friends and family back this up? Do they treat him as though he has no worth? Does anyone give him unconditional love?

ACTIVITIES

Nic finds strength to stay sober in his family, his writing, and other aspects of his life. Identify the people, hobbies, and beliefs in your own life that you rely on for strength when going through a tough time.

Tweak covers less than two years of Nic's life, yet offers a lot of insight into him as a person. Write your own memoir, choosing a period of your life that you feel represents who you truly are.

Learning CPR ends up being an important skill for Nic. Find a CPR or first aid class in your community and sign up to get certified.

Exercise is very helpful to Nic when he is sober—it burns excess energy and helps him feel focused. Dust off your bike, join a gym, go for a hike, or run around the block. Find a form of exercise that helps you to feel focused and strong.

Nic's body goes through a lot when he is in detox. Research what happens to the body when drugs are being used, and the physiology of detoxification.

Spencer believes very strongly that helping others is an important part of sobriety, as it distracts you from your own problems and desires. Look around your community and decide how you can lend a hand. Volunteer at a soup kitchen, raise money for a cause that you believe in, or even help your parents around the house.

Evaluate your beliefs about drug and alcohol use and reflect on your own experiences or those of friends.

If you are an addict or alcoholic, or are involved with someone who is an addict or alcoholic, here are some places to get help.

Al-Anon and Alateen
al-anon.org
al-anon.org/newcomers/teen-corner-alateen
1-888-425-2666

Nar-Anon
nar-anon.org
1-800-477-6291

Alcoholics Anonymous
aa.org

Narcotics Anonymous
na.org

National Association for Children of Addiction
nacoa.org
nacoa.org/just-4-teens

National Council on Alcoholism and Drug Dependence
ncadd.org
1-800-622-2255

National Institute on Alcohol Abuse and Alcoholism
niaaa.nih.gov
1-301-443-3860

National Institute on Drug Abuse for Teens
teens.drugabuse.gov

National Institute of Mental Health
nimh.nih.gov
1-866-615-6464

National Suicide Prevention Lifeline
suicidepreventionlifeline.org
1-800-273-8255

Partnership for Drug-Free Kids
drugfree.org
1-855-DRUGFREE (378-4373)

**Substance Abuse and
Mental Health Services Administration**
samhsa.gov
1-800-662-HELP (4357)

Nic Sheff is a columnist for The Fix and the author of two memoirs about his struggles with addiction: the *New York Times* bestselling *Tweak: Growing Up on Methamphetamines* and *We All Fall Down: Living with Addiction*. He also wrote for the hit TV series *The Killing*, along with the Netflix series *13 Reasons Why*. Nic lives in Los Angeles, California.